OUT OF SILENCE

OUT OF SILENCE:

Censorship in Theatre & Performance

Edited by Caridad Svich

Ꞙ

EYECORNER PRESS

Out of Silence:
Censorship in Theatre & Performance

Published by EYECORNER PRESS
Roskilde, March 2012

ISBN: 978-87-92633-14-9

Cover design and layout: Camelia Elias

Cover Photo: Michael Schantz in a scene from *Rift* by Caridad Svich directed by Seret Scott at NYU Graduate Acting Program's Shubert Theatre (2009). Photo credit: Ella Bromblin.

Photo is used with Ms. Bromblin's permission and also with permission of NYU.

Dedicated to my parents for giving me the faith to dissent...

and to the late Glyn O'Malley,
whose passionate, raging spirit was instrumental to the creation
of this volume

ACKNOWLEDGEMENTS

This book would not be possible without the practitioners and scholars who contributed of their time and energy with their work. Hedgebrook Women's Writing Retreat in Washington, New Dramatists in New York, and the Department of English at Rutgers University-New Brunswick provided practical support during editing. Thanks to Todd London, Artistic Director at New Dramatists, Vito Zingarelli, Retreat Manager at Hedgebrook, Greg Bossler at The Dramatists Guild, Cynthia Croot and Sophia Skiles at Theaters Against War (THAW), Marcy Arlin, Catherine Coray, Migdalia Cruz, Christine Evans, Randy Gener, Jonathan Kalb, Matthew Maguire, Glyn O'Malley, Adele Shank, Saviana Stanescu, Pocha Nostra and the theatre alliance NoPassport. Thanks to the photographers who provided their photos, and to Carrie Louise Nutt and Olivia Lilley for copy-editing and research assistance. Special thanks to Maria M. Delgado and Aleks Sierz. As always, my work is not possible without the love and support of Emilio and Aracely Svich.

CONTENTS

PART THREE

PART FOUR

Out of Silence

CARIDAD SVICH

[Caridad Svich is a US playwright-translator-editor and lyricist of Cuban-Argentine-Spanish-Croatian descent. She is the recipient of the 2011 American Theatre Critics Association Primus Prize. Her work has been seen across the US and abroad. Key works include *Iphigenia...a rave fable*, stage adaptation of Isabel Allende's *The House of the Spirits*, and the multimedia collaboration *The Booth Variations*. She is alumna playwright of New Dramatists, founder of No-Passport theatre alliance & press, Drama editor of *Asymptote* international literary journal, contributing editor of *TheatreForum* and associate editor of *Contemporary Theatre Review*. She's editor of several books on theatre and performance including *Trans-Global Readings: Crossing Theatrical Boundaries* (Manchester University Press, 2003), Theatre in Crisis? (MUP, 2001), and *Divine Fire* (BackStage Books, 2005).]

At this moment, everywhere from China to Indonesia to South America to parts of Africa, a woman or a man is thinking "But I daren't write it." Talent is not necessarily allied to a readiness for martyrdom or even courage. Why should it be? A good thing for writers to be talented, but to be noticed it is even better if they are in prison or fighting cancer, or like Rushdie, sentenced to death. Writers as victims, that's our mental set, but we scarcely notice the wasted or disappointed ones. [1]

---

1   Doris Lessing, "Censorship," in Lessing., *Time Bites: Views and Reviews* (New York: Harper Collins, 2004). p. 75.

In her essay 'Censorship' author Doris Lessing speaks in part about the quandary faced by writers when they meet the censor within themselves. While she lists overt instances of censorship in the old Soviet Union and South Africa as parallels to new methods of censorship that have arisen out of the dogma of political correctness, Lessing touches upon the more essential and decisive problem faced not only by practitioners engaged in free enquiry and the creative arts but by ordinary citizens at work in institutions of higher learning and the like who are silenced by a climate of fear and control (impressionable minds, you know, daren't be taught to simply love books and educate their curiosity, but to seek out only certain books who will give them the 'right' message). In 'Censorship,' Lessing muses "I wonder about books not written."[2] Although she does expand greatly upon this reflection, it is the kernel of what animates and troubles the conscience of many who face the page to write, or face the stage to make, create and sculpt figures in time and space. What happens, in effect, between the moment of yes and the moment of no? And how many no(s) tame the yes(es) that began the life of a work of art in the first place?

Practitioners often live in a state of active silence, so that the impulses and images inspired and sparked by the world around them and the dreams of what that world could be, can find the proper form in which to be contained as art. This private silence is an arena of conflict and trust. Artists obsess and toy with a multitude of images, word-scraps and thoughts before the process of making. During that private time, battle must often be done with voices of approval and/ or disapproval that may derail or discount the excitement, energy and confidence necessary to sustain the act(s) of making. These voices, outside the artist and within, can dissuade a practitioner from encountering difficult, thorny, gentle or un-charted terrain. Who will want to see that? The voice says. Who is this play, performance piece, novel, dance, film, poem, musical composition, or essay for?

Those two questions in and of themselves are central, for they may dictate what eventually is put down on the page or stage, and how the process of development and discovery will take place. Sometimes these two questions come rather late in the process, well after an initial period of lively silence where the creating and/or writing itself has not yet happened but is within the body and

---

2   Ibid, p. 74

mind of the artist. Often these questions 'Who is this piece for?' and 'Who will want to see it?' arise when the work is being developed in the practice hall or first presented in some form to an audience or a potential producing organisation. Why are these two questions of particular significance?

The assumption is usually made that practitioners have an audience in mind when making a piece, and therefore, know for whom the play or piece is intended. Of course, often neither answer is known, because the piece is for the self, or those loved and/or those imagined few the artist wishes to reach with the materials of their artwork. There is an implied hope that those loved and those imagined in the room or site of play, will want to witness the work. It is such a leap of faith that makes many an artist create in the first place, against the odds, against expectation, against any chance of a known audience or reader. The fascination and riddle of the work itself, of its possibility and impossibility, is the alchemical pull of creation. Outside of circumstances when a practitioner is making a very specific work for hire, knowing exactly who the work is for and to what purpose it will serve, short-circuits and de-limits the possibilities that arise when imagining and making art.

Thus, the two questions 'Who is this piece for?' and 'Who will want to see it?' are merely reflections of the same coin of thought. If one cannot identify the Who will indeed WANT to see it (and this is assuming of course that there is a WANT already pre-existing that has its own demands and expectations) then somehow one is looked upon as a failure. The beauty of failure, the inexorable poetics and power of failure exemplified by Beckett's theatrical aesthetic, most notably in the previous century, can be captivating and necessary for risk-taking. It can be a driving force, a mechanics of thought and will, a new way of seeing, but failure of delivering upon that WANT and being, thus, in a perceived orbit of waste and disappointment can also be a force of silence so powerful that daring to create something (and creating is above all a dare) becomes impossible, unthinkable, and unimaginable. Because the fear of creation, of daring the dare against the world of WANT, can be so strong that it can paralyze an artist's voice and debilitate vision. This fear, which is part of a larger culture of silencing, is not only damaging to the field of free creative enquiry, but also is the spectre that haunts the artist at almost every turn in the process of making, and later in seeking of access for the work.

Access is seemingly afforded to a certain few. This has always been the case. For every book published, there are hundreds unpublished, unseen. For every play produced, there are hundreds unproduced, unseen. Practitioners can work at their craft for years and indeed be considered vital voices in their community and the field without access to a public platform. Access is determined by the more mutable and dicey games of law and chance active in the marketplace. But access is also determined by the unhealthy politics of nations controlled by visible and less visible forms of oppression and repression. The state censor bearing down upon its citizens and artists is the most immediate image that comes to mind when the word 'censorship' arises. And while there is no denying that the state censor does exist in many countries around the world and actively enforces the silencing of artistic voices speaking truths to power, there are other forms of silencing that occur in the free world, which have as much to do with the market value attached to a work or a particular artistic sensibility, as they do with restraints (which govern available funding, viability of production, appropriate press coverage , publication and documentation) placed upon the form and/or content of an artistic work outside of the parameters of subjective taste and aesthetics.

There is an ethics of censorship and self-censorship that courses through the body of writing. The language of misrule and obfuscation that rose out of the dogma of political correctness, in the US in particular, has created a lexicon of terror (to borrow Marguerite Feitlowitz's phrase), an extraordinarily resourceful and insidious language of fear that displaces meaning for message. This lexicon indebted to reality-based tabloid thinking and its cultural exegesis has marked and is marking the vocabulary of art and art-making. Ageism, sexism, racism, class-ism and homophobia are operative in this lexicon of fear that stresses youth over age, enforces racial and class divisions, and turns the word 'queer' into a de-sexed, user-friendly term that evokes images of well-dressed, white men of the middle, upper or dilettante class commenting on appropriate wardrobe and interior décor on cable TV, not to mention the love-able fetishised *mestizo* boy-toy that can satisfy their outré erotic desires.

While the performance of extreme identity is overly familiar to a culture weaned on the daily antics of *The Jerry Springer Show* and other fast-food entertainments in the neo-Greco-Roman pit mode, the question that is salient to consider is what happens to artists that are continually dedicated to questioning and intervening constructions of race, culture and gender? What happens to voices that seek the quiet, gentle scene of human connection over, for example, the lurid, exploited one of human brutality? And what happens to artists whose speech is de-limited by a plastic society that chooses to only record what is politically convenient for history? What happens, in effect, to cultural memory and the legacy when so much of our lives, their mini and major histories, exist in the myopic, and therefore distorted, mirrors and compromised poetics of the blogosphere?

Voice in Culture

'When I'm in Kansas I think I hear someone behind me but I've learned by now there's never anyone outside; the sound I hear is American flags flapping in the wind. Soldiers from this state go in busloads to fight in Iraq. I look for newly dug earth in the cemetery.[3]

The idea for this book began on 11 April 2006 when I organized and moderated, through my theatre alliance NoPassport, a public panel and conversation on writing and censorship at New Dramatists in New York City, and later co-hosted with playwright Jason Grote and actor Sophia Skiles on 17 April 2006, in association with THAW (Theaters Against War) a Patriot's Day Freedom Follies at the Culture Project also in New York City. Both events were sparked by the heated debate over New York Theatre Workshop's cancellation of the US premiere of the Royal Court Theatre production of Alan Rickman and Katherine Viner's play *My Name is Rachel Corrie* (2005). The play is composed from the journal entries and e-mails of the 23-year-old woman from Washington State who was crushed to death in Gaza on 16 March 2003 under a bulldozer operated by the Israeli army. The piece had two successful runs in London in 2005. Negotiations were in place to present it at New York Theatre Workshop in spring of 2006, but the theatre company decided to postpone the US premiere indefinitely out of concerns for the sensitivities of (unnamed) Jewish groups unsettled by Hamas' victory in the Palestinian elections. The UK producers decried

3   Catherine Filloux from public statement sent via e-mail for the NoPassport 'Out of Silence' panel/ conversation on writing, censorship, funding, access and the arts moderated by Caridad Svich on 11 April 2006 at New Dramatists in New York City.

the decision by New York Theatre Workshop as 'censorship' and sought out new venues for their US premiere. For about two months in the spring of 2006 the cancellation of *My Name is Rachel Corrie* was the subject of passionate discussion in the mainstream media, blog-osphere, at theatre and academic symposia, and in chat rooms and online communities on the internet.

Six years have passed since that passionate spring in New York City, and much has changed in the sociopolitical landscape since then. The global financial crisis of 15 September 2008 has come and gone, although its effects continue to be felt, President Barack Obama is in office and up for a second term election, and the 'Arab spring' of 2011 has changed the political landscape of the Middle East for quite some time. The dark days of President George W. Bush's administration that bore witness to deliberate acts of censorship, and carefully constructed and orchestrated obfuscations of public language for the sake of political maneuvering are past. Many practitioners who spoke out for and against the cancellation of the play by New York Theatre Workshop have obviously gone on to other things and indeed many have expressed in private circles that the stances they took at the time may have been hasty and rash or, alternately, absolutely definitive. What is true regardless of time's passing and the shifting of perceptions is how for a moment once again in US theatre culture specifically there was a palpable critical mass that rose to action in defense of a play and what it stood for, and, in effect, believed that their voices could be and should be heard in culture.

At a time when the 2nd Iraq War, the genocide in Darfur, the continuing conflicts in Afghanistan and elsewhere in the Middle East, Africa and other continents occupied (and at this writing still occupy) the front and side pages of newspapers, periodicals, internet journals and blogs, the inescapable fact that a theatrical outcry over the cancellation of the presentation of the edited verbatim representation of a young, murdered US female voice from the frontlines of Gaza by a British theatre-making and journalistic team could occur in as vocal a manner as it did with statements issued to the press by such high-profile diverse voices as Harold Pinter, Kathleen Chalfant, Caryl Churchill, Vanessa Redgrave, Tony Kushner, and Christopher Shinn alongside 'lesser-profile' voices from across the arts signaled that something indeed was shifting in culture, again, if only for a moment. Marking this moment and opening up the debate to the re-animation of larger questions around how censorship thrives, de-

stroys, emboldens, and transforms theatre-making, whether it be by convention and tradition bound or through more directly interventionist means, thus,
is what has driven the making of this collection.

While some of the essays in this book refer to the *My Name is Rachel Corrie*
'incident,' many more step outside the New York-centric and transatlantic-cen-
tric mentalities that govern so much of theatre and performance studies in
Western English-language dominant cultures to explore, investigate, wrestle
with and question from myriad points of view (personal, political, emotional,
geographic, spiritual) how silence and silencing (from outside and within) factors into the languages of process and practice, especially in the era of late
capitalism.

Scholar Marvin Carlson frames the volume with a historical overview on
censorship in theatre and looks at various strategies used to enact erasure from
Plato's time forwards. Carlson's focused and useful survey approach is followed
by some quick thoughts that serve as a kind of virtual wall of impassioned graffiti from practitioners Dan Rebellato, Johannes Birringer, Marguerite Feitlowitz,
Liz Tomlin and Steve Jackson on censorship's uses and abuses. The volume then
opens up from a wide angle perspective as US scholar and cultural critic Stephen Duncombe charts the topography of how censorship is a going concern
and non-concern in contemporary and historical US culture. His lens is from the
problematic position of the progressive left in a late-age democracy overrun by
the widening structures and economies of the Information Age. For Duncombe
the difficult stance and currency of Generation Q (the quiet generation) and
previous generations X and Y are their ability to understand belief, thought and
action as separate entities that 'are no longer interlinked.' (p. 45) The erosion of
common beliefs linked by thoughts and actions affects how political art is presented and viewed and how it, in turn, affects culture at all. Rather than embrace the uncertainties of Zygmunt Bauman's 'liquid modernity' (2007) [4] and
the free construct of fictions across a matrix, Duncombe argues that the contemporary condition could use a healthy shake-up toward a re-connection to
struggles for truth (and liberty,) not as conceptual motors for 'political' propaganda but as living market-able realities that place narratives of truth at the
compelling centre of our ways of being in the world.

---

4   Zygmunt Bauman, *Liquid Times*, (Cambridge, England and Malden, MA: Polity Press, 2007).

Duncombe's call to action is followed by two essays interlinked historically by the cancellation by New York Theatre Workshop of Alan Rickman and Katherine Viner's *My Name is Rachel Corrie*. Ken Urban takes a steady and unflinching look at the censor in the mirror – ourselves – and Christopher Shinn writes on censorship, its repercussions, and the role of the artist in society (in an essay originally published in 2006 and reprinted with permission from The Dramatists Guild's in-house journal *The Dramatist*). Both Urban and Shinn's pieces pick up subtle threads from Duncombe's thoughts on the Information Age, and plea for a re-cognition of silence midst the technological noise of culture. It is, however, the illusion of secrets exposed for all to see, hear and download that is at the heart of much of the social networking communities alive on the internet, be they YouTube, Face Book, MySpace, etc. The 'naked selves' on display in virtuality are fetish-ised for their real-ness. Whether constructed as fictional selves or caught tabloid-style 'on the fly' with digital cameras, these 'naked' (i.e. exposed, unadorned, un-made-up) beings exist as entities that draw huge fan-bases from surfing and blogging communities all over the world.

Witness the phenomenon of web-based teenage series star Lonelygirl15 who became an instant celebrity as a fictional character only to be exposed as the creation of aspiring filmmakers with a viable commercial contract secured for the project. Devotees of Bree, the Lonelygirl15, of the online diary, were dismayed, but at the same time suspicions had lurked all along through side-bar online chat rooms that the character was a fake (i.e. a construct). But behind the truth and dare/truth or dare games in virtual and Second Life worlds lies the simultaneous power of fiction itself and the desire for the pre-fictive and pre-virtual to be made flesh: secrets unlocked, free from an un-mocked culture, released from the disturbed world filled with the noise of dead air.

In Stephen Bottoms' essay 'Dead Air,' the presence of emptiness is explored through an extended reflection on New York-based Taiwanese performance artist Teching Hsieh's series of One Year Performances. For Bottoms, Teching's Hsieh's commitment to opening up the body to 'new knowledge about his own physical limits, resources, and capabilities' (p. 72) through his radical performances of the self in the world – homeless, exposed in the truest most vital sense, or caged in silence – reflects a desire to be part of the eco-system and not against it. Rather than dive into the virtual, Teching Hsieh's work, according to Bottoms' thesis, is a spiritual reclamation of live-ness without need or regard for a fan base to deliberate whether or not his artistic mission is 'valid.' Unlike mediatised constructions for potential profit like Lonelygirl15 which stress the consistent, must-do 'noise' of peeping into other lives, the vulnerable presentations of the self, exemplified by an artist such as Teching Hsieh, allow us to listen to the world anew.

Focused on speech and orality, radical performance theorist Baz Kershaw posits 'Biting Tongues: eight notes and a coda on some uses of self-censorship.' Interrogating the 'monstrous' uses of the tongue, teeth, cavities, names, parts of the country and body, beards, seals, holds and what's gone missing, Kershaw constructs a disturbingly musical, poetic linguistic and spatial enactment of voiceless-ness, imprisonment, and how embedded marks of difference wound the self in society and by which other selves brutalise and wound each other. In this unconventional essay Kershaw shows the marks of pain that constitute a language of despair that has been condoned by societies that have become enraptured to grammars of violence as their moral and ethical core.

The insidious, amusing and despairing languages of corporate branding are awakened and unsettled in James Frieze's piece 'Whatever you say – Making the Monstrous Phatic,' wherein he analyses the 'small talk' of the everyday technological world through the performance of speech enacted by the duo Ridiculusmus along with a theatrically collaborative work by Will Adamsdale and Chris Branch entitled *The Receipt*. Frieze argues against the serious/trivial binary that often runs through the pre-virtual and post-virtual discourses of cultural critique. Instead Frieze seeks to illuminate the creation of new languages that exist or may be possible between branded and non-branded speech, and the successful strategies of resistance individuals can stage to maintain and expand their words and bodies from being fully co-opted. Acknowledging the inevitability of the contemporary self as cyborg, Frieze opens up the panorama of enquiry in the volume to the ways in which truths and facts collide in their quest for supremacy in the 'value' market and how manufacturing dissent (to quote Noam Chomsky) and dissent in and of itself remain two very different, though sometimes confused (as one and the same), positions.

In keeping with the theme of voice in air and time, Tim Crouch takes a playful, mordant look at the levels of censorship alive in the process of acting and responding to performance. For Crouch, there is a different grammar of violence at work in the theatre than the one Kershaw exposes in society and its stages: the veiled violence of polite hypocrisy and the subsequent masquerade enacted by actors with each other and with critics and the audience. Actor as star of a play in spite of or despite the play, for example, argues Crouch, emphasises the 'voyeuristic impulse' in an audience and the narcissistic qualities of acting itself. The actor is in a strange prison and hall of mirrors where the play (visual and/or verbal) is a secondary event to the interpretative act: the celebrity parallel that conflates the performer's identity from that of the character. Strange fictions ensue in this parallel universe and the practical and active truths of making a theatre piece work (job, practice) get skewed. Crouch insists on re-placing the voice and body of the actor in service of the work, rather than upstaging it (as has become custom).

The power of resistance of the body in performance is articulated in Carl Lavery's discussion of Genet and site-based performance viewed through a theoretical re-reading of Jacques Ranciere. Lavery argues that site-based performance produces an effect of displacement that counteracts socio-cultural 'policing,' and proposes that censorship is a type of fetish. He identifies the reality of theatre's ability to unmoor social codes and practices, and a spectator's necessary abandonment of 'place' in order to experience a work fully. Contestations of consensual logic abound in Lavery's provocative and illuminating discussion, and open up the volume to voices and bodies that have been displaced and re-situated in new landscapes and environments.

Bodies and languages in transit

'Growing up, I always asked why people failed to stand up to slavery, Indian genocide, fascism, McCarthyism, Jim Crow. But then I got older and found out that people did stand up, constantly, and that standing up is really, really hard. How far does solidarity go?" [5]

Charting the languages of bodies in transit through disparate and sometimes viably dangerous territories, this next sequence of essays stresses per-

---

5   Jason Grote from statement written for the NoPassport 'Out of Silence' panel on 11 April, 2006 at New Dramatists in New York City.

sonal testimony, meditations on geographic and linguistic displacement, questions related to issues of identity and representation on stage vis a vis the
dialectics of silence, and the intercultural, intermediary global connections
amongst artists devoted to interventionist work and cultural transformation.
Canadian and Quebecoise playwright and translator Chantal Bilodeau struggles
with the need for a figurative and metaphorical home in her essay 'Je me souviens' as she examines the many languages her mind and body inhabits, and with
which she is forced to reconcile on an ongoing daily basis as artist and citizen.
Playwright-activist Lisa Schlesinger places herself on the frontlines of fear as
she re-inscribes 'Postcards from Gaza,' and hears and mis-hears meanings in
different coded languages. Schlesinger's open-ended, poetically marked essay
is haunted by the sentence 'Fear, invariably, fucks up language' (p. 157).

Inevitably ghosted by the spectre of 11 September 2001, the policed body
has come to signify different things depending on which passport one carries.
Traveling as a US citizen through Gaza, Schlesinger is between 'unspeakable
geographies' and yet always free, ultimately, to leave. She is guarded with suspicion but also with charitable open-ness at moments least expected. Trying to
define herself to herself and to others, she finds that words beg the richness of
experience and complicated empathies she feels as an artist in the world. This
thought is sustained by both Craig Higginson and Jorge Huerta in their respective essays 'Issues of Representation in South African Theatre' and 'On Chicano
Theatre and Self-Censorship: What were we thinking' where the reclamations
against erasure and the 'official' definitions of the oppressed body are confronted by shifting regimes, in Higginson's case, and the rapidly changing demographics and ideologies of Chicanos, Mexicans, Mexicanos, and other Latino/as
making theatre and performance in the US.

As bodies and languages in transit enact various constructions of self and
culture within stratified, policed and less-policed states, Dijana Milosevic finds
the gestures to 'throw a handful of sand over the historical, cultural, political
memories of death and darkness' in her native Belgrade and elsewhere with her
ongoing work with Dah Teater (p. 140). She offers her thoughts on the 'quality
of attention' as a way to evoke the powerful necessity of speaking truth to power through acts of theatre that go sideways through consciousness, a sentiment
that is echoed in Dragan Klaic's meditation on the plight of the exiled and émigré artist in European theatre later in the section. The knee-jerk response to vi-

olation is often violence and rage, and whilst momentarily effective perhaps, Milosevic and others in this volume reinforce appropriately enough less reactionary responses to the violation of the body. The spectator as participant and mitigating observer of sites of violence is fore-fronted in Chiori Miyagawa's essay on the aftermath of Hiroshima and the problematic encounters that art-making and spectatorship are engaged with when faced with artifacts of catastrophe.

Creating the space where different voices (dialogic rather than monologic) can be heard is ultimately what many of the artists in this volume advocate. The manner in which to do so are necessarily varied though conflict resolution strategies toward peace are often at the core of the endeavours herein marked.

Sites of Performance

'You used to be born into the counter culture. If you were born gay, a transsexual, or some kind of minority, you were automatically part of the counter culture. Now, all those things have been appropriated so you can't be born into the counter culture. Now you usually have to choose it. You have to choose to be different. And people will attack you for it. You're not supposed to choose to live an alternative lifestyle. That means you're a poser. My point is that it's all drag, honey.' [6]

Out of bounds, out of range, texts, bodies, gestures and images take on divergent political life. From the story of infamous silent twins in the UK, a look at the modes of US pastiche artist Taylor Mac, staging Shakespeare in the heart of the US Bible Belt, to the denim revolution fomented in Belarus – these next series of varied and cross-linked essays and provocations in the volume move past and through bordered and un-bordered geographies to examine the many ways real-life and fictional narratives are spun against and for culture. Unvoiced appropriated private selves on display, wounded and mourned, focus Americanist scholar Bridget K. Bennett's account of the various representations on stage, prose and film of the story of the 'silent twins' who were kept/imprisoned

---

6   Taylor Mac from, as of this writing, an unpublished interview with Caridad Svich conducted via e-mail summer 2007.

at Broadmoor Hospital after committing acts of arson and violence. Aggressive, problematic, un-socialised aspects of the policed and un-policed body perform for a discomfited audience. How to view the re-enactment of a conversation taken from journal and diary entries between two sisters of Afro-Caribbean descent who created a private shell of a world and a language to go with it to resist and simultaneously reinforce their marginalisation, as an act of defiance, once those conversations, never meant to be made public, are 'used' as text to represent their lives? Which drag is best-suited to face the world and why? Nina Mankin's personal exploration through her dramaturgical relationship with US pastiche artist Taylor Mac's works renders viable the politics of the gendered body in performance. Taking us on an intimate *paseo* (stroll) though a hall of strange mirrors, Mankin lets the reader, with the use of colloquial prose - populist on principle - reflect on their own relationship to Mac's adorned and naked body as he shape-shifts from one sex to another to a third sex whilst all the while embracing and debunking traditional narrative tropes. Staging his own interventions of theatrical defiance, Mac embraces freak-ishness not as mere spectacle or assault against 'normality,' but as a wondrous acknowledgment of human variation, and in so doing calls into question how spectators routinely see themselves and those around them, and thus shape their world.

The virtue of tolerance is put to the test in Peter W. Meineck's essay on Aquila Theatre Company's tour of the US with a production of Rostand's *Cyrano* and later with Shakespeare's *Romeo and Juliet*. Meineck observes how it is not only religious fundamentalism in the US but local and federal arts funding that is dictating the production and reception of work, in this case, from the Western canon, and thus, supposedly less at-risk than other works for the theatre. And yet, Meineck notes in lucid and amiable prose how the precise apparatus created for presentation and touring in the US especially to educational institutions and venues empowers 'intolerance, bigotry, homophobia and misogyny.' (p.211).

Randy Gener traces another kind of apparatus of power and its dismantling in his insightful, journalistic essay on the Free Theater of Belarus. Gener writes about the negative space where 'unofficial theatre' rests, and how visibility and support for a revolutionary theatre is dependent upon a network of good will, solidarity and allegiance from artists worldwide. Unrecognised by the government of Belarus, the Free Theater, despite performances at Under the Radar

Festival in New York City and Arts in One World Conference at California Institute of the Arts, exists in its own 'black hole' (p. 221) and must fight on a daily basis to keep its company together and locate its sites of performance.

Zones of Contact

The first person voice gives way to two conversations amongst artists towards the end of the volume. Argentine curator Gabriela Salgado and Post-Mexican performance artist Guillermo Gómez-Peña elaborate on the concept of zones of silence: cities and countries that exist beyond the radars of the art world. Playwright Joanna Laurens and I 'speak' over e-mail exchange about perceived meanings of works, the poetic sensibility on stage, failure, neutrality and difference as operative forces in art-making and perception, and the difficulty sometimes of simply listening, really listening, to oneself and the world. Both conversations expose the nature of dialogue itself – the stops and starts, moments of flow and connection, and the interstitial points of difference that enliven and enrich our lives. In recording moments in time, an edited act of fidelity is taking place artistically in each 'transcript.' And yet the question of fidelity – which hovers largely over this entire collection (fidelity to representation, cause, political idea/stance, etc.) – in and of itself is part of censorship.

The tracing and re-tracing of wounded terrains of society, earth and conscience provides the beating heart of Matthew Goulish's piquantly sobering analysis of the act of creative writing and the consequences of murder in the chilling tale of the Virginia Tech massacre and the writings left behind by the shooter. How are we to make moral sense of a young man's rampage through a college campus when his student writings are posted without permission online for the world to see, and not only to see, but to share and use as 'evidence' of his actions on that fateful day in Virginia? What is the audience's position, in effect, when even a massacre's aftermath and its literature of mourning is ready-made for an un-sited, compartmentalised stroll through a virtual gallery?

Spiritual service to form and idea through dialogue, and against violent terrain, is at work in composer Rinde Eckert's discursive, laterally structured piece 'Making the World Strange Again.' Eckert takes on different, alternate voices to walk us through the journey of making his performance piece *Horizon* (2006).

An interrogation of faith and its consequences and an existential vaudeville on spirituality, Horizon is Eckert's freewheeling take on Reinhold Niebuhr's The Irony of American History (1952). This tracing of the piece's origins looks at the live and virtual presences that course through the blood tracks of waking and walking thought, as the piece gets made and re-made over time. Eckert finds in his dialogic, philosophical discursion a strange beast that refuses any kind of cage. The free voice - contrary, upstart, confounded and questing – is at the root for Eckert of the artistic process in concert with and out of air with the voices in culture that demand attention, and as Stephen Duncombe expresses in the first essay of the volume 'want to do something about [the truth].' (p. 49)

Concluding the collection is an eleven-part exhortation, written with cheek and wit, from critic Aleks Sierz considering the narrative of cultural liberation that pretends censorship can be abolished simply by effecting new laws. Sierz reinforces the slippery nature of silencing, from the State and from within, from the left and the right of the political paradigm, and reminds the reader of the insidious and complicated nature of silencing as well as the difficult terrain of branding that may usurp one type of censorship for another.

Parting Glance

'The newest forms of censorship should be understood against a backdrop of constant corporate muzzling of information and the countless hidden ways in which those in powerful positions (economic, political, religious) exert undue influence on who and what gets published. Fear is not confined to the knock on the door at midnight: there is the fear of losing a job, a promotion, advertising revenue, or access to power; the fear of ridicule; the fear of appearing too militant and crusading; the fear of being denied access, perks, and prizes. [7]

Six years after the 'Out of Silence' panel that sparked this volume, the world has undergone and continues to undergo change, evolution and de-evolution. The 2nd Iraq War weathers on in new fissures, fractures and contested loyalties, global warming continues to threaten our very existence, a US Presidential election changed the face of the future of US politics forever, arts funding sput-

7   Ariel Dorfman, "Fear and the Word," *Utne* (May/June 2004)

ters and spurts along for regional theatre and experimental work, and Broadway has incurred a rebound of commercial success. The Royal Court Theatre production of *My Name is Rachel Corrie* finally received its US premiere at the Minetta Lane Theatre in New York City (fall 2006) to mixed reviews despite strong work from Meghan Beals as Rachel and sensitive direction by Alan Rickman. The passion surrounding the play's cancellation in 2006 in New York City has necessarily abated and in its place remains, pockets of determined arts activism midst a quiet generation's fears. These liquid, fluid, uncertain times are nevertheless light-struck. If civilisation is founded on progress, then art needs to be part of the story of that progress. Even unrecorded, silenced art, must find a way to be witnessed, in order for the unofficial stories to finally be heard and woven into the whole fabric of a nation's voice, character and culture. A moral society "kindles genius, civilises civilisation, casts backward all that we [hold] sacred and profane, as the flame of oil throws a shadow when shined upon by the flame of light." [8]

---

8   Ralph Waldo Emerson, "Chapter II: Civilization," The Complete Works of Ralph Waldo Emerson Volume No. 7 Society and Solitude, (1870), www.rwe.org

Modes of Censorship; Strategies of Silencing

MARVIN CARLSON

[Marvin Carlson is Sidney E. Cohn Distinguished Professor of Theatre and Comparative Literature in the Ph.D. Program at the City University of New York Graduate Center. His research and teaching interests include dramatic theory and Western European theatre history and dramatic literature, especially of the 18th, 19th, and 20th centuries. He has been awarded, among others, the George Jean Nathan Prize and a Guggenheim Fellowship. His best-known book, *Theories of the Theatre* (Cornell University Press, 1993), has been translated into five languages.]

Records of attempts to silence the theatre go back almost as far as records of the theatre itself. Among classic authors Plato most famously sought to ban poets in general and theatre-makers in particular from his ideal state, primarily because he feared the power of imitation wielded by these artists could be utilised to make the people believe in falsehoods. From classic times onward theatre has been in almost every era the target of those who wished to silence it, fearing that it would lead its audiences to consider the possibility of other truths than those supported by the groups in power. Of all the arts, theatre has been particularly subject to such attempted silencing because it is the most directly social of all the arts, assembling a public to watch stories that are based upon the experiences of their own cultural community.

Moral, political, and religious material, or some combination of these, has always been of primary concern to those who wished their own view of morality, politics, or religion to be accepted without question and who feared the theatre's potential to pose such questions or, worse still, to suggest possible alternatives, precisely those "falsehoods" so feared by Plato.

Although the motive for attempting to silence the theatre has remained much the same through the centuries, the strategies of silencing have been enormously varied and the term "censorship," the word most commonly applied to such silencing, has been so widely applied that there has been no little confusion, especially in modern times, over what in fact constitutes censorship. I would like in this essay to suggest some of the ways that both silencing and censorship have operated in the theatre and I hope to clarify some aspects of the complex nature of their operations.

Most generally when we speak of censorship in the theatre we are referring to a specific historical phenomenon. Most Western nations from the late Renaissance until very recent times, had some individual or group, the British Lord Chamberlain for example, that was officially charged with the reading of plays and with the decision of whether they would be given permission to be published or performed. Clearly such an official had the power to silence unacceptable voices, and the functioning of this power was clear and publicly recognised.

Even with this familiar and relatively straightforward operation, however, we cannot always equate the terms censorship and silencing. Plays could certainly be and often were banned outright by official censors historically, but much more often the censor would not strictly prohibit a play but would require certain rewriting or modification, sometimes apparently quite arbitrary, in order to gain permission. Sometimes certain words were not allowed, such as aristocratic or royal titles during the French Revolutionary period, or in other periods words associated with sexuality, obscenity, or profanity.

In every period where there has been official censorship there are anecdotes of censors requiring changes that seem arbitrary, even whimsical. If the author was willing to make these changes, however, the play could be approved, and one can hardly speak of an author being silenced under such conditions, though his work might be compromised or diminished. Only if the play is prevented from production entirely does it seem quite accurate to speak of silencing, and even then the situation may be far from clear. Probably the most widespread and familiar example of theatrical censorship in modern times was the banning of Ibsen's controversial *Ghosts* (1881) from most of the stages of Europe. Yet even here one can hardly say that Ibsen was silenced, since the play in its printed version circulated widely and thanks to the small but highly significant free theatres and interested public, at least in a number of major theatre capitals, were even able to see the work on stage. Except for an out-and-out banning of a play, even in printed form, total silencing has not been that common, and so my discussion will on the whole be concerned not with the strategies of silencing, but rather with the modes of censorship.

One of the reasons that the theatre has proven so troublesome to would-be censors is that it traditionally operates upon two levels, both as a written text and as a performed one. Very often censors have found to their immense frustration that a text that seemed perfectly innocuous in written form can be turned by actors, or indeed even by audiences, into something quite different. This problem was extensively debated by the French Parliament in 1849, while trying to work out whether, and under what conditions, dramatic censorship should be re-established in France. The question was a volatile one, closely related to the rapidly shifting political climate. Censorship had been an accepted part of theatrical life in France under the Old Regime, but disappeared, along with a host of other restrictions on theatre, under the Revolution in 1791. As factions appeared and solidified within the Revolution, freedom of expression suffered, and the office of censor was reinstated within two years, in 1793. Napoleon continued this office, but the liberal revolution of 1830 again abolished it. Within a few months a flood of plays celebrating the departed Emperor caused such alarm among political conservatives that the office was re-established. This pattern was repeated in 1848, when once again a turn toward political openness brought the abolishing of the censor, to be followed almost at once by complaints of theatrical excesses that required regulation. It was at this point that a Parliamentary Commission was established to examine the question in detail.

One of the most interesting strategies to emerge from this study was an official distinction between two types of censorship, which acknowledged the difference between the written and the performed play. Traditional censorship (*censure préventive*) required the text to be submitted to the censor to be cleared for production, but provided no clear mechanism for closing a play once it was approved and in production, even when that production revealed or created offensive content. Some support thus developed for what was called *censure repressive*, which would allow any work to be presented, but subject "it" to censorship after its presentation if it proved offensive or disruptive.[9] Although the traditional *censure préventive* was continued when the office was re-established in 1852, *censure repressive* continued to be advocated by some officials through the rest of the century, and there were a number of times when this practice was actively followed.

The specific extension of censorship to the performed play in *censure repressive* confirms the common impression that where censorship is concerned, the various professional theatre people, the authors, actors, and producers are the common victims of an external and often unsympathetic figure representing an alien authority. Although this has been a common arrangement, the actual operations of censorship are much more complicated. Although it is rarely seen as or spoken of as censorship, the actors and other artists who produce a play have always to a greater or lesser extent engaged in the modification of the text given to them by the author. When Hugo presented his highly controversial *Hernani* (1830), he did not have to worry about the official censor, who was abolished in 1830, but he still had to suffer a kind of censorship from the actors themselves. The play contained many passages calculated to challenge and even offend the sensibilities of conservative audience members, raised upon French neoclassic drama, and on nights when these formed a vocal majority loud protests could overwhelm the play. To Hugo's considerable irritation, some of his leading actors would simple not speak the offending lines on difficult nights.[10] More famously one of Germany's leading actresses refused to perform Ibsen's *A Doll's House* (1879) - a play which, while highly controversial, was far less often openly banned than *Ghosts* - until the dramatist created a totally different ending, one in which the heroine Nora does not leave her home and children but decides to remain.[11]

Reports of Ibsen's German ending are unclear whether the reluctance of the actress was a personal matter or a fear of rejection by the public and most likely both were involved. In more recent times, as official public censors have generally disappeared, dramatists are much more likely to see their work adjusted by their presumed allies, actors and directors, than by censors. The motives for

---

9   Marvin Carlson, "The French Censorship Enquires of 1849 and 1891," *Essays in Theatre* 5:1 (Nov., 1986), 7.

10 T. Garnier, *Histoire de Romantisme* (Paris, 1874), 107.

11 Joan Templeton, *Ibsen's Women* (Cambridge, 1997), 113.

this are many, but the most common are a desire to make the work more attractive or accessible to a presumed public or, not uncommonly, to lay more emphasis upon the interpretive artist, usually the actor or the director. The dramatist is of course especially vulnerable to this sort of influence on his work because drama is only fully realised in performance and so it is in the nature of the art that the dramatist is to a certain extent always vulnerable to those who interpret his work. The degree to which interpretative artists may change what they interpret is a subject of ongoing debate, perhaps nowhere more strikingly than in theatre, where dramatists as prominent as Samuel Beckett, Edward Albee, and Arthur Miller have gone so far as to take legal action against interpretations of their plays that they considered too far from their intentions.

All of these examples deal with something closer to the sort of censorship that insists upon rewriting a contested original rather than with actual silencing, but the latter while perhaps less commented upon in modern theatrical culture, is also widespread and often clearly detrimental to the art as a whole. Of course it is true that actors, directors, and producers, once they undertake to present a play, frequently make significant changes in it which might or might not be in harmony with the playwright's original vision, but before that process even begins there is an even more basic decision, which is whether to present the play at all. Since performance is the expected realisation of a dramatic script, no play is more effectively and totally silenced than one denied any opportunity to be offered to an audience.

I remember back in the days of the Cold War discussing the matter of censorship with Russian colleagues and expressing my sympathy for their difficulty in presenting theatre under a regime where censorship was so strong and so repressive. While not belittling that problem, they pointed out to me that American theatre artists also suffered under censorship, that the market controlled and sometimes silenced their work as effectively as any state empowered censor. As time has passed I have become more and more aware of the justice of this observation. I have witnessed the difficulties facing young dramatists in the United States today, and also suffered as a theatre-goer from a theatrical culture that is so dominated by box office pressures that the theatre scene rarely departs from offering productions of crushing similarity, repeating proven formulae endlessly and stoutly resisting innovation, a process that seems to becomes more and more dominant as theatre gains in security and visibility.

This situation is today so wide-spread, and so passively accepted that the theatre-going public seems scarcely aware of it, although it is hardly news to the young and not so young theatre artists who are deprived of voice by it. Only occasionally does the process break into more general public consciousness, when, for example, a theatre calls attention to it by publicly withdrawing its support for a proposed production in what seems clearly a response to fear of offending powerful financial backers or creating a scandal that will adversely affect the box office. The cases of *Corpus Christi* at the Manhattan Theatre Club and *My Name is Rachel Corrie* at the New York Theatre Workshop are clear examples of the relatively rare public exposure of how censorship and silencing operate in today's American theatre, not by governmental interference but by the stifling effects of commercial, economic, and social forces. In most liberal Western states the once almost ubiquitous state censors have long since disappeared, and artistic freedom held up as one of the virtues of such societies. A refusal to recognise the modes of censorship and strategies of silencing that have replaced the old restraints does a great disservice to the artists that remain silenced and to the art that we all seek to encourage and support.

Some Brief Thoughts on Censorship, Dissent and Silence

[Dan Rebellato is Professor of Contemporary Theatre at Royal Holloway, University of London. He has written widely on contemporary British theatre and is currently completing a book on theatre and globalisation. He is also an award-winning playwright whose plays include *Outright Terror Bold and Brilliant, Static*, and *Mile End.*

Johannes Birringer is a choreographer and artistic director of AlienNation Co. (www.aliennationcompany.com), and co-founder of a telematic performance collective (ADaPT). He directs the Interaktionslabor (http://interaktionslabor.de) in Göttelborn, Germany, and is also founder of DAP-Lab (http://www.brunel.ac.uk/dap) which conducts research into sensor choreography, wearable computing and soft technologies.

Marguerite Feitlowitz is the author of *A Lexicon of Terror: Argentina and the Legacies of Torture*, a *New York Times* Notable Book and Finalist for the PEN New England/L.L. Winship Prize. Her fiction, essays, and translations have appeared in *BOMB, Tri-Quarterly, Salon, Salmagundi, Les Temps Modernes, Americas*, and many other magazines, newspapers and anthologies. Currently at work on a novel, she teaches Literature at Bennington College in Vermont.

Liz Tomlin and Steve Jackson are co-artistic directors of Point Blank Theatre which they founded in 1999. As writer and dramaturg respectively they have worked on the touring productions *Dead Causes* (2000), *Nothing to Declare* (2002) and *Roses & Morphine* (2005). They were co-writers on *Operation Wonderland* (2004) which was shortlisted for the prestigious critics circle award of 'Most Promising New Playwright'. The company's two new productions, *Evening with Psychosis* and *Landfill* received performances in 2008.]

DAN REBELLATO: The current incarnation of censorship seems to derive from a belief that one shouldn't offend. Political groups demand the withdrawal of *My Name is Rachel Corrie* (2005). Religious groups demand an end to shows like *Jerry Springer – The Opera* (2003) or *Bezhti* (2005) on the grounds that they offend their most deeply-held beliefs. 'We have a right not to be offended,' they declare. They don't. Rights are important things; they have to be grounded in action, defended by legislation, they must be philosophically rigorous, and they impose duties on others. There is no reasonable philosophical defence for a right not to be offended; the duties it imposed on others would be intolerable; any legislation that upheld it would be disastrous. Characteristically, rights are asserted through the language of ownership: '*I have the right'*, sing the shrill voices of the censors; '*it's my right'.* This linguistic privatisation of human rights corresponds to the individualising of politics: the individual has become so hy-pertrophied that we are all encouraged to believe that no one has the right to criticise us or even engage us in debate. Isn't calling it a right, in this instance, just a fancy way of saying '*I want*'? No one can invent a 'right' just because they wish it existed. Rights are important because they are general and – crucially – more general than the threats to our world. They are prior to corporate power, to military rapacity, to the global market, and remain a standing critique of those forces. In any case, a right not to be offended could not work, if for no other reason than the idea itself is so stupid that it offends against my deeply-held belief in human reason. A right not to be offended would offend me, thus arguing itself out of existence.

JOHANNES BIRRINGER: In the old days, one would write a manifesto against censorship and demand, as the Futurists did, the liberation of language. Parole in liberta. The manifesto writer, like a good Dadaist, assumes the free-dom to write and to expose a vision. The tone of the manifesto is revolutionary. The new theatre for the scientific age would be a total theatre, a synthetic mod-el realised by new technologies. For the last hundred years, the vision of the Futurists has progressed steadily, and as with all successful utopias, its secrets have been kept. The question of censorship is no longer disturbing the arts, as all artistic productions and the creative industries are embedded in the secrets. Truth and justice are defended by advocacy groups and human rights organisa-tions, but artists are neither advocates nor legal advisers. At best, they help to sustain the illusion that there is a freedom of the imagination, *parole in liberta,* and not just the average cynical "mocking culture" fostered by reality TV and its spectacles of (self) humiliation. In the developed countries, where the mocking-culture is produced to be exported globally, the synthetic theatre means ubiquitous computing and globalising network technologies -- our utopia embedded in digital informational technology. The cybernetic paradigm aims at a world of perfect informational flux. Within the operational system of our utopia, there are secrets that are kept from the public and then there are public secrets -- secrets that the public chooses to keep safe from itself. The late Dadaist artists may try to create noise to disturb a world without noise and the operational system of self-regulation which sustains social and political institutions, along with the mocking-culture. But how do we know that our imagination has failed? What to do with the noise that we don't know we know, or cannot acknowledge to know?

MARGUERITE FEITLOWITZ: One of the many terrible things about censorship is that it attempts to reduce the world to two categories: THAT WHICH IS ALLOWED and THAT WHICH IS FORBIDDEN, a binary opposition controlled by censors themselves. But the world is full of specifics, brimming with detail, nuance, and contradiction, events, perceptions, metamorphoses. It is exactly this abundance, this energy, that censors want us to ignore, want us to train ourselves to ignore. There is nothing so singular as a human imagination, and nothing so capable of integrating peoples of different origins, histories and cultures. Why else would it be, that during the Latin-American dictatorships of the 1960s-1970s, there were at least sixty different Spanish-language adaptations of Sophocles' *Antigone* (442 B.C.) Over the torturous 20th century, *Antigone* was revived, translated and adapted in virtually every situation of occupation, war and terror, from the pogroms of the early 1900s to Kosovo. In times of mayhem and suffering, a work thousands of years old became necessary. Far from being alone at our desks, we have the example of writers who lived before us, of writers who right now risk their lives to find their own words for what they themselves register of the world around them. Nor should our literary compatriots do without our efforts to protect them. Just a click away on the internet is PEN's Freedom to Write campaign. Censorship strives to make us dull, indifferent to the stream of life lest we make a ripple. Censors do not want us to love the world, to cherish life. But we do. And we will not be dissuaded, or dulled into a simulacrum of thought, feeling, or expression.

LIZ TOMLIN and STEVE JACKSON: To begin with a definition of *attitudinising* as meaning 'adopting an opinion for effect' clarifies that what is not being proposed here is that artists who dissent in the current climate are wasting their time. That is quite a different issue. What is being put into question is the sincerity of that dissent; the suspicion that the privileged, educated position of artists in our society makes opposition to that very society an intellectual pretension as opposed to a genuine desire. Too many artists are quick to claim marginality and hardship, when their lifestyle, whatever its difficulties, is predominantly a matter of choice, rather than necessity. There are however artists who acknowledge appalling divisions in our society and attempt to make their own enviable position within it justifiable by opposing such a condition with all the means at their disposal. This dissent may take the form of active intervention designed to share the skills and opportunities for self-expression a little more fairly than society currently allows, or it may be an artistic expression of opposition which is designed to stimulate, at the very least, an awareness of the problems we perceive within the status quo, and, at best, a desire to effect change.

The efficacy of such dissent is undeniably questionable, given the marginal nature of the live arts in today's society. We suspect, however, that in the current, political climate artists are not alone, and that the obliteration of meaningful opposition to an untouchable global capitalism is almost complete. However, if withholding dissent is synonymous with collusion then dissent remains, for me, the only honest option. Far from 'attitudinising' such a position has become unpopular and problematic to sustain an artistic climate which increasingly mirrors the political status quo in its championing of a reactionary (as opposed to a radical) postmodernism, which labels oppositional politics as no longer relevant or fashionable.

Our show, *Dead Causes* (a meditation on *Antigone*), depicts a protagonist, who protests and a chorus that dreams of it. However, our post-modern chorus is cowardly, complacent and ultimately decide that dissent is an unfashionable inconvenience. Like our chorus there are artists who dream of radical intervention (like so many politicians) when in reality their work might well uphold a reactionary status quo. Nowhere is this self-deception more evident than in live art practice where narcissism and private concern proclaims itself radical. In a climate where repressive statutes are declared radical interventions, this begins to make sense. Sadly, this appropriation and censorship of language of opposition is now upheld by many artists on behalf of the New Right. We must apologise for all left wing discourse (it is redundant). The dominant language of dissent is now fashionable but certainly not oppositional. To quote from *Dead Causes* – 'Revolution is nothing but a chain of coffee shops.'

Clearly, real dissent becomes harder to manifest in such a reactionary climate and artists like anyone else become self-censoring. It amazes us how people now apologise for referring to socialism. We replied to an arts newsgroup letter which attacked work identifying itself as socially engaged. Our response defined 'socially engaged' as naturally taking a position opposed to uncritical, unconcerned or self-interested artistic practice. Some artists were incensed that the term should be used at all; some claimed we are all socially engaged. In much the same way we can wrestle over what's meant by dissent, some artists might claim to do it, we all do it, or that nobody should do it all.

In artistic practice the ailing language of dissent is used in very distinct ways by artists of the left who increasingly self-censor or are censored by the market for their out-moded position, and by the artists of the new right where it becomes a marketing tool for a post-modern chic. In *Dead Causes*, dissent is what happens when you refuse to go on-message.

1

Censorship, So What?

New Concerns for the New Informational Age

STEPHEN DUNCOMBE

[Stephen Duncombe teaches history and politics of media and culture at M.I.T., and formerly taught at the Gallatin School of New York University. He is the author of *Notes from Underground: Zines and the Politics of Alternative Culture* (1997) and editor of the *Cultural Resistance Reader* (2002). His most recent book is *Dream: Re-Imagining Progressive Politics in an Age of Fantasy* (2007). Duncombe is also a life-long political activist, co-founding the Lower East Side Collective and working as an organiser for the NYC chapter of the international direct action group Reclaim the Streets.]

There is a paradox at the heart of the contemporary concern with censorship: we know what we're not supposed to know. We know about the flag draped coffins returning from Iraq and Afghanistan, the early warnings about 9/11 ignored by the Bush administration, and the tragic drama of Rachel Corrie, the American peace activist killed by an Israeli bulldozer. More to the point: we know that the photo images, news stories and theatre plays about these events have been banned or censored. This paradox is institutionalised in anti-censorship organisations like Project Censored. Every year for the past three decades this respected, university-based group generates a well researched, informative list of the top censored stories of the year. They then publicise this list through their website, an award-winning annual report, and press releases. This list of censored stories is then routinely picked up and broadcast by alternative newsweeklies and radio programs, and even a few national news outlets. So are these stories censored?[1]

This is not to say that government agencies and corporate entities don't routinely *try* to censor information. To find evidence of intent one merely has to consider the restrictions placed on the press during the Iraqi and Afghanistan wars. Pictures of dead US soldiers are forbidden, and even images of soldiers' coffins being returned were not allowed to be printed until the change of administrations in 2009. But in an age of 24-7 global media, and the increasing ubiquity of the Internet, home video cameras, text messaging, streaming video and pod casts it is increasingly difficult to *succeed* at censorship. Video footage shot by Iraqi insurgents of lethal attacks on US troops are loaded up on to You-Tube, while the ubiquity of digital cameras and photo-ready mobile phones in the hands of military and airport personnel made a mockery of the Pentagon's ban on pictures of the remains of returning soldiers. If I type "censored stories" into Google nearly 200,000 sources come up to choose from.

This seeming easy accessibility to ostensibly censored stories poses a troubling question for artists, intellectuals and civil libertarians, i.e. those of us traditionally worried about censorship. Is censorship still a problem? Or is the traditional liberal concern with censorship merely a comfortable anachronism, a phantom threat distracting us from far greater challenges to our understanding of reality, the value of the truth, and the relationship between power and knowledge?

In order to go forward with answering these questions we need to back up and see how we arrived at our concern with censorship in the first place. When we think of censorship we usually think of it in terms of State (or Church) authority squelching free expression. This is not surprising, for this is how it was understood in one of the first, and most famous, defenses of free expression in the west: John Milton's *Areopagitica*. Milton is better known today as an artist, the blank verse poet of *Paradise Lost* (1667), but he also wrote widely on politics and even served as an official in the revolutionary government that followed

---

1   http://www.projectcensored.org To be fair, Project Censored offers up a disclaimer stating that
there list is not of stories censored per se, but are "under reported."

the English Civil War. This new government, however, adopted restrictive practices of the old and in 1644 Milton drafted an objection to their censorious licensing act. He argued that a free flow of ideas — even wrong ideas — are necessary for the thought, debate, and expression that might lead to ultimate
Truth. It's a daring and quirky argument — he baits the would-be Protestant
censors by likening them to their enemies: the censors of the Catholic inquisi-
tion, yet defends freedom of expression for Protestants only — but the *Areopagitica* defined the debate for anti-censorship activists for centuries to come:
truth is the goal, unfettered access to information is the means, and any restrictions on the free flow of ideas must be protested and resisted.[2]

Censorship, and the fight against it, took on new importance in the age of
Democratic Revolutions that followed the English Civil War. Essential to the
idea of eighteenth century democracy was the ideal of the well-informed citizen. Citizens needed open access to information in order to make intelligent
decisions, come to rational conclusions, and thus govern themselves. Without
freedom of information there could be no democracy. For the founding fathers
of the United States, censorship was a palpable issue as the British Crown frequently censored newspapers and shut down publishers who did not toe the
line. The first paper published in the colonies: Benjamin Harris's *Publick Occur-
rences: Both Foreign and Domestick*, issued on September 25, 1690, was also the
first censored newspaper in the colonies — it was suppressed by British authorities within a few days. However, other publications with longer runs soon followed and the ideas of the new American republic were fought out in papers
and pamphlets long before any shot was fired during the revolution. Thomas
Paine's *Common Sense* (1776) may be the most famous pamphlet of the era (it is
estimated that one in five to one in ten colonists read it) but it was just one of
many publications discussing the right to rebellion and debating questions of
sovereignty.[3]

These theories of democracy and the practical lessons learned in the fight
for independence led directly to the First Amendment of the Bill of Rights of the
US Constitution:

---

2   John Milton, "Areopagitica," in *Complete English Poems, Of Education, Areopagitica*, Gordon
    Campbell, ed. (London: Everyman, 1909)

3   Bernard Bailyn, ed. *Pamphlets of the American Revolution, 1750-1776*, Vol. 1 (Cambridge: Harvard
    University Press, 1965).

Congress shall make no law respecting an establishment of religion, or prohibiting the free exercise thereof; or abridging the freedom of speech, or of the press; or the right of the people peaceably to assemble, and to petition the government for a redress of grievances.

Freedom of the press and concern with censorship is part of our political heritage.

Over the past two centuries we've extended our definition of who is part of the polis to encompass more than merely elite, white men, and our understanding of what constitutes censorship has kept pace, expanding to include new forms of informational control. Early in the past century the journalist A.J. Liebling wrote that "freedom of the press belongs to those who own one." In other words: censorship works economically as well as politically. The formal right to freedom of expression means little if you cannot afford to do anything other than rant from a soapbox. In recent years the photocopy machine, computer desktop publishing, and the Internet have drastically lowered the cost and simplified the skills necessary for the production and distribution of information, but there are still plenty of people in the world who do not have access to even these means of media manufacture.

It is also important to consider self-censorship. Just because one has the right to speak, and even the means to disseminate those words, it does not necessarily follow that one has the confidence or nerve to do it. It is foolish to expect those who society has deemed second-class citizens by reasons of race, gender, class or age, and those who have been ill-educated or actively discouraged from thinking on their own, to express themselves with the ease and confidence of those accustomed to being regularly listened to. There is no need to censor someone too unsure of themselves to speak up.

But these definitions of censorship, old and new, rest upon a number of suppositions. First, that there is a scarcity of information, its every expression is precious, and if it is censored it will be lost. Second, that there is *intrinsic* value in being exposed to a diversity of ideas and a range of facts, and with this information we can – and want to – reach some sort of truth. And finally, underlying all concerns with censorship is a faith that, in the words of Jesus (or his 1611 King James interpreters): "Ye shall know the Truth, and the Truth shall make you free." That is: truth makes something happen.

At one time there was a legitimate basis for these suppositions. For millennia the informational economy *was* one of scarcity and information *was* precious. In Ancient China literacy was aligned with power within the state bureaucracy and thus reading and writing were severely limited. In Medieval Europe the Catholic Church controlled access to the Bible, thereby managing the whole cosmology of the common person with this monopoly on The Word. As with any other controlled and coveted resource those with access to information had power over those without. The Protestant Reformation, in this light, was as much an informational revolution as a religious and political one. The Protestant demand to be able to read and interpret the Bible for oneself struck at the heart of the Church's power. It's no coincidence that assaults upon the monopoly of knowledge like the Protestant Reformation were followed by assaults on the monopoly of power like the English Civil War and the American and French Revolutions. When the monopolies over information crumbled the structures of power that were built upon them collapsed too. They were integrally connected: knowledge equaled power.

But we live in a vastly different informational world: a world of info-abundance. This is an historical process which began with the struggle for access to The Word in the sixteenth century, picked up power with the steam press and universal education in the early nineteenth century, and has arrived today with Google and Wikipedia. We still need to guard against censorship, especially in this age of perma-war and "emergency measures," as the old world never completely disappears, but the forces of globalisation, which brings with it the spread of communication and information technologies that even the corporate and political elite themselves cannot contain, has also nullified many of the traditional concerns about censorship. It is impossible to monopolise information in the way the powers-that-be once routinely did. The truth is out there, on the Internet, and it's easy to access.

But...knowing the truth doesn't have the same power it once did.

At no other time in history have more people had more access to information. In no other era has it been easier to publish and disseminate one's ideas. It stands to reason that we should be entering the Golden Age of democracy and egalitarianism, with hierarchies of power laid as flat as the structures of knowledge now seem. But this is not the case. National and global economic inequality has actually increased in the past few decades, and the United States has taken its place as arguably the most powerful empire the world has ever seen. Something has gone terribly wrong with the equation of knowledge equaling power; it no longer adds up. Faced with this seeming disconnect between an equality of knowledge and inequality in matters political and economic, we need to ask a different set of questions and consider a different set of problems.

Our problem is no longer one of access to facts. Today we are awash in facts – but what we often lack is the meaning with which to make sense of them. Picking up the business section of *The New York Times* I read that unemployment is up and so is the Stock Market. Is this a good economy or a bad one? To be honest, I really don't know. I don't know because although I have access to the facts I have no way to order them, no way to give coherence to the data I'm provided each and every day. What I need is a sort of meaning map that can help guide me through the data swamp, pointing out that this is an important fact here, letting me know that I can overlook that one over there, reassuring me that this is a solid fact that I'm perched on right now, and offering a key for interpreting the bit of information right in front of me. Otherwise I'm lost, slowly sinking into the info-muck.

In recent years conservatives have been doing a much better job than liberals at creating these sort of meaning maps.[4] I may not want to follow their direction, but I do have to respect that they have a sense-making plan: government is bad, markets are good, strength is respected, God is essential. You can come across almost any errant fact and this meaning map will help you to find your way to some sort of coherent sense. People are poor? It's because they have become dependent upon the government. Too much sex on the airwaves? Not enough God in the schools. Threatened by terrorists? Invade a country. And so on.

The conservatives have also learned to do something else: use their meaning maps to direct people toward some sort of activity. It's not enough to know how to order the information I come across, I have to know where to go with it. Conservatives provide a clear direction with which to move with their meaning: into the church or the Republican Party. Liberals, on the other hand, have made

4   George Lakoff has been working on this problem, attempting to create a meaning map – or frame – that gives coherence to progressive politics. George Lakoff, *Moral Politics*, 2nd edition (Chicago: University of Chicago Press, 2002) and, more recently, *Don't Think of an Elephant* (Vermont: Chelsea Green Publishing, 2004)

a fetish of following their own paths in recent years. In fact, they are currently arguing that this inability to agree upon any one direction is the strength of their party: a commitment to diversity and debate. Consequently, as a liberal, you are not provided with coherent meaning. You make up your own sense – or you wander aimlessly not making sense at all.

There's another problem we face today: the detachment of action from information. In 1881 Frederick Douglass wrote a memoir in which he recalled learning to read as a young slave. Douglass remembers how his master's kindly and naïve wife taught him how to read by parsing out words from the Bible. Inevitably, however, his master finds out about these lessons and lays down the law to both his wife and Douglass. "Learning will spoil the best nigger in the world," the master lectures. "If he learns to read the Bible it will forever unfit him to be a slave....If you teach him how to read, he'll want to know how to write. And this accomplished, he'll be running away with himself."[5] Which, of course, is exactly what Douglass does: running North to freedom to become an anti-slavery activist and one of America's greatest orators.

What's remarkable to me about this passage is the *assumption* that both Douglass and the slave master, with all their differences in race and power, share: that thought leads to action. They, like many people of their time and before, fervently believed that knowing something meant acting upon it. It's only with this understanding, for instance, that the hodge-podge of freedoms guaranteed in the First Amendment make any coherent sense. To the framers of the Constitution the freedom of religion, press and assembly – that is: *belief, thought and action* – were of a whole, inextricably linked to one another. This was common sense.

In our times, however, it is not. Belief, thought and action have become separate and distinct entities that are no longer interlinked. Why? Partly because of the ascendancy and domination of another shared map of meaning and activity: consumerism and spectatorship. With the growth of the consumer/spectator economy we have learned another model of relating to ideas and expressions, to facts and data. We watch or buy them. Our activity vis a vis ideas is limited to our consumption or possession (and paying the cable bill). In

---

5   Frederick Douglass, *The Life and Times of Frederick Douglass,* (London: Christian Age Office, 1887) p. 79

46

short, information has become a commodity – a package we consume, enjoy, horde or throw away. In fact, going to an art exhibit or sitting down in front of the TV is usually considered a relief or release from activity: it is *leisure*. Parenthetically, this is why much of what is referred to as "political art" is anything but political. Instead of moving us toward action, it safely binds politics up into a nice, pristine package to be "appreciated."[6]

Perhaps the problem we face is even greater than this. It just may be that we, as a people, don't really care about de-censoring facts, uncovering reality, or discovering the truth nowadays. In fact, we may very well prefer fiction – as long as it is well told. At one point, not too long ago, a majority of Americans believed that Saddam Hussein was directly connected to the terrorist attacks on September 11th. Some of this had to do with state propaganda and the unrelenting repetition of this spurious connection by every top official in the Bush administration. But this propaganda was created with an astute understanding of how we frequently find comfort in compelling narratives and change the channel when confronted with messy facts. If Osama bin Laden is elusive and al-Qaeda ephemeral, Saddam Hussein and the easily recognised nation of Iraq seemed made for prime-time trouncing. When the Iraqis didn't welcome us as liberators and catching Saddam proved anti-climactic, no matter: there was always *Saving Private Lynch*. My hunch is that many people knew that the Bush administration was spinning out a fantasy and didn't care. They liked the story.

It's not as if the truth was hard to access: NPR, the *New York Times*, any international news site on the Internet – even the CIA – issued long, detailed reports making the case that there was no relationship (other than a hostile one) between al-Qaeda and Saddam Hussein. But people didn't want to know the facts; they wanted a story that helped them make sense of their world. Maybe this is basic human modus operandi. It's no accident that Jesus' commandment that "The Truth shall make ye free" was set within the compelling narrative of the New Testament. Jesus rarely lectured; instead he told parables. Perhaps this penchant for the story over the fact is the more modern result of being weaned on endless movies, ads, sitcoms and pop songs, each of which tell a mini-story. The result is the same: people desire engrossing narratives not revealed reality.

6 The cathartic consumption of 'political' art was something that both the theorist Walter Benjamin and the playwright Bertolt Brecht were deeply worried about.

There is a liberal, Enlightenment faith that people are out there waiting for the Truth to be revealed, and that once people have access to this truth, the scales will fall from their eyes and they will see reality as it truly is (and, *of course*, agree with us). But revealing reality doesn't amount to much if no one is paying attention. And the state, church or corporation doesn't even need to censor when people prefer to watch the lie.

Central to the struggle against censorship is the belief that it is critical that people have access to the truth. What I am suggesting is that today we do have this access...and that it doesn't really matter. We don't know what do with the truth, we don't act on it once we have it, and we may even find comfort in lies. This doesn't mean we are irrevocably screwed, but it does mean that we have to think differently about the problem. If we are sincerely concerned about information and power then we need to move past (though not abandon) our older concern with censorship *per se* and instead look seriously and think critically about what sorts of controls operate when people have full access to information. This is what I've tried to do, in a cursory manner, above. Following my own advice, however, I don't think it's sufficient to end this essay with a revelation of the Truth that the truth doesn't really matter, so here are some suggestions for what we might do to make the truth mean something again.

We need to create new meaning maps. There's another word for these maps, one we usually don't use in polite society, it's called *ideology*. Ideology, with its connection to the lockstep thinking of Fascism or Communism, has negative connotations in a society like our own. But ideology need not be dictated from above, or hardened into dogma, it can be generated from below through a process of debate and discussion and it can be modified to fit different contexts. (This is something that both the Italian Communist Antonio Gramsci and the American Pragmatist John Dewey understood.)[7] Belief does not have to be divorced from thought. Creating a democratic ideology – and creating ideology democratically – will not be easy, but it is necessary, for without it you are left without meaning, power or direction.

We need to reconnect thought to action by creating institutions that facilitate this progression. Having the facts or knowing the truth means nothing if

---

7   John Dewey, *The Public and Its Problems* (New York: Henry Holt & Co. 1927); Antonio Gramsci, *Selections from the Prison Notebooks*, Quinton Hoare and Geoffrey Nowell Smith, ed. and trans. (New York: International Publishers, 1971).

people don't know what to do with these things. OK, the war in Iraq is an unmitigated disaster. We now know this. But without a structure that operationalises that truth into "peaceable assemblies and petitions to the government" (to quote the U.S. Constitution) this knowledge is impotent. In practical terms this means that all of us who are passionately interested in the truth need to take it to the next step by acting upon it. And, I would argue, one of the most important tasks in acting upon the truth is setting up political institutions that help other people act upon it as well.

We need to make information into an activity. The digital revolution has opened up previously unimaginable possibilities for expressing ideas and then disseminating them. While this isn't a solution in itself, it's a start – for it moves information out of the realm of something you consume and into a thing you produce. This Do-It-Yourself ethos, shared by underground musicians, fanzine writers and colonial pamphleteers, has ramifications outside the media. The division of labor of producer/consumer, creator/spectator, politician/citizen reproduces the hierarchies that the informational revolution was supposed to undermine. An activity of amateur production challenges these very divisions and hierarchies by making, in the words of Walter Benjamin, "readers or spectators into collaborators."[8] Once information becomes something you can do yourself, it's also a much smaller step toward demanding direct participation in other arenas, be it DIY politics or DIY economics.

Finally, and most importantly, we need to make our own compelling narratives about the truth. Intellectuals and artists of a liberal, enlightened bent love to refer to the quote from the Bible that I, myself, quoted above: "Ye shall know the Truth, and the Truth shall make you free." To them, it's an assurance that knowing the truth in itself is some sort of power. But what I find revealing about Jesus' words is the nature of the truth he is referring to. Truth, for Jesus (and his interpreters), is not a fact or a bit of data, it's a story. The Truth is the story of

---

8   Walter Benjamin, "The Author as Producer," in the *Cultural Resistance Reader*, Stephen Duncombe, ed. (New York and London: Verso, 2002) p. 78. It's also useful to consider that John Milton, when arguing against censorship, was not arguing for access to truth as a thing. Instead he believed that one needed access to ideas in order to engage in a dynamic discussion which might lead us to truth. "Truth," he writes, "is a streaming fountain." That is, truth is a process – not something fixed and given; truth arises out of a dialogue -- not received from a monologue.

God told through the narratives of the Old Testament and the parables and bi-ography of Jesus in the New Testament. It is, as it's been called, *the story of stories*. We can learn from this. Those of us who are concerned with the power of knowledge must never be satisfied with mere access to information. We must weave stories around it, make art of it, organise protests about it. It must be communicated in new ways and marketed so that it sells. It must be yelled from the mountaintop. If we really care about the truth then we need to make it into something people want to pay attention to and want to do something about. For truth makes no one free by itself.

The Censor in the Mirror

KEN URBAN

[Ken Urban's plays have been produced and developed by Moving Arts, Lincoln Center Theater Directors Lab, Soho Rep, Target Margin, Son of Semele Ensemble, and The Chocolate Factory. His plays can be found in *New York Theatre Review*, *Plays and Playwrights 2002*, and *The Best Women's Stage Monologues 2001*. He is the Artistic Director of The Committee and he makes music as Occurrence. He teaches at Harvard University.]

For those of us opposed to the practice, Anthony Neilson's play *The Censor* (1997) depicts a familiar unmasking: the revelation of the censor's hypocrisy. In Neilson's play, the lead character spends his days in a basement office watching films that he will ban because of their pornographic depiction of sex. He is in a loveless marriage and has toiled in this job for six years, still waiting for a fabled promotion; in other words, he is the picture of normality. But when a female filmmaker challenges his ruling on her sexually explicit film, the play's events reveal the censor's dark secret: he is impotent. The cause of his ailment is intense shame stemming from his fantasy to see a woman defecate. The man who catalogs sexual acts in order to ban them is a secret lover of scat.

We who oppose censorship have a definite image of those who support it. The men and women who wish to restrict and repress, we imagine, are they themselves repressed and restricted. In this Freudian formulation, the banned sexual imagery reveals a desire hidden deep in the censor's heart; the censored political content contains a truth that the forces of censorship must eradicate before it spreads like a contagion. It is undoubtedly a singular pleasure seeing the self-proclaimed guardians of decency and fairness revealed as indecent and hypocritical. Understanding censorship as the purview of others unwilling to face reality is seductive. Its seduction comes precisely because it locates the forces of censorship as existing outside of us. Those of us who champion free speech defend it from those who wish to suppress it: a noble battle of the good against the misguided, the Left against the Right.

Certainly, the history of censorship is one of artists being persecuted by forces who despise a work for content that is deemed un-representable. However, institutional censorship, while by no means extinct, is fading quickly into distant memory in England and America. The Lord Chamberlain's Office ceased censoring the British stage in 1968, and the operations of the once-mysterious British Board of Film Classification are now increasingly transparent, even liberal in its ratings, since 1999. In the United States, a country always slightly uneasy with institutional mandates, calls for censorship do not largely come from government, but from individuals and grass-root groups, typically speaking on behalf of religious organisations. Recent controversies over plays like *My Name is Rachel Corrie* (2006), *Corpus Christi* (1998) and *The Vagina Monologues* (1996) stem from perceived slights at the state of Israel, the Catholic Church or a sense of propriety that forbids public use of the V-word. The result is a small but sometimes-noisy set of individuals picking up placards, writing letters and making phone calls, and theatres, in some cases, capitulating to the demands. In the case of *Rachel Corrie* in New York City, such tactics were initially successful, but it was a short-lived victory. Quickly following its cancellation at New York Theatre Workshop in the spring of 2006, the play opened with little fanfare for a commercial Off-Broadway production in the fall. I image plays like *Rachel Corrie* and *Corpus Christi* will be read by bemused future generations who will find them so inoffensive they will wonder what all the fuss was about.

Truth is, time is never on the side of the censor. The forces of censorship always fail in the long term. The controversial image, the impolitic film, the shocking play: they eventually win, no longer ostracised, but circulated, taught, even canonised. Hindsight has a way of making those who call for censorship appear out-of-step, a throwback to a less enlightened time, the future punch line for a joke. The truth is American and British theatre artists rarely worry about being censored. We have been granted complete freedom, at least in theory. In Neilson's play, for instance, a woman shits on a newspaper for the erotic pleasure of an impotent censor, and no one in the British theatre world bats an eye. In those rare cases when censorious picketers come out of the woodwork, the result is more often a rise in ticket sales and a ten-fold increase in the cultural cache of the play.

There are notable exceptions, of course. The closing of *Behzti* (*Dishonour*) by Gurpreet Kaur Bhatti at Birmingham Rep in December 2004 because of the violent protests of some local Sikh groups is a reminder of how conservative religious groups can still organise to censorious effect when a work is perceived to slight their faith. Despite the theatre's attempts to reach out to the local Sikh community before the show's opening (or perhaps, in retrospect, because of those very efforts), the protesters succeeded in terrorising the theatre. The Rep, no longer feeling they could protect the audience or the actors, cancelled the remaining shows of the run. Though the play has many supporters, it remains unclear if Bhatti will ever allow future productions of the play. The case of *Rachel Corrie* in New York initially appeared to be a similar victory for censorship. The production at New York Theatre Workshop was "postponed" (the theatre's term) because of imagined protests that they felt would occur should they pursue the production. The furor created by the cancellation made many quickly rush to the play's defense, even when some questioned the play's artistic merit. This case is more emblematic of the current function of censorship in American theatre.

Instead of dispiriting, cries for censorship actually embolden theatre makers, for it makes us feel alive. When you work in an art form so often marginalised by mainstream culture, if the work is actually noticed, discussed and debated, it energises the whole of the community. As a result, we love the battle against the censor. Even while censorship is often no longer a real threat, we treasure the idea of offending the blue hairs in the hopes they will want to suppress our artistic freedom. The battle against the oppressive outsider remains alive because like any good sentimental fiction, it comforts us.

But I fear this romantic model of censorship is far from accurate or comprehensive. The dominant strand of censorship thriving in American theatre is far more nebulous, far more diffuse, and far more oppressive. The social process of censorship is alive and well in theatre, but its primary vehicle does not come from outside, but instead the source is ourselves. The most dangerous censor is the person we see reflected in the mirror. Every time I subjugate art to economics, or decide that I cannot write that kind of play because I am a certain kind of person, or force a play into a prescribed or expected statement of meaning, an act of censorship has taken place. We have internalised the censorious impulse and the result is the wide-scale foreclosing of our theatrical imagination.

As a playwright and director working in the US, primarily in New York, I observe three major sources contributing to the proliferation of self-censorship in the American theatre: the economics of playwriting, the reification of identity and the reduction of art to argument or message. This essay will elaborate these three areas of concern and provides a possible solution to this dilemma.

Economics: We live in a moment when to imagine an alternative to capitalism feels almost laughable. Capitalism's grasp feels almost complete, and in the arts, there is a widespread embrace of the corporate model. The playwright is always writing for a marketplace, for an industry that spends big money for a show that is seen by relatively few people when compared to a movie. But as theatre producers and artistic directors see budgets tighten and tighten, their aesthetic choices grow increasingly conservative. This is hardly news. (Playwright Jeffrey M. Jones has written convincingly about the impact of subscribers on the economics of theatre and presents a possible solution to attracting subscribers to "difficult" theatre.9) But what is especially depressing is how this situation affects new writing. Before even beginning a new play, we sit in front of the pad or computer screen and think, "Well, my agent says that comedies with five people or less are hot right now." "This play requires eight actors, but I know a theatre won't pay that many actors, so maybe it really is a three person play." "Theatres are wary of politics in the theatre unless it is written by a journalist or a Brit, so...." And so on and so on. The marketplace appears so closed off to anything that doesn't fit a specific prescription that young writers find themselves foreclosing possibilities before they even begin: "I will wait to write that play about Iraq until I have a few successes under my belt." The result is the marketplace has censored the creative impulse, but the economic forces barely lift a finger, for the squashing desire has been internalised by a generation of

---

9   See Jeffrey M. Jones's essays, "Geezer Theatre" (in *Performing Arts Journal*, September 1994: 123-133) and "Thinking About Writing About Thinking About New Plays: Or, How the Visual Arts Audiences Got Comfortable with Radical Innovation, While Theatre Audiences Didn't" (in *American Theatre*, October 2005).

writers who cannot imagine the possibilities of the Off-Broadway movement of the 1960s and '70s.

Identity: While undoubtedly identity politics continues to allow a diversity of new voices to enter American theatre, the drawback is that identity has now been reified to the point that abstract and constructed ideas like race and ethnicity appear as truths beyond question. In the theatre, a bastardised identity politics rears its ugly head at the level of authorial expectation. If you are, for instance a Black writer, there is a specific kind of play you are expected to write; certain subjects must be raised in certain ways. At the 2007 No Passport Dreaming the Americas conference at the Martin Segal Theatre Center in New York, audience members spoke passionately about the demands of artistic directors and theatre professionals to make a play "fit" the identity of the writer: "Wouldn't this play be better if the family was Latino?" (Though if you are surprised that an Artistic Director would say something ridiculous, you'd better brace yourself if you plan to stay in this occupation.) I have been on the flip side of the coin. As a white writer who often writes roles for non-white actors, I have felt forbidden to tackle certain subjects. When I began *Sense of an Ending*, my play about the Rwandan genocide, I envisioned it as a play for an all Black cast. But when it came to writing the first draft, even though I saw the play in my head one way, I felt compelled to make the main character a white journalist. No one told me that a Black cast was off limits, but I felt it was. As a result, the play languished for a bit because I knew something wasn't right. It was only after I stopped censoring myself that the play took off, when I ceased worrying about what was responsible or appropriate, and just wrote and saw where it took me.

The Message: I have never learned anything from a talkback or post-show discussion. That's not the say I don't enjoy them, or that they aren't interesting. But in truth, if a theatre experience is really powerful, it silences conversation, at least for a few hours after the performance. In the world of play development, however, talkbacks are supposed to serve a higher function for the playwright. That is, they are supposed to help playwrights "fix" their play. But it is an operation doomed to failure. The reason: plays aren't things to be fixed. New play development is obsessed with the idea that a play has a message or an argument that it is putting forward to an audience and the goal is to make that statement as clear as possible. This has a trickle-down effect on audiences and new writers. I am always amazed when I am working with student playwrights and they express a desire to tidy up all the loose ends. They feel a need to reduce their plays to a singular idea or statement. They look at me in terror when I suggest it is the asking that matters and that if they already know the answer to the question, the play will suffer as a result. In a world as fractured and complicated as ours, our theatre needs to reflect that and we cannot censor our imaginations all in the hopes of the unified argument that will sum it all up. A play is not the transcription of a nice rational argument. My advice is to leave that to the debate team.

These three areas that create an environment of self-censorship operate, of course, in mutually reinforcing ways. This outline merely serves to capture what I see as the greatest threat to new writing. It is not the lack of opportunities, the conservatism of theatre institutions or the paucity of money alone. Yes, these are all real concerns, but it is the closing of the theatrical imagination that must be resisted at all costs, the internalisation of these censorious impulses fostered by these material conditions. We can complain endlessly about the state of theatre in this country, but it is crucial to recognise our hand in creating this environment.

I am optimistic about the possibility of resisting since I think right now is a great time to be a playwright, despite all the hardships. There are a lot of small theatre companies across the US that are interested in producing new plays by new writers, not merely throwing together a reading series in order to "develop" new plays. More and more playwrights are producing themselves, forming theatre companies and getting their work seen. But I am also a realist. The economics of the theatre will not change in the foreseeable future, hackneyed conceptions of identity are unlikely to disappear, and the demand for coherence and narrative is as strong as ever. What are we to do then?

Foremost, we must forge a path that resists both cynicism and naïveté. Cynicism turns any possibility for change into something unattainable. Though cynics long for change, they deny even imagining its realisation. That, of course, is a sure-fire recipe for unhappiness. And honestly, who among us really wants to dwell in the naïve's state of excessive simplicity? Instead, writers must cultivate what German theorist Peter Sloterdijk calls kynicism, a state of cheekiness in the face of earnestness. For Sloterdijk, it is Diogenes, not Plato, who should be lionised:

Diogenes who picks his nose, farts and masturbates in the face of the Platonic ideal.[10] I do not, obviously, mean we should literally act as Diogenes did in the Athenian marketplace. For playwrights hoping to get gigs at South Coast Repertory Theatre in California or the Public Theater in New York City, institutions that actually pay living wages to their artists, I doubt such bold bodily indiscretions would win over many literary managers, especially not at the former where they ask for plays with no swearing or male nudity for fear of upsetting their elderly west coast audience. (And what *really* exciting play, I ask you, does not have swearing or nudity?) But the spirit of Diogenes – laughing in the face of adversity, refusing to squash the bodily for abstractions, embracing irony's powerful cheekiness – is an incredibly useful way to fight the censor within. There is nothing wrong with pursuing work at theatres that have the institutional wherewithal to financially support new work, but that must be pursued with a kynical eye. It cannot be the end all and be all.

As idealistic as it might sound, playwrights must take up the mantle of speaking truth to power. We do this by creating work invested with personal truth. This does not mean more plays about our parents. But more work that does not shut itself off from what we need to express, no matter how painful, which in writing, inspires us to laugh and laugh hard. When theatres demand four-person comedies, give them a four-person comedy that is really a critique of the Iraq war in disguise. When theatre institutions shut you out or doom you to endless bout of development, start your own theatre company that rejects the corporate model. Let indie-rock and electronic laptop music be inspirations, not a regional theatre system programmed for endless mediocrity. The only places worth having plays done are not big institutions, but smaller companies who consistently do good work, theatres like Moving Arts and Theatre of Note in Los Angeles, Salvage Vanguard in Austin, and Annex Theatre in Seattle. Rethink your personal definition of success so that it does relish in quick affirmation over long-term artistic achievement. Smaller companies will do good, often amazing, productions, but they can't pay you much, so that means day jobs to get by, and that can be discouraging. Of course, don't stop working on get-

---

10 See Peter Sloterdijk's wonderful *Critique of Cynical Reason* (Trans. Michael Eldred, Minneapolis and London: University of Minneapolis Press, 1987), a book that masterfully weaves together neo-Kantian philosophy and fart jokes.

ting a producer to drop a cool million for an Off-Broadway run which will inevitably lose everyone money. Don't use all means possible to find a writing gig that might actually pay rent for a few months. But in the end, we can't wait. You don't get bitter. And don't let the inner censor shut down the good plays lurking inside you just because such plays aren't marketable, politically correct or easily digestible.

Part of the hard work ahead is relinquishing the comfort of the censorship narrative: where the oppressive forces are out there and that the battle for artistic freedom in the theatre is a case of us against them. The problem is not the occasional blue hair with manufactured outrage over depictions of a gay Jesus or a play slightly sympathetic to the Palestinian cause. If only, this was true. It is we the artists that often shut down possibility and succumb to censorious impulses that block the progress of the theatrical imagination. Thanks to years of training, we have internalised those desires. If this call-to-arms sounds like another variation of radical individualism, rest assured: it is not. The best way to smash the censor inside is to ban together with other artists who likewise want to energise the stage. Judging by the number of people I see at downtown theatre in New York, there is a renewal of excitement about the theatre and, dare I say, even a community of artists who don't see theatre as a means to an end (i.e. film and TV). There are more and more of us working towards re-energising the stage despite all the odds, which is why this is not a time to despair but a perfect time to get to work.

It Starts with Us

CHRISTOPHER SHINN

[Christopher Shinn's plays have premiered at the Royal Court, Lincoln Center, Manhattan Theatre Club, Playwrights Horizons, the Vineyard Theatre, and South Coast Rep, and have subsequently been performed all over the world. They are published by TCG, Methuen, and DPS. Christopher is presently on the faculty at the New School for Drama, and has taught at Columbia and NYU. Awards and grants include an Obie and a Guggenheim Fellowship. This essay was originally written for The Dramatists Guild's in-house magazine *The Dramatist*, and is reprinted with their and the author's permission.]

Early in 2006, a planned staging of Alan Rickman and Katharine Viner's play *My Name Is Rachel Corrie* was cancelled. The one-person show, about a 23 year-old American woman's political activism on behalf of Palestinians in Gaza, had played without incident in London and was now coming to America. According to an official statement, the decision to cancel the play was justified "because of the nature of the subject and the possibility that it could offend many people."

Were these words issued by Jim Nicola, the artistic director of New York Theatre Workshop? No, they are the words of a spokesman for the Miami-Dade County School District. When a planned student reading of *My Name Is Rachel Corrie* was cancelled by a local high school principal earlier this year, the spokesman for the district said, "Because of the nature of the subject and the possibility that it could offend many people, the principal decided to take it off." This is more or less the same explanation that Nicola offered when he cancelled a production of the same play at his theatre this past March, in a decision that drew criticism from Harold Pinter and Tony Kushner, as well as emerging theatre artists from around the world. Explaining his decision to the *Guardian*, Nicola said, "In our pre-production planning and our talking around and listening in our communities in New York, what we heard was that after Ariel Sharon's illness and the election of Hamas, we had a very edgy situation. We found that our plan to present a work of art would be seen as us taking a stand in a political conflict, that we didn't want to take."

Exceptions abound, but New York Theatre Workshop's actions point to a trend: the institutional narrowing of what the theatre is, what it can talk about and deal with. To many artists who publicly and privately expressed outrage at New York Theatre Workshop's decision to cancel *My Name Is Rachel Corrie*, what was especially confusing was that this was a theatre whose mission statement in part read that it was committed to "challenging and unpredictable new theatre" that explores "perspectives on our collective history and responses to the events and institutions that shape our lives." The contradiction between its words and actions seemed obvious to so many artists; how could the theatre's leaders miss it?

This past year has given us many opportunities to mull over that general question, and many related ones. Theatrical work is coming under attack in school districts in "red" states and in the most progressive cities in the Western world. *My Name Is Rachel Corrie* is only one of many works to come under attack. Consider these incidents from the last year:

- American high school productions of *Grease*, *Ragtime*, and *The Crucible* came under fire from religious leaders and conservative activists, leading in the former cases to softened language and cuts, in the latter case to cancellation.

- In Spain, playwright Pepe Rubianes pulled his play about Federico Garcia Lorca after receiving death threats from far-right political groups.

- In Paris, the Comedie-Francaise cancelled a production of a new play by the Austrian writer Peter Handke because of statements he made about Slobodan Milosevic, prompting the Nobel-Prize winning writer Elfriede Jelinek to say, "By not putting on this play, the Comedie-Francaise, with its rich past, is following in the worst tradition of cultural institutions under dictatorships, who throw out artists who cause trouble and condemn them to silence."

- In Germany, Berlin's Deutsche Oper cancelled a three-year-old production of Mozart's *Idomeneo* because it included a scene that showed the severed head of the Prophet Muhammed. (After months of widespread and diverse criticism, including from Chancellor Angela Merkel, this decision was reversed.)

In a sense there is not much more to say about this. We have already heard many respected artists and intellectuals argue that these works should have gone on, that freedom of expression is important whether we agree with the expression or not, that the decisions to postpone, cancel, or change these works were cowardly and self-defeating, etc. So if most reasonable members of the artistic community can agree on these points, the question becomes, why were the decisions made in the first place?

It is difficult to answer this question definitively, since in most cases those who made the decisions offered banalities and obfuscation in their defense. Some seeking a deeper analysis have speculated about the fear artistic organisations have of offending conservative subscribers, as well as individual, private, and government funders. Others have invoked the dangers theatres face when they produce controversial work, in light of the murder of filmmaker Theo Van Gogh by a member of an Islamist militant organisation, and the deadly protests that followed the publication of twelve Danish cartoons that depicted the Prophet Muhammed.

If we take these speculations as reasonable, or at least as partially illuminating of the anxiety artistic leaders around the world are feeling, the question then shifts from how these factors affect artistic institutions to how they affect the artists those institutions serve. John Patrick Shanley made a statement about this subject on New York Public Radio's Brian Leher Show on March 22nd of the year 2006, shortly after New York Theatre Workshop's cancellation of *My Name Is Rachel Corrie*. What he had to say points us in an interesting direction:

> The motives of the people who were going to produce this play Off-Broadway in New York are not adequately known and I think that they should be aired...But it highlights a larger phenomenon which is an international gangsterism towards

the arts at this time. I consider the *New York Times* not publishing the cartoons about Muhammed to be an act of editorial cowardice and inappropriate--obviously it was major news--and this idea of it being 'sensitive' to religion, respectful to religion, not to air differences, not to air slurs, not to air slights, is just giving into intimidation of different kinds. Now the theatre in New York may not have been afraid that they were going to be killed, they may have been afraid they were going to lose funding from somebody, that I don't know. But I do know there is intimidation across this country in the arts, where plays like Grease are being vetoed by local organisations as being too racy and cartoons are being called unworthy of publication because the sensitivities of people of a certain religion trumps the need of people of every persuasion to know. And I think it has to be looked at. There's a certain degree of cowardice involved and I think people are going to have to get used to the idea that doing these things--like what happened to Van Gogh in the Netherlands--may lead to them being killed.

Shanley is criticising arts institutions that display "cowardice" in the face of the various dangers that taking a political risk threatens to bring about. He more than implies that artists and those who serve them may have to be willing to die if they wish to create politically engaged works in a world where the threat of terrorism, particularly from Islamic extremists, is very real. Shanley does not explicitly make the link between Christian fundamentalism in the United States and the controversies surrounding high school productions of *Grease, Ragtime,* and *The Crucible*; nor does he explicitly examine how American writers might be affected by New York Theatre Workshop's cancelling of *Corrie,* whether the reason be that which was initially proffered by Nicola, or the one Shanley offers when he wonders if fears of loss of funding motivated the decision.

But his statement leads us to those questions. To translate it into practical terms, let us imagine what a political playwright today might have to think through before she sits down to begin writing a new play. "How do I write truthfully if I feel I can't make a decent living doing so, or may not even be allowed to live if I do so? Do I want to write truthfully and struggle financially and perhaps be hurt or killed, or do I want to write less truthfully and prosper and live safe from threats?"

To claim that these questions are histrionic is legitimate, but one need only point to the above examples to show that, while extreme, they are not in fact ridiculous. (Even before 9/11, these questions were something a political playwright might have thought about; one need only recall the fatwa issued in 1999 by Sheikh Omar Bakri Muhammad and the British Islamic group Al-Muhajiroun against Terrence McNally, when his play *Corpus Christi* opened in London.) Breaking these questions down into their component parts sheds even more light on the task facing a political playwright as she begins work on a new play. Let us imagine her thought process in simple language:

- What should I write about in my experience of the world? Should I write politically?

- What kind of audience is there if I write politically; does it exist?

- What kinds of theatres exist to put on my political plays; will they be able to pay me a living wage?

- How am I to make a living as a writer in Hollywood given the concerns that I express in my political plays; are there TV and film producers who will hire me based on these plays, so that I can make a living writing?

- What kind of chance do I have that there are regional theatres across the United States that will produce a political play following its initial production?

- Are there people who have financial ties to these theatres that may not want to hear what I have to say about certain political issues, and will an artistic director be thinking about their concerns when program- ming a season?

- What kinds of people are out there who might threaten or try to harm or kill me if I write political plays?

- *Why should I write plays that put me at mortal or financial risk?*

How do concerns such as these, however conscious or unconscious they may actually be, affect what we write? To argue that these concerns have no effect on our work, or that we may override their effect in a willful act of decid- ing to do so, is a naïve position. We are made by history as much as we make it. Some things simply cannot be transcended, even in America, a country built on the idea that any and everything can be overcome. (There is a profound difference between overcoming and overlooking, though it is shocking how often the latter is confused with the former.)

If we accept that we are bound to be affected by the pressures and realities of contemporary life in composing our plays, what can we realistically expect of the institutions that serve us? It would seem that an increasing conservatism, perhaps cloaked as a particular aesthetic sensibility, is inevitable. Some would say it's already here, in force.

But it is easy to criticise theatres who fail playwrights who take political and artistic risks. It is much more difficult to sustain our asking the difficult questions of ourselves, when our lives and livelihoods are at stake. It is hard enough to simply write a good play; to consistently confront oneself with the disappointments and deprivations one may face as a playwright verges on the impossible. To imagine the deeper forces at play in oneself in the process of creating a work of art can lead one to the brink of despair.

And yet I believe that this is the work we must do: get to the bottom of our artistic selves, our fraught relationship to the times we live in, to the communities we speak to and derive our income from. This work delivers us to our tragic core, to the wound that made us want to be artists in the first place. It brings us back to the writers who first disturbed us, to the Greeks, to Shakespeare, to Ibsen, to Brecht, to those who had the courage to say what they felt and to sing about the dark times; it painfully links us to the horrors of history, to the demands of tradition, to, in Robert Pinsky's great phrase, "the responsibilities of the poet." This is not an easy thing, but I think it is an essential thing. Maybe it is the only thing.

If one needs a bit of hope at this point, I think that there is always the hope that if we do our part in this task, the institutions will do theirs. The cynic would say that I'm a fool for believing that, and the cynic might be right. But at the very least even the cynic must admit that this work cannot start with the institutions; it has to start with us.

Be Silent

STEPHEN BOTTOMS

[Stephen Bottoms is Professor of Drama and Theatre Studies at the University of Leeds, England. He is the author of *Playing Underground: A Critical History of the 1960s Off-Off-Broadway Movement* (2004), *Albee: Who's Afraid of Virginia Woolf?* (2000) and *The Theatre of Sam Shepard* (1998). He is co-editor with Matthew Goulish of *Small Acts of Repair: Performance, Ecology and Goat Island* (2007).]

Silence is usually figured in the popular imagination as a passive state, a condition of lacking—lack of sound, lack of information—rather than as an active or creative condition. Indeed, this association with passivity is secured in the English verb form, "to silence," which explicitly bespeaks a silencing of someone or something else: a person is silenced, is to be silenced, and the language itself seems to forbid (to silence) the possibility that this person might opt for silence of his or her own volition. The nearest we can get is the adverbial "to be silent"—but even that seems to connote a silence imposed rather than chosen (quite unlike linguistic parallels such as "to be heard", "to be seen", or "to be fashionable"). The title of this book, *Out of Silence,* might be taken as advocating an end to silence, a finding of voice by those who have been silenced by one means or another. This short chapter, however, starts from the presumption that silence need not always be something imposed on an unwilling victim—and indeed that, precisely because it is apparently devoid of information, silence possesses a disorienting power all of its own.

I'm explicitly not referring, here, to the frequent silence of those in power and authority when called upon to account for themselves. Anybody who has played improvisational "status games" in drama workshops knows that a confidently maintained silence is one of the best ways to demonstrate a status level higher than that of one's chattering counterparts. Yet while silence can certainly be a tool for affirming existing social circumstances and hierarchies, I'm interested here in the ways in which it might also be deployed to question or destabilise such norms. Indeed, in a mediatized culture dominated by incessant noise and chatter (and now twitter), silence can possess an uncanny potential to disrupt the flow of "normal service." Eric Bogosian's drama *Talk Radio* (1987) hinges on the appalling fact that Bogosian's shock-jock anti-hero is finally lost for words, mid-broadcast: "This is dead air," his producer whispers to him frantically, as his unanticipated silence deepens, "dead air!"[11] Yet the panic prompted by this silence suggests a *liveness* rather than a deadness in the air. Sometimes, perhaps, silence contains just a little too much liveness—interrupting the regulated routines of quotidian time to remind us of our mortality. And so we rush to fill the "dead air" with noise.

Even as short a period as four minutes and thirty-three seconds is, it would seem, too long for an assembled group of people to reasonably tolerate silence. When John Cage's famous anti-composition *4'33"* (1952) was performed by a full orchestra at London's Barbican Centre in 2005, the conductor Lawrence Foster chose to mark the transitional stages between its three temporal "movements" of silence by having every musician turn a blank page on his or her music stand. The resultant flutter of paper was accompanied, during both interim moments, by a loud chorus of coughing from the packed audience—as though in protest at having had to be quiet for more than a minute. Foster even prompted peals of laughter by theatrically mopping his brow after his (non-)exertion during the first movement. At the end of the performance, the audience offered an ironically sustained round of loud applause to the orchestra, who duly stood to acknowledge the acclaim. In effect, this rare performance of an avant-garde milestone seemed to function as an opportunity for tongue-in-cheek mockery of its "pretensions," but those involved thereby underlined Cage's central point . . . that there is no such thing as true silence.

---

11   Eric Bogosian, *The Essential Bogosian* (New York: Theatre Communications Group, 1994), p.76.

Something comparable, though perhaps more complex, occurred in 1998 when the British performance company Blast Theory staged its piece *Kidnap*. Having initially planned to make a theatre piece *about* kidnapping—and the enforced deprivations and silences it entails—the company eventually resolved to conduct an actual kidnapping. To keep this legal, the two victims were in fact volunteers—chosen from among the many respondents to a questionnaire which had invited them to describe their fantasy kidnap scenario (every respondent also sent in a £10 entry fee to secure for themselves a place in the kidnap selection lottery). Yet the company were less interested in people's fantasies than in the banal realities of confinement: the two "lucky winners" were snatched unexpectedly out of their daily routines, and placed in an unfurnished, wooden-boarded room barely larger than a cupboard for a period of forty-eight hours.

During this time they were provided a functional minimum of food, and liquids were fed to them through a straw protruding through the hardboard wall. Both captives knew they had the legal option to request an end to their captivity at any point, and to their credit both stuck it out—but as one remarks in a video documenting the performance, 'it was with my consent but against my will.'[12] The experience seems to have been both radically disorientating (the captives had no idea where they were, having been hooded in transit) and utterly tedious: deprived of the people, places and activities around which they would normally co-ordinate their lives and experience themselves as themselves, they were made to experience a period of "dead air" in the usual flow of time. That experience, moreover, was web-streamed live to the internet, thanks to their constant surveillance by CCTV cameras. Since the event was well covered in the news media, the website was visited by large numbers during the forty-eight hour window of imprisonment, but for most of the time, the live feed simply showed silent footage of a man and a woman awkwardly inhabiting a small, bare space.

Clearly, the silence was too much for many: the online chat-room discussion accompanying the video feed was filled with demands that the kidnap victims be made to *do* stuff. Why weren't the monkeys performing? Yet for Blast Theory,

12 *Kidnap*, video produced by Blast Theory, London, 1998. For further information see also web pages at www.blasttheory.co.uk/bt/work_kidnap.html

part of the point of the piece was to question, or at least intervene in, the relentless flow of mediated spectacle by broadcasting 48-hours of near-dead air: they were looking to disorientate the viewers as well as the viewed.

Blast Theory's *Kidnap* proved oddly prescient. Just two years later, in 2000, the UK's Channel 4 television station broadcast the first series of its hugely popular "reality show" *Big Brother*, in which carefully selected members of the public are held in captivity and under surveillance for weeks at a time. In this instance, though, the production company Endemol were more than happy to make the monkeys perform—providing pointless tasks a-plenty to keep them spectacularly occupied.

The notion of captivity as media entertainment was taken to a bizarre extreme in 2003 when the American illusionist and attention-seeker David Blaine had himself suspended in a Perspex box above the South Bank promenade of London's River Thames. He (apparently) remained there for a period of forty days during which he (apparently) received no food. It was an image of ascetic fasting, or of hunger strike, reconceived as media sideshow—the endurance artist as messianic hero. Alone in his box, Blaine himself remained verbally silent, but the whole event was conceived as a performance with and *for* the babble of contemporary media (hundreds of channels with dead air to fill). The British public also made their presence felt—attending the site of Blaine's suspension to cheer at him, egg him on, or (predictably as popular) to hurl abuse. There is very little silence to be heard in the still-available YouTube footage of the event.

Blaine claims to have taken some of his inspiration from the durational performance art tradition of the 1970s and '80s, but his noisy self-aggrandisement is thrown into sharp relief when compared with one key example of such work— the *One Year Performance* that the Taiwanese artist Tehching Hsieh enacted between the Septembers of 1978 and1979. Informally known as "the Cage Piece," this involved Hsieh imprisoning himself inside a metal cage, situated in his Lower Manhattan loft-studio, and remaining silent for a year. He gave himself a bed, and a small amount of space to move about in, but intentionally deprived himself of the opportunity to read books, to listen to music, watch television, or even speak to other people. His friend, Cheng Wei Kuong, brought him food and removed his waste (itself an extended performance of quiet humility), and Hsieh simply remained in his cage, doing (almost) nothing, for a year. He was, he tells us, thinking about art—as if converting the notion of conceptual art, an art of thought processes, into a stubbornly literal reality. However, since he has chosen not to reveal anything of what he thought about, we can only respond to this silence with thinking of our own.

One immediate train of thought might lead us to contemplate the extreme personal isolation that Hsieh's performance entailed: unlike Blaine, hanging there with London to look at, and with London looking at him, Hsieh had only bare walls and a floor, and very little company. His completion of the assigned task was verified not by the permanent presence of observers but by seals on the door of his cage, signed by lawyers and confirmed by them as unbroken on the day of his "release." Members of the public were permitted to view the piece on one day in every three weeks, throughout the year, but since there was very little to see—and no response to be gained from Hsieh—even the most curious of viewers did not hang around long. The rest of the time, Hsieh simply served his self-imposed sentence in quiet solitude. One can only imagine that, deprived to such an extreme degree of the kind of outside stimuli with which we usually distract ourselves, Hsieh's mind and body became peculiarly attuned to the minutiae of his surroundings and his relationship to it – the degree and quality of light in the room, for example, or the physical processes of sitting, standing, lying down, walking around. Yet what Hsieh experienced in that context – what he *knows*, physically and mentally and emotionally as a result – must surely remain unfathomable to the rest of us. There is a silence at the heart of the piece that still troubles: could *I* have put myself through that kind of mental quietude without driving myself crazy?

Hsieh's daily enactment and experience of isolation seem to have stemmed, in part, from the fact that isolation had been a prominent factor in his life ever since arriving in New York five years earlier, in 1974. He had voluntarily exiled himself from his native Taiwan, which at that time was run by the autocratic Chiang government (driven off the Chinese mainland by Mao's Communists, the regime still impotently proclaimed sovereignty over all China). Hsieh had been forced to undergo compulsory military service, and more generally, as a young artist, he had found "the whole environment in Taiwan very oppressive;

there was little chance to catch exciting avant-garde art from the Western world."[13]

Yet the irony was that, having experienced one kind of cultural isolation, his relocation to New York (in search of the avant-garde) occasioned quite another. Speaking very little English, and confronted with an art establishment whose gaze was still myopically trained on the activities of white males, Hsieh found that the only way he could exhibit his art was by finding ways to do it himself.[14] Moreover, as an illegal immigrant without employment papers, he had to eke out a living in low-paid, cash-in-hand jobs: in *Cleaning Up*, a short film he made in 1978, Hsieh documented himself performing his nightly routine in a SoHo restaurant—stacking chairs on tables, washing and waxing the floor, then un-stacking the chairs again. As he explains, such experiences led with a certain logic toward the extended silence of his first *One Year Performance*:[15]

> Culture shock and the language gap deepened my experience as an illegal im-migrant. During the first four years of living in New York, instead of being a prac-tising artist, I was a thinking artist—a frustrated person who stayed in the studio thinking about life and art. . . I thought, "why don't I make the process of thinking about art in my studio an artwork, and present it using a long duration?" I had spent a lot of time in this situation of isolation, as if I was doing time. . . . My *One Year Performances* present my different perspectives of thinking about life, but they are all under this same premise: life as a life sentence. (319, 324)

If the cage piece alludes to the experience of imprisonment – perhaps po-litical imprisonment – Hsieh's second *One Year Performance* seems to invoke the "life sentence" of dehumanizing regimentation experienced by manual work-ers. In this piece, completed between 1980 and 1981, Hsieh punched a factory

---

13   Tehching Hsieh, "I Just Go In Life" (trans. Liao Mei and Qinqin Li), in *Out of Now: The Lifeworks of Tehching Hsieh*, by Adrian Heathfield and Tehching Hsieh (Cambridge, Mass.: MIT Press, 2009), p. 322. Subsequent quotations from Hsieh are from this source, with page numbers noted parenthetically.

14   In 1985, an exhibition titled *An International Survey of Painting and Sculpture* was held at New York's Museum of Modern Art. Of the 169 contemporary artists featured, only 13 were female, and fewer still were non-white. The grotesque selectivity of this exhibition prompted the formation of the feminist artist-activist collective, the Guerrilla Girls.

15   Hsieh does not offer an explanation as to how he afforded to live for a year without working: presumably he either saved up the bare means for survival, or was blessed with support from an understanding patron.

time-clock in his loft on the hour, every hour, for one year. Given this restrictive frame, he could never sleep, or leave his loft, for more than 59 minutes at a time (although in practice, he did sleep through alarms on around 100 occasions, out of a total of 8,760 clock punches scheduled for the year).

Hsieh gave himself license to work, read and converse during the periods between punchings, but the overwhelming fact of his appointments with the clock must have prevented him from conducting anything like a normal life, and forced him to keep his own counsel for much of the time. Significantly, the key piece of documentation for the piece is a silent film that Hsieh made by expos-ing one frame of film with each, hourly punching of the clock. At 24 frames (or one day) per second, the year boils down to just over six minutes of screen time, during which Hsieh's hair grows out from an initially shaven head to form a long, shaggy mane. Appearing as a kind of jerky, stop-motion animation of sped-up time (behind Hsieh's near-static figure, the hands of the timeclock it-self whir around at a dizzying rate), the film is a partly comical, partly unnerving meditation on the way that routinised time structures impose their own impris-oning influence on all of us.

Mere months after completing this second *One Year Performance*, Hsieh embarked on a third—the so-called "Outdoor Piece." Between the Septembers of 1981 and 1982, Hsieh spent a year in New York City without shelter, never al-lowing himself to go into or under any roofed structure – a criterion which en-compassed not only homes, shops, even public toilets, but also cars, buses, bridges and subway tunnels. Clearly, again, there is the suggestion of social content here, an identification with the excluded. Yet Tehching Hsieh did not simply make a piece about being homeless, he *made himself homeless*, albeit for delimited period of time, in what was then one of the most dangerous cities in the world.

Hsieh spent the year vulnerable to attack, to extremes of temperature (he endured what turned out to be one of the coldest New York winters on record), and to the pitying or disgusted looks of passers-by who saw him as just another street bum – just like all those other street bums whom we presume to know are "just street bums." His work, in the words of Steven Shaviro, has always re-quired "an extraordinary willingness to let go: to give oneself over to time and chance and materiality," and this is nowhere more clearly demonstrated than in the Outdoor piece.[16]

Indeed, almost as if courting the possibility of disaster, Hsieh arranged to have an earlier artwork exhibited in a group gallery show during his time on the streets. This was the first public exhibition of his poster piece, *Wanted by U.S. Immigration Service*, in which he had constructed an imagined facsimile of the document the immigration service might have had on its files. The poster, which details Hsieh's physical appearance, as well as displaying his 1974 passport photograph and all ten fingerprints, was in effect his first "coming out" to the art world (and to the extended public) about his status as an illegal alien. It was also during his time on the streets that Hsieh abandoned his previous artistic pseudonym, Sam Hsieh, and embraced his illegal identity as Tehching Hsieh. He had broken cover publicly, but was not to be found at his usual address. Nobody, he notes, came looking for him on the streets.

Nevertheless, in a bizarre twist of circumstance, it was the legal system that forced Hsieh to break his self-imposed rules by forcing him indoors on one occasion during his outdoor year. Having been provoked into a confrontation by a passer-by on the street, Hsieh was arrested for carrying a concealed weapon (not unwisely, he kept nunchaku in his rucksack for self-defence), and was dragged into a police station literally kicking and screaming. This striking disruption of his habitual calm, captured on Super 8 film by a friend who had come out to find him, was clearly prompted by his unwillingness to break his own commitment to remaining outside—but perhaps also by his fear that legal interrogation would reveal his immigration status (and thus lead to forced repatriation). In the event, though, Hsieh's luck held. Nobody asked to see his green card, and when his case eventually came to trial, it was heard by a judge who had read about his work in the *Wall Street Journal*. Permitted to remain outside the courthouse, in recognition of the integrity of his art, Hsieh was eventually sentenced to "time served."[17] It remains delightfully unclear whether this referred to the fifteen hours he had spent in police custody, or to the time Hsieh had imposed on himself.

16 Steven Shaviro, "Performing Life: The Work of Tehching Hsieh," essay accompanying Tehching Hsieh: One Year Performance: Art Documents 1978-1999, DVD-ROM published by the artist, 2000.

17 Adrian Heathfield discusses the legal circumstances in revealing detail in his excellent, extended essay "Impress of Time." See *Out of Now*, Heathfield and Hsieh, pp.44-45.

These incidents may have been the most "dramatic" of his year outside, but the real story of those months surely lies in Hsieh's willed acceptance of near-powerlessness—in his voluntary surrender to circumstances which must have tested his own physical and emotional resources to the limit. Hsieh made himself dependent for survival on the potentially hostile environment surrounding him: he sought out and charted places where he could safely sleep, eat, bathe, shit, hide money, and so on—and each day, he carefully annotated his progress through the city on a fresh copy of the New York street map. I have no way of confirming this, but I imagine that Tehching Hsieh knows things about the urban ecology of New York City that nobody else does.

I imagine him spending that year exploring nooks and crannies that most of us would never even notice, examining pore by pore the surface of the skin of the body of land that is Manhattan. A year was not enough, of course: as his mappings make clear, he did not see even a fraction of the total picture that year, staying mostly in and around the Lower West Side so as to orient himself around certain fixed locations. Yet he must have become familiar with his surroundings in a kind of microscopic detail. Hsieh had begun his artistic career as an abstract painter, and I wonder if, for that year, the city became for him one giant Jackson Pollock canvas: I see him standing there, up close, just millimetres from its surface, losing himself in the smallest details, the tiniest curl or glob of paint, tracking single splash marks from here all the way to there, intricately annotating the traces of other bodies previously present in this same physical space.

But I'm becoming a little fanciful. A little verbal. The key thing to remember here is the silence. Indeed, by the mid-1980s, when Hsieh's year-long pieces had made him moderately well-known in the tiny environs of the performance art world, he quite deliberately removed himself from view, as if to silence even those who wished to speak about him. From July 1985 to July 1986 he undertook a *One Year Performance* (his fifth) involving "a year without art" (1985-86)—an anti-performance for which, of course, no documentation exists.[18]

---

18 Observant readers will note that I have myself remained silent on the subject of Hsieh's fourth *One Year Performance*, during which he remained tied by a short rope to fellow artist Linda Montano, while avoiding physical contact with her. The issues of intimacy and relationship raised by this piece fall beyond the scope of this short essay—though I may also be performing an avoidance of my own.

He presented only a poster in which a silent black square hovers above a calendar of the year's dates; a blank space filling the place where, on posters for previous performances, he had placed photographs denoting his year's constraining activities. Then, shortly after completing this year without art, Hsieh announced a thirteen-year performance that would take him up to the turn of the millennium, during which—he explained—he would make art but not exhibit it publicly. He then disappeared from view. Not only that, he also attempted to remove all trace of himself and his previous work from public records and art collections. He stole himself away until, at a gathering of the curious in Greenwich Village's Judson Memorial Church on 1st January 2000, Hsieh reappeared to present documentation relating to the previous thirteen years. Anyone expecting a fulsome explanation would have been disappointed by his unveiling of a small poster bearing words collaged together from newsprint like a kidnapper's ransom note. It read simply: "I kept myself alive. I passed the Dec 31, 1999."

This can be read as a joke, perhaps, at the expense of his witnesses—those who had not quite understood, as yet, that Hsieh had by now blurred the line between his art and his life to the point of total erasure. But it was also a statement whose profundity lies precisely in everything that it does *not* say—in its almost complete silence regarding thirteen years of an individual's life story. The New Year's Eves of 1986 and 1999 also marked Hsieh's 36th and 49th birthdays, and during the interim period the world at large—while appearing curiously the same—had changed enormously (the fall of the Berlin Wall, the end of the Cold War and of apartheid, the first Gulf War, the massacres in Bosnia and Rwanda, the advent of the internet . . .). Hsieh's work, I would suggest, is not only filled with silences, but is *like* silence—insofar that it is both empty of and pregnant with significance. Or, more precisely in this last case, the silence is significant because (paradoxically) it seems to bespeak a certain lack of significance: Hsieh simply kept himself alive, as indeed did all of us who lived through that period of time, and he makes no claim to anything remarkable occurring to him. Certainly there was incident (he discusses a little of what he got up to in the interview with Adrian Heathfield previously cited in this essay), but there is incident in any life: the thirteen-year piece seems, with hindsight, to emphasise the ordinariness and everyday-ness of his previous one year performances, rather than the extremity of their constraints. He just got on with living. It may or may not be significant that in 1988, just over a year into his thirteen-year time frame, Hsieh won legal residency status in the United States. His disappearance from public view coincided more or less directly with his no longer needing to remain "invisible."

Whenever I introduce Hsieh's performances to students, the reaction is invariably a blend of intrigue and outrage—usually outrage at the very idea that Hsieh did these things and called them performance. I have found, though, that the more outraged the student, the more she or he wants to talk about Hsieh's work—as if to fill in the "dead air" around it. They want to talk because something about it bugs them, like an itch, and they want to explain it away. And yet they find that, unlike "bad art" that can simply be dismissed as unworthy of attention, Hsieh's sustained commitment to his endeavours somehow disarms their criticisms. Conversely, even those students most taken with the accounts of Hsieh's work find it hard to know what to say about it. As Hsieh himself puts it, with a simplicity borne of experience, "yes, you see something in it, but still something is missing" (326).

It is tempting, of course, to ascribe Hsieh's performances to the facts of his biography—to assume that his experiences of marginalization led him to identify with the marginal; with the prisoners, the workers, the homeless. Yet to reduce his work to being "about" these things is also to do it a great disservice—not least because such a perspective tends to emphasise the notion of victimhood, of being done unto, rather than the fact that Hsieh purposely chose to submit himself to a series of lengthy ordeals. His life experiences of isolation and cultural silencing may have led him towards this work, but the sheer magnitude (conceptual and actual) of the active silences in Hsieh's *One Year Performances* seems greatly to exceed anything that can be said to have prompted them. We are left speechless.

In the end, Hsieh's performances can be about nothing other than the experiences themselves. Those of us who did not live them can never really understand them, and the artist has never attempted to rationalise, explain, or contain them through words, because the banal extremity of what Hsieh put himself through in these pieces renders interpretive commentary of any shade inadequate. Imagine, if you will, a one-year performance in which Hsieh sits and listens to a team of critics critiquing the one-year performance in which he sits and listens to a team of critics. Before long – a week or two, perhaps, maybe a month at the outside – the critics would run out of things to say, and be reduced to silence. But Tehching Hsieh would still be sitting there, listening—to the shuffling of papers, the awkward coughing and mumbling. Or listening, perhaps, as John Cage once did in a soundproof chamber, to the sound of his own body circulating its fluids.

There is no such thing as dead air.

Listen.

Biting Tongues:

eight notes and a coda
on some uses of self-censorship

BAZ KERSHAW

[Baz Kershaw is Professor of Performance at the University of Warwick, UK. In 1960 he was a member of the North West CND (Campaign for Nuclear Disarmament) Committee of 100 in Manchester, pledged to civil disobedience and held in Strangeways Prison following an anti-nuclear demonstration. In 1980 he became an associate of the performance group Welfare State International, continuing though to 2006 when the company was archived. In 2000 and 2001 he made research visits to Australia, studying the impact of 19th-century immigration for a performance project on the Bristol-based heritage ship, the SS *Great Britain*.]

1. Tongues

The sardine can has just levelled out to drone along at thirty thousand feet for the next eight hours, re-circulating a fresh bunch of bugs and viruses brought on by the replacement bodies at Singapore. One of them is sitting beside me, a burly moustachioed man of uncertain age who to begin with seemed taciturn, determined to fill out the window seat with the air of a souring king. This was my second trip to Australia and past paranoia had driven me early to Heathrow to bag legroom in an emergency exit row, stupidly unthinking about the extra in-flight trials that might award. There was something more than faintly faux in the Aussie orders issued in broad Strine to the female attendant, who smiled archly at the well-worn routine. And plus two bottles of the red, love. Each. Leaning toward me. Alright, mate? She laughs at my overdone double take and stammered decline, but delivers them anyway. The wallet comes out with the first slimly ironic Chin chin, mate! exposing two chubby kids in unkind close-up. Suburban Adelaide. Good cook for a wife. Three cars in the drive, one is classic. Can't wait for the winter warmth after the Indonesian heat. Just grown the hairy upper lip because his boss had. Whendya start grawing yer beard, mate? I bite my tongue, lightly.

2. Teeth

In Samuel Beckett's Not I only a mouth, teeth and a tongue are seen, lit very precisely with a spotlight. Everything else is blackness.[19]

The hole is an evasive one, as it speaks compulsively without ever using the first person pronoun and regularly denies it is speaking about itself, apparently without ever wanting to admit to being anything but disembodied sounds. The voice seems squirming to escape what it means to be a soul, a person, an identity, what one will. Like a flittering kite, tethered by invisible lines in a gale. There is a story that for the first production in England, at the Royal Court Theatre in 1973, the actress Billie Whitelaw asked to be tied on to a stepladder to do the play.[20] Restraint is the principle of freedom. Hold hard back, making lots

---

19 The text of Not I indicates the onstage presence of a shadowy 'Auditor', though Beckett chose to omit the figure from his own productions as he came to consider it 'an error of the creative imagination'. James Knowlson, Damned to Fame: the Life of Samuel Beckett (London: Bloomsbury, 1996), p. 591.

20 In fact it seems that 'she allowed herself to be strapped in a chair called an "artist's rest" on which a film actor wearing armour rests because he [sic] cannot sit down. Her entire body was draped in black; her face covered with black gauze with a black transparent slip for her eyes and her head was clamped between two pieces of sponge rubber so that her mouth would remain fixed in the spotlight. Finally a bar was fixed which she could cling to and on to which she could direct her tension.' Wikipedia, Not I: http://en.wikipedia.org/wiki/Not_I (12.1.2007)

vacant. Anything to survive the double bind of speaking an absence: no options but utterly unacceptable ones.[21]

3. Cavities

The youth stood naked between the prison warders. There were three of them with light blue shirts, dark blue ties, black pressed trousers and big-soled boots. A man in a white laboratory coat stood beyond them in the gloom, observing. One of the warders stretched and pulled on a pair of white medical gloves. Bend over, said another. The youth shook his head, almost imperceptibly. We can easy make yer, said the third, routine orders. The youth bent as bid, wincing slightly as the gloves probed, then unfurled his back to stand. Yer just 'ave to tell us yer name and it's done. The youth stood silently still. Open yer mouth. No response. The third held his arms by the elbows from behind, pulling them towards each other so they crooked. The second reached from the side and pinched his nostrils together. When his mouth opened the first gripped his jaw and with the other gloved hand, the one that had fingered below, searched the cavity. The youth wretched deeply, doubling over as they let go of him. White-coat perked up: What did you say your name was, friend?[22]

4. Names

First they were debugged. Then debriefed. Where were they from? When did they leave there? How did they get here? How long did it take? How much did it cost? Who organised the boat? Did they bring any relatives with them as well as the children? Have they had any illness? What are their names? What is your name? The name always last, when it was the first thing that mattered. All

21 Samuel Beckett, *Not I* (London: Faber, 1973); see also: http://www.english.emory.edu/DRAMA/beckettnoti.html; http://ubu.wfmu.org/video/Beckett-Samuel_Not-I-Whitelaw_1973.avi (12.1.2007)

22 Baz Kershaw, *The Radical in Performance: Between Brecht and Baudrillard* (London: Routledge, 1999), pp. 126-7.

through an interpreter who's English often was not up to the job. The Government will hold you until your case can be considered, we cannot say for how long. Actually they will be kept by ACM (Australasian Correctional Management), a private company paid by taxes to run this refugee and asylum seeker's detainment centre. Managing corrections always *starts* with naming. Asia, *or* Australia. Drilled in like filled teeth or blood infused soil. This place was marked for 400 people but in 2002 it holds over three times that many. About 450 are children, some of them unaccompanied. The average detention time for children is one year, eight months, eleven days. Most of the inmates are Afghans and Iraqis first fleeing oppressive regimes then President George W. Bush's war on the Axis of Evil.[23] Name hell, you make heaven.

5. Parts

Way below stretched the deserts of the Northern Territories, from the air-conditioned cocoon looking hot and beautifully bronzed. He has drunk four or five 250cl bottles of the cheap airline wine, plus a couple of whiskey doubles. He loves driving, both golf and the car kinds and his best game combines both. He has a great trick going for the vehicles east to west. The classic in the drive is a Morris Minor Traveller. Fifties goldmine, mate, he says. Over a million built. He doesn't know how many are left in Limey, but – sotto voce – enough to keep his Indonesian mate Baharputra (he pronounces it Bey-hair-poot-raw) busy making new spare parts in his hut. He's organised all the manuals and sourced the drawings to set him up, like. Good raw metals brought in from Japan. Finished items to the Adelaide three-car bungalow for quality control, sent to another mate in Kent, UK for dispatch. He taps the side of his nose, twice, and just to make sure winks at me. I almost splutter up the acid wine. Golden hole in one,

23 Wikipedia, Woomera Immigration Reception and Processing Centre: http://en.wikipedia.org/wiki/
    Woomera_Immigration_Reception_and_Processing_Centre (12.1.2007); for 'Axis of Evil' see The
    White House, President George Bush, State of the Nation Address, January 29 2002:

    http://www.whitehouse.gov/news/releases/2002/01/20020129-11.html (12.1.2007)

he smirks, raising his third whiskey to the hissing air-vent, Cheeeers Baharputra mate![24]

6. Beards

The youth could never have imagined the horrid twinkle in a warder's eye, the stab of degradation in the slightest smirk, the venom in a friendly voice. The unspoken exchanges nurtured a toxic seed of utter corrosion, stripping away self-knowledge, leaving just an empty rimless hole. The cell of course had no mirror for checking the loss. But worst was having no way to speak a name to others, nominated as nothing in a subtly excessive game of power, just a hollowness at the heart of everything.

Lying at night on the hard pallet, the youth whispered it out loud, compulsively, but the mantra was utterly vacant of meaning. Without a witness it was wasted breathe, an absent agent. Yet as his shorn head shifted against the canopy of the grotty blanket its electric prickle induced a tiny spark of bodily anger, suffusing a resistance so deep and dispersed as to be almost unknowable. Somewhere in the emptiness of his foetal curve something had decided to grow a beard.

7. Seals

There are demonstrations in three of the compounds and, here, a 19-year-old Afghan man has climbed into the razor wire. Got people up on roofs of buildings in three compounds. The man on the razor wire says that if he can't see the Department of Immigration about his visa, he'll kill himself. He starts cutting his arms with a razor.

For another man, it's the day he's been waiting for. He's just been given a visa. But these days, this celebration is an exception. There are now 189 people on hunger strike. 62 have sewn their lips together, including two women and

---

24 Wikipedia, Morris Minor: http://en.wikipedia.org/wiki/Morris_Minor (12.1.2007)

five children. ACM staff making this video are clearly disturbed by what they're seeing. I see the compound all the time. I see hundreds and hundreds of people begging and crying, and I see people dehydrating in the sun. I see people with sewn lips and buried in the ground, 'cause that's what they did. Four Corners has obtained the computer records of the thousands of official reports written by ACM over the last three years and given daily to the Department of Immigration. They document the relentlessness of hundreds and hundreds of self-harms and suicide attempts. It was that, the visa process, which caused most stress for detainees. In particular, the Refugee Review Tribunal was seen as arbitrary. Despite its name, each tribunal was made up of only one person. Last month, Woomera was closed. In the end, 80 per cent of those detained there were found to be genuine refugees and given temporary visas.[25]

8. Holds

The nose of the sleek sardine tin begins to tip downwards for the long run in to Sydney. He's been deeply asleep for the past two hours, sometimes a light snore ahead of a long exhalation flowing below the fuzz of the moustache. I shake his arm gently, as requested, and he starts awake, in one fast move slipping up the window blind looking out and down and wheezing Ta, mate. A frightening recovery, then a stretch that extends everywhere. Exporting body parts. Earlier, with the slightest of slurs, he'd asked what I did for a living and I said Engineer of the Imagination, public spectacle like opening the Olympics but not as big. He seemed to like that. Well, it was true for some of the time.[26] He said he'd admired the army for the way it organised that kind of stuff. Tenta-

---

25 Australian Broadcasting Corporation, *Four Corners...About Woomera*:
http://www.abc.net.au/4corners/content/2003/transcripts/s858341.htm (12.1.2007); see also: Michael Dudley, 'Contradictory Australian national policies on self-harm and suicide: the case of asylum seekers in mandatory detention', *Australasian Psychiatry* 11, s1 (October 2003); also summarised at: www.psychology.org.au/members/ current_issues/michael_dudley2.pdf (12.1.2007)

26 Tony Coult and Baz Kershaw (eds), *Engineers of the Imagination: the Welfare State Handbook*, rev. ed., London: Methuen, 1990. The 2000 Olympics took place in Sydney. In the opening ceremony an Indigenous Australian, Kathy Freeman, lit the Olympic Flame. Wikipedia, Kathy Freeman: http://en.wikipedia.org/wiki/Cathy_Freeman

tively, I batted back his question. Not at liberty to divulge, mate, he said. I shrugged an OK. He swivelled in his seat and stared at me, just a little blurrily. Let's jus' say I carry on where Canoot left off. Canoot? Ahh, Canute! I risk a quizzical look. His lips part for the whisper. Holding back the tide.

9. Missing

Speak, gentle niece. What stern ungentle hands
Hath lopp'd, and hew'd, and made thy body bare
Of her two branches – those sweet ornaments
Whose circling shadows kings have sought to sleep in,
And might not gain so great a happiness
As half thy love? Why dost not speak to me?
Alas, a crimson river of warm blood,
Like to a bubbling fountain stirr'd with wind,
Doth rise and fall between thy rosed lips,
Coming and going with thy honey breath.[27]

---

27 William Shakespeare, *Titus Andronicus*, III, IV, 16-25.

"Whatever you say...":

Rendering the Monstrous Phatic

JAMES FRIEZE

[James Frieze is a Senior Lecturer at Liverpool John Moores University and a creator of devised performance. His essays and criticism are published in a variety of journals, and his book *Naming Theatre* published in the year 2009 looks at performances that relate theatrical enunciation and citation to naming within medical practice, military code, corporations, archival taxonomy, cybertechnology and critical theory.]

"For most of us," writes poet Michael Pollick, "an average day is filled with phaticcommunication and we never even notice":

> We may call it small talk, but in reality we would be lost without [the] phatic...
> Sociologists suggest that phatic communication, such as discussing the weather,
> opens up a social channel. This, in turn, can lead to more substantial or factual
> communication. Very few people start and end conversations with straight
> facts—phatic communication such as a handshake helps set the stage first.
> Some people are simply not comfortable with the idea of making meaningless
> 'small talk'. Others seem to embrace the social ritual of phatic communication,
> even to the point of avoiding much factual conversation with others. Communi-
> cation experts suggest finding a middle ground, using phatic communication as
> a means to open up more substantial conversation. Too much emphasis on small
> talk can make a person seem unfocused or chatty, while too little can make

someone appear stern or unapproachable. The trick lies in finding a proper balance between factual and phatic communication.[28]

In reading the performance of speech in works by the duo Ridiculusmus, along with a collaborative work by Will Adamsdale and Chris Branch (*The Receipt*), I will argue that these pieces of double-act devising extend and complicate the traditional linguistic/sociological characterisation of the phatic rehearsed by Pollick.

Behind the idea that effective talk consists of "a proper balance between factual and phatic" lies an abiding linguistic orthodoxy that speech consists of kernels of information surrounded by a variety of other tonal and lexical elements that indicate relationships between and attitudes of speaker and listener. "Finding a proper balance between factual and phatic" implies that the serious business is the passing of the kernel of information from speaker to listener, while the role of the phatic is to "open up a social channel" through which the kernel may be passed. And behind this view lies a binary between serious and trivial that continues to hold sway over all kinds of communication, including theatre.

In reference to a group of works performed at the 2006 Edinburgh Fringe Festival, Joyce McMillan applauds their serious engagement with the apparently trivial:

> As cities burn and displaced children run through shell-shattered streets, it's hard to give a damn about people who feel oppressed because the office equipment's not working, they can't get a boyfriend, or they're not famous by the time they're 25. So it's all the more impressive, against this backdrop, to find a clutch of fine Fringe writers and performers who have discovered ways of reflecting on yuppie misery and alienation that give these tales a wider meaning, and a sense of connection to the bigger story of our times.[29]

McMillan's assertions, which question but confirm the serious/trivial binary, are made in a glowing review of *The Receipt*, which went on to win a Fringe

---

28 Michael Pollick, "What is Phatic Communication?" (2007), posted on the online knowledge compendium wiseGEEK http://www.wisegeek.com/what-is-phatic-communication.htm.

29 Joyce McMillan, "*The Receipt*", *The Scotsman* (9 August 2006), accessed http://edinburgh-festivals.com/reviews.

First.[30] If The Receipt needs to be defended against the charge that it is an amusing tale of "yuppie misery", binary logic dictates that Say Nothing, by Ridiculusmus—an irreverently satirical romp about life in Derry, a hot-spot of "the Troubles" in Northern Ireland—be defended against the opposite charge: making light of the horrific.

On the back of their successful adaptation of Flann O'Brien's At-Swim-Two-Birds (1994), Ridiculusmus (David Woods and Jon Hough) were invited to become the resident theatre company at the Playhouse Theatre in Derry, a city keen to celebrate its links to O'Brien. Hough and Woods both had Irish ancestry, and were proud to regard themselves as part-Irish; since London was proving an impossibly expensive place to run a small theatre company, they decided to take up the offer. Though they remained in Derry from 1994 to 1999, they found the city's embrace to be less than whole-hearted. During their five year residency, they felt a thinly veiled hatred toward Brits and British accents from many quarters, compounded by a widespread suspicion of theatre's, and particularly new theatre's, propensity to express feelings and ideas. It wasn't until they left Derry in 1999 that Woods and Hough felt settled enough to reflect on what they had experienced there.

The title Say Nothing alludes to a Seamus Heaney poem about the Troubles: "Whatever you say, say nothing".[31] The 1998 Belfast Agreement, aka the Good Friday Agreement, was heralded as a new dawn for peace in Northern Ireland. It was a sun, felt Woods and Hough, that drove bitterness further below ground. Throughout Say Nothing—which toured the U.K. and Ireland at the dawn of the twenty-first century—Woods plays Kevin, a thirty-something born in Ireland but resident in England since boyhood. As field work for his PhD in Peace and Conflict Studies at a college in Goole, England, Kevin goes to Derry, but is forced to escape to Donegal after upsetting the locals during a sing-along. The other characters are all played by Hough: Sally, who runs the guest house in which Kevin is attempting to stay; Frank, the explosive manager of the dubious "centre" where Kevin is working on a conflict-resolution project called Hands Across the Barricades; and fellow project worker, the excrutiatingly fey Dan, with

---

30 The Fringe Firsts are awarded each week during the Edinburgh Festival Fringe by a team of critics for The Scotsman newspaper. The Receipt received won in the first "batch" of 2006 awards. It subsequently won the 2006 Total Theatre Award for Innovation.

31 Seamus Heaney, "Whatever You Say, Say Nothing", North (London: Faber and Faber, 1975), p.59.

whom Kevin attempts to jointly facilitate a forum to allow border residents space in which to heal and reflect.

Space, as a metaphor for openness, is always invoked sardonically in *Say Nothing*. The "action", more accurately described as inaction, takes place on a sizeable playing area, but only a tiny rectangle in the centre is used. The duo perform the play's many episodes on a rectangle of fertile, if soggy, turf. The grass seems to have spewed from an open suitcase that forms the border of this tight inner stage. Kevin's "conversations" with both Frank at the centre and Sally at the guest-house take place in liminal, hallway spaces. Feeling at home is a luxury Kevin is never able to attain, despite the overbearing welcome he receives from Sally, Frank and Dan—all of whom restrict and intrude on his personal space while accusing him of trespassing on theirs. Sally, the guest house owner, insists that Kevin sleeps outside in his car until the completion of work on his room, the exact nature of which is only vaguely explained. Forcing him to pay rent for six weeks to retain the room, Sally compensates Kevin every morning by bringing to his car, and forcing him to eat, a huge, "traditional" cooked breakfast. Craving room, meaningful work, and escape from the monotony of compulsory small-talk with Sally, he goes to the venue where the conflict-resolution forum is to take place. Emerging from the sanctuary of the toilet, he tries in vain to explain to Frank, the centre's irate proprietor, that it is kids and not he who are responsible for flicking shit around the bathroom. Sounding like a vitriolic preacher stung by a bee, Frank claims to know nothing about any conference and attacks Kevin for leaving his car in the car-park, making him pay an arbitrary charge, which they then negotiate. Asking for 50 pounds and quickly settling for 50 pence, even Frank himself seems unsure what he's after in the negotiations, just whatever he can get that feels like a deal.

Kevin and Sally trade in nouns: names of places with which they are both familiar, an attempt to literally and metaphorically locate common ground. At the start of the play, they seem to be meeting for the first time. A bit awkward, Kevin tries to open a channel by enthusing about Donegal, which he describes as Derry's "huge, vast, raw back garden".[32] He says he feels "drawn to" Done-

---

32   Quotations are from a video of *Say Nothing* in performance at the Traverse Theatre, Edinburgh in August, 2000, provided by Ridiculusmus and by Gloria Lindh for the agency Your Imagination.

gal: "it's, like, my spiritual home". Emboldened by Sally's phatic nodding, he enthuses that Inishowen "is like a macrocosm of Donegal". A mumble of assent encourages him further: "Of the world, even." Still, though, no real dialogue is taking place, so Kevin—to draw Sally out and avoid the embarrassment of silence—begins to list names of places in Donegal, as if to indicate his credibility as something more substantial than a tourist. Sally indicates little recognition of the places named, and chips in other names that are not in Donegal, either not understanding the rules of the list or not very familiar with Donegal. Bemused, but without any hint of openly questioning Sally's apparent lack of knowledge, Kevin asks how long she has been there:

SALLY: 15 years. Before that I was in Birmingham.
KEVIN: Oh right, I've just come from England myself, from Goole.
SALLY: Oh yes, Goole, lovely place. *[Pause]*. Where is that exactly?
KEVIN: [*attempting to map it with his hands*]: It's in the North, sort of, here.
SALLY: Ah, Bronte country.
KEVIN: No, no, Bronte's [*busily adjusting his hand-map*] more... here.

Sally begins to spout names she associates with the part of the country he is indicating, each wrong association causing Kevin to re-draw the increasingly complex map. Sally's proffered cultural landmarks shift from literary to televisual and from high-brow to popular: James Herriot, Catherine Cookson, Melvyn Bragg, Brookside, Queer as Folk, Hollyoaks, Coronation Street, Eastenders. Once Kevin has completed the map, neither one knows what to say for a moment. "Originally I'm from Crookhaven" offers Kevin, switching the focus back across the water. "Oh yes, Crookhaven, lovely place". "Yeah, yeah, it's, er, got great, er.. roads".

Say Nothing is about what Hough and Woods call "the circulations of the Peace Process",[33] the word "circulations" tracing both circularity and flow: the circularity of negotiations and the flow of ire and angst that is as strong as ever when forced underground. Something strange happens when the above en-

33 David Woods, "An analysis of the current practice of Ridiculusmus theatre company", M.A. thesis, University of Kent, 2003; p.108. Copy of thesis provided by Woods.

counter—like that with Frank about the shit-spray in the toilets—is enacted for a second, and then a third time. Laughter wanes with repetition. A reflective atmosphere fills the theatre as the audience perhaps considers the purpose of the repetition, the significance of small textual variations and differences in tempo and gesture. There is something sinister about the repetition; or, more precisely, about the cyclical, circular, counter-active structure of the action in which repetitions play a part. Mirroring Woods and Hough's feelings about the peace process, Kevin's stay begins with an initial period of euphoria, is followed by pragmatic adjustments, then sinks into a destructive phase where differences are not just unresolved but wearingly re-affirmed. Six weeks after arriving at the guest house, Kevin continues to sleep in his car. His conversations with Sally and Frank are either repetitive or repeated—it is hard to tell which.

This is not the progressive, jazz-like repetition and revision (or "rep and rev") that characterises, say, Suzan-Lori Parks's plays[34]: *Say Nothing* is repetition and entrenchment. Whereas Parks's characters might slowly grapple with realisation, their myopia gradually lifting, breakthroughs in *Say Nothing* are not so much epiphanal as exorcistic, violent purgations of sedimented anger. That vitriol is unleashed on romanticism, sentimentality and hypocrisy—all of which help to maintain the habits that paper over entrenched divisions. While Frank is the most immediately objectionable of the three characters played by Hough, his upfront unpleasantness gets him off the hook. It is the more ingratiating characters, Sally and Dan, who are on the receiving end of Kevin's outbursts. Sally is always pressing Kevin, whose frustrations she doesn't quite get, to have a nice cup of tea. After she does so for the sixteenth time, Kevin, with building dementia, waxes lyrical about the "traditional Irish cup of tea, traditional Irish Bailey's, traditional Irish Jameson's, traditional Irish Bushmills, traditional Irish hatred, traditional Irish kneecapping, traditional Irish punishment beating ...."

Say Nothing is partly a riposte to Marie Jones's plays *A Night in November* and, in particular, the multi-award winning *Stones in his Pockets* (directed by Pam Brighton) which played in the UK to packed houses and great acclaim be-

---

34 Parks's particular play with repetition and revision is documented, for example, in Alisa Solomon, "Signifying on the Signifyin': The Plays of Suzan-Lori Parks", *Theater* (Summer/Fall, 1990), pp. 73-80 and in James Frieze, "Imperceptible Mutabilities in the Third Kingdom: *Suzan-Lori Parks and the Shared Struggle to Perceive*", *Modern Drama* 41.4 (Winter, 1998) pp. 523-532.

fore returning to Derry.[35] According to Woods, Jones's jovial account of tensions within an Irish village was loudly booed by those angry at what they saw as (at best) the play's liberal guilt and (at worst) a desire to cash in on a romanticised view of Ireland by pretending that even Protestants are really nationalists at heart. Lambasting them for secretly kowtowing to leading republicans, he describes Jones and Brighton as "a breed of non-native catholic-protestant more passionately Irish than the Irish, more nationalist than the nationalists".[36] They typify, for Woods, the absurdly contorted identities that permeate the borderlands.

Allegiances here are routinely paradoxical, as evident in descriptors such as "West-Brit", "native German Irish", and "Pinko-Provo". Being ethnically in transit while pretending to be settled is the norm, with many German, American, and British visitors making intense effort to speak in local accents. Woods reports: "In the six years of our residency in the province we were followed by the IRA who suspected our giveaway accents as possible SAS integrators - stories of SAS (pronounced "sass" in Derry)...[although] death threats in the end came from the Loyalist faction the LVF, who gave a blanket 'get out or be shot' warning to anyone engaged in peace and reconciliation work in 1997".[37]

It is through this quagmire of suspicion, hostility, and disguise that Kevin, doctoral student in Peace and Conflict studies, attempts to move. I first saw *Say Nothing* in 2001, when I was completing my own PhD, and wondering whether the ground-clearing, future-oriented, epistemologically re-centring discourse that I studied in graduate school in the mid-90s had done more than plaster over cracks between epistemes, and between academia and social realities of difference. Watching *Say Nothing* made me think of an iconic performer of the 90s, Anna Deavere Smith. One of the many ironies attendant upon the reception of Smith's work was that, while she spoke against the idea that actors should see themselves as "special vehicles", she was herself often endowed

---

35 *A Night in November* was originally produced in 1994 and *Stones in his Pockets* in 1996. Both productions were directed by Pam Brighton for the Belfast-based DubbelJoint Theatre Company. Texts of the plays are published together: *Stones in his Pockets/A Night in November: Two Plays* (London: Nick Hern Books, 2000).

36 Woods, 108.

37 Ibid., 109.

with shamanic/voodun/preternatural powers.[38] While Smith directed her audiences to "search for American character"[39] in the *gap between* the real person and her attempt to seem like them, it was a different gap that caused the most heated debate about Smith's work: the gap between her project's vaunted transparency and the contingencies of interviewing, editing, and staging within which her performance of openness was bound. Particularly contentious, her rendition/pursuit of the hesitations and non-fluencies of her interviewees was perceived as the mark of purity by some and unacknowledged prejudice by others.

Whereas Smith's *On the Road* project presents itself as open, *Say Nothing* presents itself as bitterly cynical. And yet, the portrayal of closure in *Say Nothing* left me more optimistic about theatre as a seeing-place than Smith's performance of empathetic listening. Maybe this says a lot about my own scepticism; maybe it is about changes in structures of feeling during the 1990s.

A different site of dysfunction was scoured in Woods and Hough's next show, *Ideas Men* (2003), about two "creatives" under pressure to come up with "the next big thing".[40] The office in which they work is the hub of the only department in a factory-based corporation that is left in the UK once the entire manufacturing operation has been exported to the Far East. *Ideas Men* taps into the dark side of role-play, an activity highly valued in the corporate world as a conduit for creativity. Mike and Liam are sick to death of their role-playing

---

38 "Not So Special Vehicles", delivered as a plenary speech to the Association for Theatre in Higher Education (ATHE) in 1993, was published in *Performing Arts Journal* (17: "The Arts and the University", 1995), pp. 77-89. The framing and self-framing of Smith in the early 1990s is a tissue of contradictions. She emerges as a natural scientist and a spirit channel; a non-author who is supremely interpretative; a Black woman in touch with the material reality of the streets but who is quasi-transcendentally objective and culturally liminal; and as deeply vulnerable yet above human foibles. Richard Stayton claims in "Anna Deavere Smith" (*American Theatre*, July/August 1993, pp.21-22) that she "seems to tap into your mind"; a television critic, reviewing the television version of *Fires* broadcast as part of the PBS series *American Playhouse*, describes her as "a chameleon and an exorcist" (John Leonard, "The Search for Signs of Intelligent Life in Brooklyn", *New York* 3 May 1993 p.68). A review of *Fires* in *Theatre Journal* claims: "Perhaps more than any other human being on the planet, [Smith] carries Crown Heights within her" (Attilio Favorini, "*Fires in the Mirror*", *Theatre Journal* 48.1, March 1996, pp.105-107).

39 *Fires in the Mirror* (1992) and *Twilight: Los Angeles, 1992* (1993) are parts of a series of works that Smith collectively titled *On the Road: A Search for American Character*, as outlined in her introduction to Anna Deavere Smith, *Fires in the Mirror* (New York; Anchor, 1993), pp. xxiii-xli.

40 All quotations in this paragraph are from Charlotte Cripps, "The Commodification of Ideas", *The Independent* (London) (29 September 2003), an interview article about Ideas Men accessed http://www.findarticles.com.

and in desperate need of some real inspiration. They cannot do without the games because they cannot face the possibility that there is nothing but the game. As in *Say Nothing*, dysfunction is a cycle that drives and is driven by denial: the games *make* them "frazzled, overworked, dried up," but allow them to avoid *confronting* the fact that they are "frazzled, overworked, dried up." Also as in *Say Nothing*, the devising process is layered with the product, the fictional with the autobiographical.

Research found them "hanging out in the City and with business students on an MBA course," wearing "suits so we didn't look like outsiders, and becoming fluent in office slang" such as "EBITDA: Earnings Before Interest Taxation Depreciation Amortisation... Then we made up a few ourselves, such as ICARUS: I Can Achieve Real Unparalleled Success," useful when they presented their ideas at a Unilever-sponsored creativity contest. What creativity means to Ridiculusmus seeps into *Ideas Men*. The pressurised role-play of Liam and Mike parodied in parallel to the pressure Jon and David feel to provide a conventional dramatic plot, hinting at their struggle to reconcile the desire for success with their belief that experimentation is key to personal and artistic integrity.

A similar struggle is at the heart of The Receipt, in which actor/deviser/ stand-up comedian Will Adamsdale narrates and plays protagonist Alan Wiley, while sonic artist Chris Branch produces a battery of sound effects from a Moog synthesizer and a couple of filing cabinets. Wiley works for a company called RotoPlas, though what they actually do is not clear. As well as being a company, RotoPlas is also the name of the building in which a range of other, apparently unrelated, companies are housed. Who is pulling whose strings is difficult to determine. It is a world of pseudo-transparency, full of rules, protocols and agendas that purport to systematise communication and prescribe the navigation of space. To pass through one arbitrarily demarcated area to the next, Wiley is asked to present 'an entry docket' or 'an exit docket' before being buzzed in. Things begin to go wrong for Wiley when he is sent to NeuCom to get a portable presentation surface called a BusiWall. Arriving at NeuCom, he presses the intercom and a voice answers, "NeuCom":

> WILEY: I've come to pick up the BusiWall.
> INTERCOM: No, mate, this is DivertEntry:HerenotHere.
> WILEY: Yeah, I've come to pick up the BusiWall.

92

> INTERCOM: No, the building's closed, mate; this is
> DivertEntry: HerenotHere. *[Pause]*. I'm not here.[41]

NeuCom's intercom system meets the needs of the visitor to the closed building by connecting them to someone hundreds of miles away who tells them when the building will be open. The someone that greets Wiley is, as they converse, also rearing chickens in a farm near the coast. Ironically, it is with the intercom chicken farmer that Wiley enjoys the deepest encounter he has in the entire play. Explaining his career choice to Wiley in avuncular fashion, DivertEntry: Herenot Here tells him: "It doesn't matter what you do, mate, just find something and stick to it."

Having gained access to the BusiWall, Wiley finds he cannot move it in one piece despite the assistance of the BusiHandle, a BusiWall product designed to make the BusiWall more portable. Returning to RotoPlas with only the base, which he intends to take upstairs before returning to NeuCom to pick up the other segments, he is told he cannot leave it in the lobby as he doesn't have an object docket. As he wonders how he will ever get the whole of the BusiWall up to his office, Wiley's boss informs him that RotoPlas are to go into business with BusiWall, the people who make the BusiWall. "You know what this means don't you, mate? We're going to do the BusiWall presentation to BusiWall! And you know what that means, don't you, Wiley? I'm going to need you to take the BusiWall to the BusiWall building, mate."

Other than moving BusiWalls, Wiley's work consists largely of answering phone calls asking what RotoPlas do. He seems well drilled:

> Hello RotoPlas; space up. Well, you've probably heard of us from the space management stuff? OK. Let me play a little game with you. When you think of "space" what do you think of? No, no, you can't be wrong. Well: people talk about space to work, space to live, here at RotoPlas, we like to talk about space to dream. That's what we do.

Wiley's dreams come to an end when he fails to master the subtleties of the RotoPlas switchboard, inadvertently hanging up on a client, who, unbeknown

---

41 *Receipt* quotations are from a DVD of a performance at the Assembly Rooms in Edinburgh in August, 2006. The DVD was provided by Will Adamsdale and the agency Fuel.

to him, is Alain Fête. Who Alain Fête is remains a mystery; hanging up on him, though, is clearly a sacking offence. Wiley's boss (barely distinguishable from Branch's many other roles) dismisses him with the rationale: "You can't hang up on someone like Alain Fête, Wiley. It's a busy time for us, mate, what with the re-branding."

After being let go by RotoPlas, Wiley begins a new and, to everyone except him, disturbingly random line of work: the search for the rightful owner of a crumpled piece of paper he finds in the street— a receipt for a glass of chardonnay. Wiley hopes that if he can reach the first target, the bartender noted on the receipt as Server 8, this will lead him to the actual purchaser behind the encrypted credit-card information— customer 241482. The quest is both a surrender to irrational personal obsession and a symbolic rite of passage that takes Wiley beneath the veil of consumer culture. Coming home from his first day of work on the receipt, though, he suffers a setback when he finds himself evicted from his flat, which, it turns out, is owned by RotoPlas. He resolves to live in the self-storage locker in which all his possessions have been crammed. Unfazed by being cooped into a tiny space with no amenities, he appears liberated by self-employment as he recalls the advice of the chicken farmer—"just find something and stick to it."

His quest takes to (as Branch insists it is pronounced) *drincoffee*, the running-together of the two words integral to the aura of the brand. It is a cheeky merger that leads Adamsdale to ponder other consumer items, which, on the contrary, are one thing impishly disguised as two— such as a shirt with a false layer that appears to be two shirts. After *drincoffee*, he realises he must go to a branch of another bar chain owned by the same company, Indel. bar_*space*_bar is a collocation of estate agency, café and nightclub, catering ingeniously to the previously unrecognised needs of those searching for property and a drink at the same time while saving space and maximising mood possibilities. Wiley, who just wants to wait until Server 8 comes in, struggles to master bar_*space*_bar's esoteric policies about which piece of paper, or "space tab," will enable him to buy the kind of drink necessary to allow him to sit in the daytime. Just as he seems to be defeated by Indel bureaucracy, he remembers to utter the name of Alain Fête and doors magically open.

The Receipt, like *Ideas Men* and *Say Nothing*, is an enterprise in which the handling of language and of space pits theatrical solutions against business solutions. From the start, unwanted sonic contributions from Branch impede Adamsdale's attempts to progress— a dynamic reminiscent of double acts such as Abbot and Costello, Laurel and Hardy, Morecambe and Wise. Branch's undermining of Adamsdale takes us into territory that devised theatre so frequently visits these days: the labour-intensive telling of a story about the impossibility of telling a story. But *The Receipt*, like *Ideas Men*, exemplifies another brand of contemporary storytelling: the anthropological study of life in workplaces in which no meaningful work is actually done. Whereas *The Office* (BBC, 2001-2003) was television that parodically quoted television documentary, and *Nathan Barley* (Channel 4, 2005) was television infected by and satirical of new media art platforms, *The Receipt* is very much a piece for the stage. Adamsdale's Wiley is mobile, animated, demonstrative. Using direct address, and switching with felicity between narratorial and actantional modes, he enjoys an empathetic complicity with his audience, his innocent, Martianist tone poses insights as questions for spectators: "Why is technology increasingly named after fruit? Are you on Apple? I mean, I'm on Apple too, but it works better if you're on Orange as well." Struck by the volume of paper that supports and surrounds office machinery, he asks whether machines weren't supposed to limit the need for paper, rather than generate it? Branch, in contrast, is physically static, always seated and side-on to the audience, always largely shielded by his keyboard stack. He occasionally chips, in but mostly remains detached. As Adamsdale's stress levels climb, Branch remains irritatingly untroubled by the beeps, buzzers, alarms and bits of muzak that are the soundtrack to Wiley's alienation, his mundane tone and side-on efficiency the perfect foil.

The playing by one performer of multiple, luridly antagonistic roles is a common feature in political satire on stage and on film. Stanley Kubrick's deployment of Peter Sellers in *Dr Strangelove, or How I Learned to Stop Worrying and Love the Bomb* (1964), draws on a theatrical tradition and is itself referenced in plays such as Paula Vogel's *Baltimore Waltz*.[42] What is different about *The Receipt*, is that, rather than going for vivid signification of type, as Hough's performance of Frank, Sally and Dan does in *Say Nothing*, Branch's performance is strikingly mild-mannered and not (in Kirby's terms) matrixed. At the

---

42 *The Baltimore Waltz* was first produced in 1992 at Circle Rep in Manhattan, directed by Anne Bogart. The text is published in *The Baltimore Waltz and Other Plays* (New York: TCG, 1996).

same time, it is not non-matrixed, but closer to what Kirby calls the "symbolised matrix," in which "the referential elements" of a world are applied to, but not acted by the performer.[43]

Ambiguity about the matrixing of Branch's performance creates the image of the corporation as impalpably demonic. While having one person play an entire corporation seems like a flight of theatrical fancy, it should be remembered that corporations have, for centuries, been masquerading as individuals— a point made in *The Corporation*,[44] a film documentary which shows how laws designed to help freed slaves counter discrimination were exploited by nascent corporations. To this day, a system that allows corporations to function legally as individuals, limits responsibility by masking power. *The Receipt* parodies the personification of the corporation that enables actual individuals to mask themselves as they carry out corporate work.

In *The Philosophy of Horror*,[45] Noël Carroll conceives the horrific in a way that resonates with Wiley's journey through the corporate world. Though one barely has time to notice if they do their job properly, monsters (claims Carroll) are monstrous by virtue of their structurally transgressive ontology, what he calls their "fantastic biology." His two main types of fantastic biology are fusion and fission. Fusion monsters are individual entities in which categories normally opposite and exclusive, such as living/dead, are unified in figures like zombies, vampires or mummies. The prototypical fusion monster is what Freud calls the collective figure or condensation, frequently found in dreams. In Vogel's *Baltimore Waltz*, it is in the extended daydream that the condensation figure appears, and when the playwright's alter-ego wakes up, we glimpse a more mundane reality but one infused by the consciousness of the dream. In *The Receipt*, as the RotoPlas slogan promises, there is space to dream, but it is not a dream we are ever fully immersed in or suddenly wake up from: the condensation fig-

43 Michael Kirby, "On Acting and Not-Acting", originally published in *TDR: The Drama Review* (16.1, 1972, pp. 3-15) and reprinted in Phillip Zarrilli (ed.), *Acting Re(Considered)* (London: Routledge, 1995), pp.43-58.

44 *The Corporation* is written and directed by Mark Achbar, Jennifer Abbot and Joel Bakan. It had a fairly wide cinema release, was released on DVD in 2004, and has been shown on Channel 4 television in the UK.

45 Noël Carroll, *The Philosophy of Horror*, or *Paradoxes of the Heart* (New York: Routledge, 1990).

ure remains throughout, in the person of Branch, uncannily singular and multiple, real and fantastic.

Whereas fusion monsters unify opposing categories, fission distributes them. If fusion is about collapsing, fission is about splitting. It can be temporal, dividing characters over time within one body, as in Dr. Jekyll/Mr. Hyde or a werewolf; or it can be spatial, as in the doppelganger or alter-ego, in which one, self-contradictory entity is distributed over different bodies. While fusion and fission create the underlying logical deviance needed to make a monster, monstrosity is intensified and specularised by operations that include self-replication and extreme changes of scale (cloning and massification), along with startling changes in demeanour.

Fusion, fission, cloning and massification thrive in the corporation-governed world depicted in *The Receipt*. It is a world in which many companies, some invisibly incorporated, can share, or appear to share, the same space; a world in which estate agency can merge with binge drinking; in which outlets of different natures can be controlled by the same corporate body; and in which previously exclusive categories of human and machine merge to create an intercom chicken-farmer. Though Carroll's focus is on horror, the structural logic he describes bears more than a surface resemblance to what I will call the "genealogies of takeover" that can be found in Naomi Klein's analyses of branding,[46] analyses which parse mergers, acquisitions, incorporations, lateral monopolies and multi-platform synergy— a lexicon as structural and as formalist as Carroll's in *The Philosophy of Horror*.

Carroll focuses on how, in philosophical terms, monsters work. But what makes monsters charming are the ways in which, in practical terms, they *don't* work. Zombies, for example, being both living and dead, tend to move incredibly slowly. Confusion and bluntness are the decoys that make corporate schemes seem more innocent. When it comes to creating a brand like RotoPlas, a job like space management, and a system governed by "dockets," evacuation of substance passes as provision. The non-communicative language and non-service services alienated in *The Receipt* are potent ways for corporations to restrict social channels.

---

46 Before *No Logo* (London: Flamingo, 2000), Klein wrote for many years about corporations and global markets for *Village Voice* and many other newspapers and magazines.

Like the BusiHandle, the Baudrillard is a tool that tends to evade the grasp, but we should persevere, as it is useful for portability. In *The Transparency of Evil*— a misleading translation of the more literal *Trans-Apparency of Evil*, which is akin to opacity, not transparency— Baudrillard examines the stealthy evacuation of substance satirised in *The Receipt*. He describes a world in which "every individual category is subject to contamination, substitution possible between any sphere and any other...Politics is no longer restricted to the political sphere, but infects every sphere— economics, science, art, sport, which is no longer located in sport as such, but in business, in sex, in politics, in the general style of *performance*" [his italics].[47] For Baudrillard, performance is a "style" that supercedes substance. Thanks to this supercession, "value" is allowed to roam free of structures that used to contain it. Historically, he states, objects had a natural or use-value; then, in the commodity stage of culture, they had exchange value, which could be determined by reference to a logic, or system, of commodification; later, they had structural value as signs, determinable by reference to a set of codes. In the fourth stage, which Baudrillard calls fractal, viral or radiant, there is no law of value, but a dispersal or haphazard proliferation of value. As Wiley is reminded during his detective work by several employees of Indel (perhaps Indel is short for Indelible?), the receipt has no natural value, no commodity value, and no structural value. The receipt is a valuable project precisely because it is just another discarded piece of paper. It is as if value, for Wiley, can only be determined by escaping the values of a world in which value itself refuses to be quanitifed. In such a world, the chicken-farmer's advice makes sense to Wiley: "It doesn't matter what you do, just find something and stick to it."

For Wiley, as for Baudrillard, contamination between spheres like estate agency and clubbing is alarming. He is perplexed by the "obscure origin and questionable utility" of haphazard mergers, since the corporations seem helpfully to be reminding us, as if we have forgotten, exactly what should happen where. "Eat this," they tell us, offering pointers like brown bags that say "E.A.T." or "Medium Brown Bag." Showing us the sections of the Saturday *Guardian* newspaper one after another, he wonders if we need to be told what a "Family,"

---

47 Jean Baudrillard, *The Transparency of Evil: Essays on Extreme Phenomena* (Bath: Verso, 1996), p.8.

"Work" and "Travel" are.[48] Such supplements convince us that we have lost our memory: that we can't do without their aid. At its most (if I may so term it) "evacuous", corporate culture is not, in old money, phatic but purely factual.

In satirising commodified creativity and vitriolic vacuity, the double-acts I have re-presented take severe theatrical issue with the idea that genuine communication "lies in finding a proper balance between factual and phatic," between information and the padding that seals the channels along which value-rich information flows.

---

48 This section of the show, about the phatic function of paper bags, newspaper supplements and other consumer items, was not in the original production at the Edinburgh Fringe from which I quote elsewhere. It was added as an opening monologue by Adamsdale in the version I saw at the Unity Theatre in Liverpool in February, 2007 as part of a tour (New York, Melbourne and various U.K. venues). I am highly grateful to Josephine Large, with whom I saw the show in Liverpool, for her insights.

'darling you were marvellous'

TIM CROUCH

[Tim Crouch is a playwright and performer, based in Brighton, UK. Plays include *My Arm* (Prix Italia, 2005), *Shopping for Shoes* (Brian Way Award for children's playwrighting, 2007), *An Oak Tree* (Glasgow Herald Angel, 2005, Obie Special Citation, 2007) and *England* (Scotsman Fringe First, Glasgow Herald Archangel and Total Theatre Award, 2007), and *The Author*. He is an Education Associate of the National Theatre and Associate Artist of the Franklin Stage Company, New York.

Here's an exercise to break the ice at the start of a theatre workshop. It's good for novices and professionals alike. I found it went down particularly well in prisons. It's called "Darling You Were Marvellous." Introduce it by saying that all actors need reassurance. Paint the picture of going backstage after a particularly grisly time in the theatre and greeting a member of the cast – a friend, maybe, someone whom you consider responsible for much of the grisly-ness to which you have just been subjected. Approach them with a confident step, outstretch your arms flamboyantly, envelop them inside your voluminous span, kiss the air an inch from each cheek and declaim for everyone to hear the immortal words: "Darling, you were marvellous!!!" Get your workshop participants to try this out with a partner. It feels good, doesn't it? Then get them to move around the room and greet everyone else in the same way. Within seconds, the air becomes thick with the sound of deflection and deception.

This, you tell your workshop participants, is how you talk to actors after you've seen them in a show you didn't like. It works every time with even the most hardened realist in the most terrible of plays. Tell them they were marvellous and, despite all evidence to the contrary, they will believe you. A little bit of the gloom will lift. "Really?" they'll say. "Thank you so much!" With one swift act of duplicity, you've restored their faith in themselves and you've effectively neutered any chance there ever was of an intelligent, open and free discussion with them about the nature of what you've just seen. You then go to a bar with some fellow audience members and rip the show to shreds.

This is the language of direct performance criticism that pervades the actor/audience relationship even amongst the brightest and the sharpest. I've seen university professors do their own version of 'darling you were marvelous.' There is no freedom of speech. People who speak freely to the actors after a performance are seen as self-regarding and insensitive. No, we are cagey about what we say after the show. We eye each other up, we read each other for signals. We censor our inner thoughts until we are able to escape to a safe place, a haven; somewhere where we know we can speak freely and without persecution.

I'm not talking about the stuff of pamphlets and articles and chapters in books. I'm talking about the real day to day stuff. This is in the 'field': in the theatre lobby, at the stage door, in the bar. It is the awkward, fumbling exchanges where true thoughts and feelings are suppressed beneath the diplomatic flags of sensitivity, caution and politeness. We don't want to hurt anyone's feelings and, by not wanting to do so we impede the progress of theatre criticism. How do we do that? We leave it to the professionals.

The rise of the professional critic (paralleled with the rise of the professional director) has removed the need for us to have an opinion of our own. It removes from us any responsibility for what we see. The critic can tell the actor that they stank. The critic can tell the director where they went wrong, where the playwright screwed up. By leaving it to the critic we can comfortably renege on our duty as audience members to sustain the critical debate. "Darling, you were marvellous," we can say to the actor, in the knowledge that somebody else will tell them what we really thought. We hand the critics an authority and thereby disengage the language of theatre criticism from the everyday of human exchange. The most we can expect as actors from an audience member is, "How did you manage to learn all those lines?"

*

My play, *An Oak Tree*, brings me into contact with these dynamics of criticism and free speech every time it is performed. At each performance I bring a
different actor on stage with me – an actor who has neither seen nor read a
word of the play they're about to be in, but who plays an equal character in the
story. This is a delicate, vulnerable process for both of us. Before each show I
talk with the second actor. I tell them a little about the devices that the play will
use; I invite them to be open and to take their authority on stage. I tell them
that in the play they can doing nothing wrong. I also tell them that throughout
the play they will get continual support and praise from me. "Fantastic." "Beautiful." "You're doing brilliantly." I tell them that most of these encouragements
are scripted, but also that I will mean every word. My aim in the show is never
to allow the second actor to feel doubt-ridden about what they're doing. Doubt
is an enemy to the creative process. It can be the death to open-ness. If the
second actor starts doubting themselves, then they stop feeling able to trust
their instinct, they close up and my play suffers. In the spirit of 'darling you were
marvelous,' I know that the merest suggestion of success (even if scripted) is
enough to lift the actor to a place of self-confidence. *An Oak Tree* is explicit in
this respect. "You told me I was doing brilliantly," the second actor's script in-
structs them to tell me. "That was just a thing to say," my scripted line replies,
"to encourage you."

So how do we find an objectivity? How do we talk to actors? Do we just not
bother? Do we repress our opinions? Do we admire their line-learning abilities?
Do we just tell them that they're great? Out of fear of destroying them, do we
just say 'well done'? They'll find out that they stink when their work dries up,
when the reviews come out, when the audiences stop coming. Would it were as
simple as that.

This fragility of ego is the stuff of art; it's what makes a performer watch-
able, a brush stroke compelling. Success through vulnerability is the best kind
ever, but contingent on that vulnerability needs be the ever-present chance of
failure. Success without some degree of doubt is brash and tawdry and hard to
watch. So we must be equally careful of our praise. As soon as an actor starts
to believe their own hype, then the rot sets in. How do we achieve that balance? I had an actor in *An Oak Tree* who, from the outset, was completely closed
down. He stood on stage and smirked at the audience. He did what he was in-
structed to do but he responded neither to the given circumstances of the story

we were telling, nor to my red-faced exhortations to 'act', to 'make it you own,' to 'take your authority.' True to my word, I praised his efforts; "You're doing brilliantly". Here, however, was a tone of desperation in my voice. I was in a double bind. I needed to praise him to attempt to unlock him from his closure. But my praise only made him think he was succeeding – he believed his own hype. He listened selectively. He didn't hear my encouragements to change; he just heard the headline praise, and that confirmed in his mind that what he was doing was right. So he just smirked some more. Here was a performance when I should have ditched the velvet gloves and told him to start acting... I should have told him what I thought, spoken my mind freely. It would have done us both the world of good. But because I'd only met him an hour before, I didn't know what damage that would do.

This is where we are in the everyday of lay theatre criticism: we walk on egg shells, disempowered to say what we feel, and mindful of the egos we could so easily destroy. We are censored.

Some theatres have taken the processes of audience response in hand. They create audience feedback forms – questionnaires which give the impression that the audience's views are valued. They suggest that the audience can really voice an opinion. Forms with questions like, "Did the production live up to your expectations?", "What did you enjoy most about the show?" "What was your least favourite aspect?" Hidden within these forms are the marketeers' needs: "How far have you travelled to get to the theatre tonight?" "How did you hear about tonight's show?" "Would you like to be on our mailing list?" Often these documents are created at the request of the funding bodies that need to know how their grants are being spent: "Did you think this evening's performance constituted value for money?" I was working in a theatre recently and next to the laundry basket in my dressing room was a pile of these completed feedback forms – yellowing and abandoned. They seemed a fitting symbol for where we've got to in terms of talking about theatre after the event.

How else do we encourage free critical exchange? Many people are now turning to blogs to vent their opinion, but this still feels like a poor substitute for face-to-face. Bloggers can hide behind their anonymity. Speaking one's mind is still seen as an act of aggression. Bloggers are covert operators whose freedom to say what they like is born from their being removed from the process. They do no enter themselves into a genuine live dialogue. BAC in London set up a more structured approach to enable audience members to speak their minds. Their "Scratch Nights" attempt to open up the process of works in development to an audience of interested and articulate theatre-goers. The work is shown, the feedback forms are filled in and space is given to meet the artists and talk after a performance. Even within this carefully supported environment there is still a terrain of awkwardness and artificiality. The effort to organise something that should be a natural process often leaves these discussions feeling stilted. Theatre is a complex experience. The dominant critical mode, however, is constantly trying to reduce it to a base level of entertainment, and leave all the detailed analysis to the experts.

*

I suggest that one reason for this level of critical trepidation is the current ambiguity of the 'idea' in acting. We've lost the map to its location. Actors are primarily seen as skilled impersonators of observed behaviour. They are not encouraged to think about the 'idea'. Often, from my experience, they are not encouraged to think, period. Their honed memetic skills separate them from the ideas of the plays they are in. We have been trained as audiences to take enjoyment from an accurate impersonation. A judgment of an actor's work has become whether they can be a convincing 'character,' a plausible 'other.' A schism is established where we can distinguish 'good acting' from a 'good play.' "The play was terrible, but the actors were great." What does that mean? How does one judge a performance independent of its context? This feels wrong to me. The fact that we can make such a split is an indication of a disconnect. Rather than recognise the role their work serves in the transmission of the active ideas of the play, actors are encouraged to offer themselves up to a voyeuristic imperative. Acting is then seen as a process of personal and intimate revelation and mimicry which swamps any objective critical standpoint towards the play as a whole. As a consequence of this, actors become absorbed in notions of 'personality' and the language of actor criticism is reduced to the banal and platitudinal. "You were really convincing!" Because the mimetic imperative becomes central to the way we talk about acting, the playwrights write plays that pander to that imperative. And the drama schools train actors to successfully fulfill that imperative. It's a vicious circle that keeps the audience preoccupied with the wrong thing. We either 'believe' the actor or we don't – but we're not encouraged to question what the bigger truth is.

I test this emphasis on mimicry with *An Oak Tree*. Each actor, whether male or female, old or young, black or white, plays the same character – a 46 year old father. There is no rehearsal, no chance for psychological research or physio-logical transformation. There can be no attempt from the actor to 'simulate' a physical truth to this character. As such, the distinction between performer and idea is clearly stated. The actor becomes a much more articulated vehicle for the idea – which thereby alleviates the audience of its obsession with imperson-ation and allows them a clearer critical standpoint to the play as a whole. An-other example of this process is in my first play, *My Arm*. This, ostensibly, is a first person autobiographical piece about a boy who puts one arm above his head and then never takes it down. I deliver the story as my own – up to the point of my death. But at no point in the proceedings do I ever raise my arm. This is not a performance with which I want to dupe an audience into uncritical silence. I want the idea of the play to be foregrounded and the performance of the actor to be secondary. By achieving this dynamic I hope I liberate an audi-ence into a sense of their own critical authority. I want to give them their voice.

*

Before I started to write plays, I acted for a living. I worked for other people on other people's plays. In that sense, I was employed as an interpreter; a trans-lator of other people's ideas. Because the ideas were not mine (or rather be-cause I was never authorised to 'own' the ideas) my only focus was on my act-ing. I had to be a 'good actor,' whatever that meant. I had to embody the language, be realistic in my responses to the given circumstances in which the play placed me, I had to do what the director told me – and that was about it. When I was an actor, it meant little to me if the critics rejected the play I was in. So what? But I would be mortified if they didn't like ME. My whole *raison d'etre* was to be seen as a good actor, a good interpreter. Even if I was in a bad play, I would make it my mission to salvage my reputation; I would come out of it un-scathed. The writer and director could concern themselves with the ideas; I just wanted people to tell me 'well done.' I created a critical environment around my work which was predicated on me getting through untouched.

At some point in my career I began to doubt the shallow simplicity of this critical transaction. I can pinpoint the beginning of that doubt around the time of a 1996 revival of Caryl Churchill's *Light Shining in Buckinghamshire* (1976) which I did at the National Theatre in London. Here is a play rammed full of ideas about performance and governance and belief. Set during the English Civil War, with our production touring Britain around the time of the 1997 General Election (the one which got rid of the Tories). A political play at a political time, and yet we approached this play as 'actors.' We broke it down into psychological objectives and units of intention. We assiduously found transitive verbs for everything our characters said to one another. We explored the history of the period, to attain an historical verisimilitude. On the road, however, this play became a political rally. There were talk-backs and post-show discussions, and it was the actors' job to host them. None of us had a clue. Here was the disconnect. Where were the idea people when we needed them? We were just the actors. Where was the writer and the director? How could we be in such an ideological play, and not have an idea? And nobody seemed to be all that interested in our acting. Something more important was happening on the stage. We were serving it well, but we didn't know what it was.

As I started to write, and as I began to perform the things I wrote, my approach to my acting began to change. Acting was no longer the end in itself. It had become the means to the end. The end, now, was the transmission of an idea: the idea I had placed inside a play. Fortunately for me, my plays were also about 'performance' (which play isn't?) – and so there was an even clearer connection now to my acting. My acting became an idea as well – not the confusion of techniques I had picked up at drama school – but an active idea reflected in the thesis of the play. At last I started to know what I was doing. In the process of this transition I stopped obsessing about the critics; I no longer needed the personal approbation from the audience. I could handle the post-show discussion. Whether I was 'marvellous' or not was no longer the point. The point was the play, and what the play required from me to successfully communicate it. My quality of performance became 'outward facing.' I hope that, in the process, my audience has become enabled to tell me what they think. There is no longer the precious self-revelation in my performance work. Rather a robustness of an idea in action. And an idea is up for grabs far more readily than an actor's ego.

This transmission of idea is connected to giving the audience its own authority in relation to the debate. Whilst theatre continues to be tangled in notions of ego and psychological and physiological realism, then the audience will continue to be disempowered in the critical debate around it. The 'idea' of each

play is never far from the surface, but it has been obscured. Scratch a practitioner and you'll find a theorist. How can it not be otherwise? There is no practice
without an idea supporting it, no matter how submerged that idea is. Scratch
an audience and you'll find an ideology. But by placing the audience in a dark
space, by getting them to sit still and quiet whilst we subject them to indulgent
and impersonated fantasies – this is an abuse of power.

Police on my Back:

Or How Site-Based Theatre Can Outwit the Censor

CARL LAVERY

[Carl Lavery teaches theatre and performance at Aberystwyth University in Wales. He is the co-author of *Jean Genet: Performance and Politics* (2006), *Sacred Theatres* (2007), and *Walking, Autobiography and Performance* (2008, forthcoming). He is currently writing a book for Manchester University Press about Jean Genet and the modernization of Paris in the 1950s and 1960s. The book is called *Spaces of Revolution*.]

> Just across the straits, away from the river, off the beaten path, at the end of the subway line, there lives another people (unless, it is, quite simply, the people). (Rancière, 2003 p. 1)

Normally, when we think of censorship, we think in terms of particular cases, such as, for instance, the Lord Chamberlain's decision to bar Jean Genet's play *The Balcony* from public theatres in UK in the 1950s,[49] or, more recently, the famous National Endowment for the Arts scandal that took place in the US in the early 1990s.[50] In the two examples mentioned above, censorship is best

---

49 Genet's play was staged, privately, in the Arts Theatre Club in London in April 1957. Genet was savagely critical of the production by Peter Zadek.

50 In the wake of severe criticism that followed the National Endowment for the Arts (NEA) support for the transgressive photographs of Andres Serrano and Robert Mapplethorpe in 1989, the board decided to revoke, in 1990, the grants it had made to four performance artists, Holly Hughes, Tim Miller, Karen Finley and John Fleck, on the grounds of obscenity. Although the artists later took the NEA to the US Supreme Court in 1993 and had their grants restated, Congress effectively used

understood as a delimited activity, an operation played out in a confined field. However, as with every ideological operation, the particular case veils an invisible, more generalized rationale that remains concealed within the actual act of censorship itself. Like the commodity, then, censorship is a type of fetish that obscures a hidden set of values and assumptions.[51] In order to bring these assumptions into the open, so to speak, I intend in this short intervention to draw attention to the larger political logic that subtends all specific acts of actual censorship in the arts through the French philosopher Jacques Rancière's notion of the police. Before I start I want to make it clear here that I am dealing with censorship in what for some might be a too simplistic or crude sense: namely, as an operation performed on behalf of a dominant group or State jealously interested in guarding its own hegemony.[52]

In *Disagreement: Politics and Philosophy*, the foundational text for his later political and aesthetic thought, Rancière is careful to distinguish the empirical police from what he calls police logic:

> The word police normally evokes what is known as the petty police, the truncheon blows of the forces of law and order and the inquisitions of the secret police. But this narrow definition may be deemed contingent....The petty police is just a particular form of a more general order that arranges the tangible reality in which bodies are distributed in community....The evolution of Western societies reveals...that the policeman is one element in a social mechanism linking medicine, welfare and culture. (1999, p. 28)

Despite the Foucauldian resonances here, Rancière insists that, for him, police logic is not to do with 'disciplining' bodies; rather it is a process or law that

---

the scandal to prevent the NEA from funding individual artists. Tellingly, the practitioners mentioned explored alternative notions of sexuality and gender, while critiquing, in their largely autobiographical work, heteronormative structures of normality.

51 For Marx, the commodity both conceals and reveals alienated labour. The same logic pertains to censorship. In my view, the censored object simultaneously shows and hides the dominant values in any society. The act of censoring, in other words, is often, for me, an attempt to maintain hegemony by transforming culture into a spurious nature. However, the very decision to censor something (be that an opinion or a work of art) is, necessarily, a sign of the very contingency which existing power structures strive to repress.

52 See for instance Janelle Reinelt's categorization of five different modes of censorship in her recent article 'The Limits of Censorship' (2007, p. 6.). For Reinelt – and it is difficult to disagree with her – censorship is not always a bad thing: hence the consciously constructed sense of ambiguity in her title.

governs their 'appearing' in what he calls 'the distribution of the sensible' (ibid., p. 29):

> The police is, essentially the law, generally implicit, that defines a party's share or lack of [power]. But to define this, you must first define the configuration of the perceptible in which one of the other is inscribed. The police is thus first an order of bodies that defines the allocation of ways of doing, ways of being, ways of saying, and sees that those bodies are assigned by name to a particular place and task: it is an order of the visible and the sayable that sees that a particular activity is visible and another is not, that this speech is understood as discourse and another as noise. (ibid.)

Rancière's claim that police logic determines what can and/or cannot be seen or said transforms censorship from a relatively limited activity into the very stuff of politics itself. To put this another way: censorship, as its etymology suggests, is inextricably bound up with the notion of consensus, the attempt, that is, to establish a sense of false harmony over the entire social field.[53] In Rancière's thinking, consensus or policing is radically opposed to politics proper, which, as he sees it, is forged in dissent and antagonism between those who have a share in the distribution of the sensible (all the elements and representations that produce (and reproduce) the status quo), and those who are excluded from it, and whom he calls 'the part with no part':

> I reserve the term politics for an extremely determined artistic activity antagonistic to policing: whatever breaks with the tangible configuration whereby parties and parts or lack of them are defined by a presupposition that, by definition, has no place in that configuration – that of the part of those who have no part. This break is manifest in a series of actions that reconfigure the space where parties, parts, or lack of parts have been defined. Political activity is whatever shifts a body from the place assigned to it or changes a place's destination. (ibid,. pp. 29-30)

---

53   As Reinelt highlights the 'censor was a Roman official who had two tasks: to count the population and to regulate the morals of that population' (ibid., p. 3). From a Rancièrian perspective, the censor is effectively a policeman, but not a member of the petty police. His role is to regulate what can be seen and heard and to make sure that all the population is counted and accounted for, that is to say, located in its proper place.

For Rancière, the antagonism between politics and 'policing' gets to the core of official censorship, which, as we know only too well, generally uses a rhetoric of impropriety to repress discordant forms of representation that challenge hegemonic configurations of the sensible.

Rancière's notion of politics as a dispute over the sensible places aesthetics – and in particular theatre – at the very heart of political emancipation. Not only is theatre a representational machine which allows bodies and voices to take place and 'appear', but its taking place is always in public. Theatre makes politics palpable both on the stage and in the stalls. Just as the performer evades any attempt to tie herself to one body or voice, so spectators, too, escape their social moorings. To be a spectator is quite literally to abandon one's place, to enter into a physical relationship with other people from different classes and walks of life. Theatre then is a space where placelessness takes on physical form. This is underlined by the UK philosopher Peter Hallward in an excellent article on what he calls Rancière's 'theatrocracy':[54]

> Peopled by multiple voices, the theatre is likewise the privileged site of a more general displacement – a place for the out-of-place. Every theatrical experience undermines the great police project, which is also the ambition of historians and sociologists – to see people 'rooted in their place and time'. (2006, p. 5)

If every theatrical experience, to cite Hallward, has the potential to disrupt the consensus of space and time, then site-based theatre, theatre that takes place outside of the auditorium, would appear to be particularly suited to producing a politically uncensored stage. This is because site-based theatre, to return to Rancière, 'changes a place's destination' by asking its spectators to stop, look and think about their surroundings. Crucially, Hallward notes that such stopping and looking is what police logic is concerned to avoid:

> [T]he counter-political action of what Rancière calls the 'police' is first and foremost anti-spectacular. Against Althusser, Rancière insists that 'police intervention in public spaces does not consist primarily in the interpellation of demonstrators but in the breaking up of demonstrations'. Rather than solicit a submissive recognition or response, the police dismantle political stages by tell-

---

54 The term 'theatocracy' is taken from Plato's Laws. Where Plato uses the word pejoratively to connote a sense of the unruly mob or demos, Rancière appropriates it for positive ends.

ing would-be spectators there is nothing to watch. They point the obviousness of what there is, or rather, of what there isn't. "Move along! There is nothing to see here". Where political actors turn the streets into stages, the police re-establish the smooth circulation of traffic' (ibid., p. 12)

Like the political demonstration or public gathering, site-based theatre cannot help but transform the city into a stage. As a consequence, site-based performance makes visible what police logic is so concerned to repress: the lack of any natural fit between a place or site and the people who inhabit it. Let's be clear about this. I am not simply suggesting that site-based theatre's capacity for disrupting consensus, or what amounts to the same thing, censorship, is found in its content or form. Rather I am proposing that its capacity for creating dissensus is found in its ontology, or what the art critic Rosalind Krauss might call its 'medium specificity' (1999). At the same time, however, this is not meant to suggest that all forms of existing site-based performance necessarily exploit the disruptive potential inherent in the medium.[55] As critics such as Rosalyn Deutsche (1996) and, Miwon Kwon (2004) have pointed out, many examples of site-based art actually function to bolster the status quo and to affirm consensus. However, despite the very real validity of Kwon's and Deutsche's objections, their reservations do not alter the essential point of my argument: namely, that site-based theatre has an inherent capacity, if used for such a purpose, to dislocate and to unsettle the relationship between place, function and identity.[56]

Think here for instance of the UK artist Graeme Miller's on-going sound piece *Linked*.[57] In this performance, Miller invites solitary spectators to walk alongside the M11 link road in North East London (E11), and to listen to the testimony of the ex-residents who were forcibly evicted from their houses to make way for the road in the mid-1990s. In Miller's work, London – or at least the four miles that run from Hackney Wick to Walthamstow – is transformed into a ghost city, as the walker-participant listens to the stories and mashed up fragments of sound that are broadcast from the transmitters strategically

---

55 I am grateful to Charles Campbell and Gülgün Kayim for reminding me of this in their engaged reading of an earlier draft of this essay.

56 This is apparent in the political potential Deutsche and Kwon reserve for alternative, more resistant forms of site-based art.

57 For a detailed account of the effects and affects of Linked see Lavery (2005) and (2007)

placed on the footpath that skirts the link road. As the cars buzz by in a banal blur of non-place transience, the narratives on the headset speak of snow in London, of cooking in the kitchen, of laughing with neighbours, of shared memories, of slower pleasures, and of organizing collectively to fight the contractors and bailiffs sent by the then Conservative government to appropriate their dwellings in order to ensure the smooth circulation of capital. The City of London, with its 'chemical' banks, stockbrokers and status symbol architecture, is only a mile or so away, as the crow files. By making mute things speak and summoning spectres, Miller contests the consensual logic which, as the US art historian W. J. T. Mitchell cautioned in his seminal collection *Landscape and Power*, is always at work in our perceptions of place. In this way, *Linked* reminds us in the most physical way possible – we have to walk the work, after all – that landscape is a verb as well as a noun, a process which produces the present by silencing the past and, all too often, erasing 'the scene of the crime'.

In this context, it is surely no coincidence that *Linked* should act as a sonic memorial to the bitter and sometimes bloody battle for 'Leytonstonia' that took place between the (empirical) police force and a dedicated band of local road protestors and eco-warriors in the 1990s. To this extent, *Linked* is, then, best described as a testimony to dissensus and an act of dissensus in and by itself - its function is to question accepted notion of place and territory by sending its participants out into the city and by asking them to hear and to see what police logic strives so desperately to conceal. As a consequence, it disrupts what the censor always wants to prevent: the possibility that things could be different, that the distribution of the sensible is always open to change and reconfiguration.

Another piece of site-based performance that challenges the logic of consensus, albeit in a different way, is *The City Itself*, a marathon triptych by the Minneapolis collective Skewed Visions, whose very name appears to celebrate dissensus. As Charles Campbell, one of the founder members of the company, along with Gülgün Kayim and Sean-Kelly Pegg, puts it: 'The name Skewed Visions refers to the plurality of visions within the company and the individuality (or skewd-ness) of where these visions come from' (in Jakovljevic, 2005, p. 96). *The City Itself* is a site-specific and time-based performance that took place in Minneapolis between September and November 2004. Unlike Fiona Templeton's influential performance *You-The City* which took place in Manhattan in the late 1980s , *The City Itself* sought to draw attention to how urban and spatial practices affect and impact us in and by themselves. The work consisted of *The Car*, three intimate performances staged in the closed space of three cars as they snaked their way through downtown Minneapolis; *Side Walk*, a Janet Cardiff-esque sound piece and *The House*, a domestic performance that took place in a home in South Minneapolis.

While each of these performance was conceived as a 'material intervention and resistance to established structures of belonging' (2007), the first part of the triptych *The Car* seems to have produced an especially strong sense of dis-identification for its audience members. Writing in *The Drama Review*, Branislaw Jakovljevic, for instance, describes how the three performances in *The Car* – 'The Prostitute', 'The Wild Ride' and 'The Taxi' – were doubled by the performance of the city itself. For Jacovljevic, the performance acted as an aesthetic frame which, by suspending our conventional modes of urban perception, made the city appear strange, unreal, skewed:

> This is a performance that actively engages audiences physically without ever insisting on participation. Pushing the non-existent brake pedal is as much part of the experience of *The Car* as keeping an eye on the changing street lights behind the backs of the three performers – who are simultaneously changing their clothes and urging the driver to run the red light. Where does acting stop and driving begin? And furthermore, where is the boundary between watching the performance and navigating the road? *The Car* poignantly reminds us how much our bodies are involved in the act of perception, regardless of the site-neutral's theatre's attempts to immobilize it and lull it into a perceptual slumber. (ibid. 99)

Jakovljevic's questions here are revealing: they hint at the ways in which site-based theatre can politicize our surroundings by aestheticizing them. Or to continue where Jakovljevic stops: they allow for a different configuration of the sensible. Like the nineteenth-century French workers who, in Rancière's book *Nights of Labour: The Worker's Dream in Nineteenth- Century France* (1989), became revolutionaries by using their nights and free time for aesthetic pursuits (reading poetry, going to Chartres Cathedral), spectators in *The Car* are encouraged to look at things differently, to become aware of urban practices, to put the time and the space out of joint.

Although I did not experience the performance at first hand, I can imagine driving through downtown Minneapolis in the dusk, and gazing out of the window, in a moment of silence or tension in the performance, and suddenly seeing the people that the police wish us to forget: addicts, immigrants, the homeless, the working classes. In my hypothetical reading, these visions of what Rancière quite simply calls 'the people', although part of the show, would not be picturesque figures stationed to provide local colour like the farm labourers and milking maids of eighteenth- century landscape artists. Rather, I think that the aesthetic frame provided by the performance would allow me to rerealize them, to bring them into visibility; and in a manner akin to Ingrid Bergman in *Europe '51*, Roberto Rosellini's sombre 1952 film about post-war poverty in Rome, I like to imagine how such an experience might provoke a displacement in consciousness and leave me open to an alternative form of 'impossible identification' with those who make up the 'part that has no part'.[58] This surely is how Campbell's comments about wanting to make work that interrupts conventional 'structures of belonging' would play itself out. That is to say, he sees site-based theatre as a performance medium that encourages its spectators to reflect on how space, identity and representation function together to producing a certain configuration of the sensible.

By provoking such a reflection or distancing, Skewed Visions, like Graeme Miller, contest the logic that resides behind every act of censorship. For, as Rancière notes, political consciousness or what he calls subjectification 'decomposes and recomposes the relationships between ways of doing, of being and or saying that define the perceptible organization of the community, the relationship between the places where one does one thing and those where one does something else' (1999, p. 40). Or to paraphrase: where the censorship performed in the name of police logic always allocates a certain task to a certain place, site-based performance allows 'all that is solid to melt into the air' by producing what Rancière describes as 'moments when the real world wavers and seems to reel into appearance' (1989, p. 19). In these intense 'moments' the consensus of the censor is undone and dislodged for the sake of what Jean Genet, in a famous essay on theatre, censorship and urbanism, defined as 'a breathtaking liberation' (2003, p. 104).[59]

---

58 Rancière's essay ' A Child Kills Himself' (2005) provides a brilliant 'dissensual' reading of Europe '51.

59 In the essay 'That Strange Word', Genet demands that his play about the Algerian War, The Screens, be staged in a cemetery in the very heart of Paris. See my 2006 essay 'Theatre in a Graveyard: Site-Based Performance and the Revolution of Everyday Life' for a detailed discussion of Genet's attraction towards a site-based aesthetic for this work.

References

Campbell, Charles, Personal email to author, 15 November 2007.

Deutsche, Rosalyn, *Evictions: Art and Spatial Politics*, Cambridge: MIT Press, 1996.

Genet, Jean, 'That Strange Word', in *Fragments of the Artwork*, trans. Charlotte Mandell, Stanford: Stanford University Press, 2003, pp. 103-112.

Hallward, Peter, 'Staging Equality: On Ranciere's Theatocracy', *New Left Review*, 37, 2006, pp. 1-12, Accessed on-line, http://newleftreview.org/?issue=271, 15 November, 2007.

Jakovljevic, Branislav, 'The Space Specific Theatre: Skewed Visions' *The City Itself'*, *The Drama Review*, 49: 3 2005, pp. 96-106.

Krauss, Rosalind, *A Voyage on the North Sea: Art in the Age of the Post-Medium Condition*, London: Thames&Hudson. 1999.

Kwon, Miwon, *One Place After Another: Site-Specific Art and Locational Identity*, Cambridge: MIT Press, 2004.

Lavery, 'The Pepys of Ell: The Politics of *Linked'*, *New Theatre* Quarterly, 82, 2005, 148-60.

———, 'Theatre in a Graveyard: Site-based Performance and the Revolution of Everyday Life', in *Jean Genet: Performance and Politics*, eds. Clare Finburgh, Carl Lavery and Maria Shevtsova, Basingstoke: Palgrave Macmillan, 2006, pp. 95-105.

———, 'Performance Writing, Narrative and Walking', in *Theatres of Thought: Theatre, Performance and Philosophy*, eds. Daniel Meyer-Dinkgrafe and Dan Watt, Cambridge: Cambridge Scholars, 2007, pp. 95-110.

Mitchell, W. J.T. ed., *Landscape and Power*, Chicago: Chicago University Press, 1994.

Rancière, Jacques, *Short Voyages to The Land of The People*, trans. James B. Swenson, Stanford: Stanford University Press, 2003.

————, *Disagreement: Politics and Philosophy*, trans. Julie Rose, Minneapolis: University of Minnesota Press, 1999.

————, *Nights of Labour: The Worker's Dream in Nineteenth- Century France*, trans. John Drury, Philadelphia: Temple University Press, 1989.

Reinelt, Janelle, 'The Limits of Censorship', *Theatre Research International*, 32:1, 2007, pp. 3-15

2

Je Me Souviens

CHANTAL BILODEAU

[Chantal Bilodeau is a playwright and translator originally from Montreal, Canada. Her last play *Pleasure & Pain* was presented at the Magic Theatre in San Francisco and in a Spanish translation at Foro La Gruta in Mexico City. She has translated work by French Ivory Coast, Congolese and French-Canadian playwrights. She lives in New York City.]

At twenty-nine, I decided it was time for a change. I left my apartment, my job, my partner, my country, my culture and my language and moved to the U.S. At the time, I thought this was an exciting but temporary adventure – a journey with a beginning and an end that would eventually take me back home. But twelve years later, the adventure continues. I have spent a great deal of time trying to figure out what triggered such a bold move; I did not fall in love, was not offered the job of a lifetime and certainly was not running away from poverty, human rights abuses or civil war. Then what was the underlying drive? As I explore the relationship between cultural identity and the politics of language – which, as a wordsmith, has become an interest of mine – I see that my desire for change may have stemmed, at least in part, from the way French-Canadian identity is defined and how we, *Québécois*, internalize it.

Je me souviens (I remember) is the official motto of the province of Québec. It is found on the coat of arms and on Québec license plates. No one knows its exact meaning but one story suggests that the full quotation "*Je me souviens que né sous le lys, je croîs sous la rose"* (I remember that born under the lily, I grew under the rose), refers to the floral emblems of France and England. Although the quotation may at one point have expressed an admiration for the British parliamentary system, it has, over time, taken on a nationalist flavor. Ask any *Québécois* today and they will tell you that the motto stands for "I remember my French history and heritage" or even, "I remember what the English did to the French."

The history of Québec is the history of a people fiercely defending their French-Canadian culture in a country where the overwhelming majority is of English descent. From 1608, when Samuel de Champlain founded Québec City, to today, the task of preserving a distinct cultural heritage has been an on-going struggle. Traditionally, wealth and positions of power have been the exclusive privilege of a minority of English-speaking citizens. (Until the 1950s, the majority of French-Canadian workers lived below the poverty line.) Local radio stations, cable networks and movie theaters have long been dominated by American material. And despite Canada's two official languages, as recently as in the 1950s, a French-speaking salesperson serving a French-speaking customer in an English-Canadian department store in Montréal, had to speak English for fear of losing her job.

In the 1960s, things started to change. Conservative Premier Maurice Duplessis, who, with the support of the Roman Catholic Church had dominated Québec politics for sixteen years, was finally defeated. Under new Premier Jean Lesage, liberals who had formed an intellectual opposition against Duplessis' regime started to put in place the dramatic social and political changes that were going to define the next two decades. What became known as *La révolution tranquille* (the Quiet Revolution) saw the decline of Anglo supremacy in the Québec economy, the decline of the Catholic Church's influence, the creation of social health insurance and welfare programs, and the emergence of a pro-sovereignty movement. Other changes also included the creation of a Ministry of Education and Ministry of Cultural Affairs, massive investments in the public education system and the unionization of the civil service.

The Quiet Revolution, in conjunction with the rapidly growing nationalist movement, allowed a new generation of artists to emerge whose primary objective was the affirmation and celebration of French-Canadian identity. It was an exciting time, a sort of cultural emancipation for a society that had never had a voice. Suddenly, we were governing ourselves, managing our resources and had access to power. And just as suddenly, there were songs and plays and novels and even films celebrating self-determination, personal freedom, and an assertion of independence from English Canada. In school, we were studying the history of Québec and the geography of Québec and were reading *Québécois* authors and seeing *Québécois* plays. Singers like Robert Charlebois and the group Beau Dommage created a new soundtrack for our lives. And with the arrival of Michel Tremblay, the first playwright to make *joual* – the linguistic features generally associated with French-Canadian working class – acceptable, we discarded any remaining doubts about the value of our culture and developed a rock-hard pride in it.

Prior to 1950, Québec writers produced very few plays of significance. Although the art form enjoyed a short golden age between 1895 and 1910, most of the plays presented during the first half of the century were from the French classical repertoire. Government and church censorship confined *Québécois* playwrights to religious and historic plays, light comedies and melodramas that enjoyed a certain popular success but did not withstand the test of time. It took the talent of actor, playwright and director Gratien Gélinas with his play *Tit-Coq* in 1948 to see the emergence of a real national theatre. With simple but colorful language, the play tells the story of Tit-Coq, a bastard child now soldier in WWII, who, through his upcoming marriage to his friend's sister, hopes to find the family he never had. Critics saw in *Tit-Coq*, which was hailed a masterpiece, a play with deep popular roots that was sure to be a hit on international stages. Reality proved otherwise but Tit-Coq became nonetheless the first *Québécois* tragic hero and paved the way for the strong nationalist movement that was going to define the theatre of the 60s and 70s.

In 1968, with his play *Les belles-soeurs*, playwright Michel Tremblay gave *Québécois* theatre its voice and the sense of identity it had been longing for. Exposing the myth of the French-Canadian mother – standing at the stove on a cheap linoleum floor, an apron tied around her waist, a wooden spoon in her hand, a baby propped up on her hip and two or three young kids pulling at her skirt – *Les belles-soeurs* was the ultimate cry of despair of the French-Canadian woman. It stirred up a storm of controversy by attacking the deeply religious patriarchal society, clearly signaling that theatre was stepping away from tradition and from the control and censorship exercised by the clergy. Revolutionary in its construction, it also set out to prove that the language of the streets was beautiful. Despite some early negative reviews, *Les belles-soeurs* became a classic. It was Tremblay's first professionally produced work but his working-class, French-Canadian characters soon crossed borders and languages making *Les belles-soeurs* his most produced and most often translated play.

The same year *Les belles-soeurs* was presented at the Théâtre du Rideau-Vert in Montréal, the Social Democratic political party *Parti Québécois (PQ)* was formed. Its leader René Lévesque became Premier of Québec in 1976 and a year later, introduced *La charte de la langue française* (the Charter of the French Language). Often known as Bill 101, it made French the official language of the state in the province of Québec. It also made French the normal and habitual language of the workplace, of instruction, communications, commerce and business allowing the advancement of French-Canadian towards management roles and the creation of a French-Canadian middle class.

Increased income, increased access, increased representation: it was a good time to be *Québécois*. During the Quiet Revolution, literary production more than tripled, the market share for Francophone music peaked at 25%, and many institutions – including the literary journal *Parti Pris* and the theatre organization *Centre des auteurs dramatiques* – were put in place to support *Québécois* artists. In the theatre, in addition to Michel Tremblay, playwrights like Jean-Claude Germain, Jean Barbeau and Françoise Loranger fueled the nationalist flame, using experimental approaches – including improvisation and collective creation – *joual* and parody to comment on official culture, high art, institutionalized religion, and other embodiments of social pretension which excluded the working class. This highly prolific artistic period culminated with the 1980 Québec Referendum. Called by the *PQ*, it asked *Québécois* whether Québec should pursue a path toward sovereignty and secession from Canada. The proposal was defeated by a 60% to 40% margin and the heydays of Québec nationalism came to a grinding halt.

People of my generation, who grew up during those years, remember life as culturally vibrant and filled with a sense of possibilities. Our parents' access to positions of power provided the majority of us with a comfortable middle-class upbringing. And since education was free and readily available, we were sent to university *en masse* with the mandate of becoming the teachers, artists, scientists and engineers who would keep the culture strong and carve a place for it among the international community. After all, the city of Montréal had already hosted the 1967 International and Universal Exposition (or Expo 67), considered the most successful World's Fair of the 20th century, and the 1976 Summer Olympics. There was no reason why we could not capitalize on what had been achieved and continue to move forward.

But this strong sense of identity was based on the existence of a remarkably homogeneous society with the vast majority sharing ethnic origins, religion, language and socio-economic background. Immigrants and English-speaking *Québécois* represented a small percentage of the population (which became even smaller after thousands of Anglophones left the province in reaction to Bill 101) and were mostly found in Montréal. In suburbs and rural areas, people were – and still are to this day – direct descendants of the original French settlers. The government contributed to maintaining this uniformity by imposing strict language laws. Bill 101 restricted citizens' linguistic school choice by forbidding immigrants and *Québécois* of French descent from attending English-language schools. (Rudimentary English was taught in French schools but one had to wait until college to be allowed to go to an English institution.) Although this measure was meant to be empowering, it was also dangerously limiting – effectively restricting the concept of *Québécois* culture to a narrow and fixed definition.

The loss of the 1980 referendum suddenly created an identity crisis. While the idea of being a separate country had seemed like an essential condition to the preservation and flourishing of our culture and language, the referendum made it abundantly clear that this was not the will of the people and that no matter how strong the nationalist ideology, doing away with certain economic realities was impossible. Another important factor was our changing demographics. The fertility rate for French-Canadian women went from 3.9 children/woman in 1960 to 1.4 children/woman in 1986 (a rate 20% lower than in other provinces), suddenly raising concerns about relatively low if not negative population growth and rapid aging. To counter the threat of population decline and to continue funding extensive social services that relied heavily on taxes, Québec had to open its doors to immigration. Throughout the 80s, new immigrants from all corners of the globe, including the Middle-East, Haïti, Eastern Europe and Asia, made their homes in Québec. Their arrival and gradual integration rendered obsolete the die-hard *Québécois* identity that had been the linchpin of the Quiet Revolution. Showing remarkable adaptability, Québec redefined it-self as a pluralist society, encouraging immigrants to share their heritage, par-ticipate in common public institutions, and jointly help to build a modern, plu-ralist, French-speaking nation. Nationalism shifted from being based on ethnicity to finding its roots in the shared experience of a territory and, most importantly, of a language.

This influx of immigrants, added to the emergence of a middle class, in-creased access to education and the migration of workers from rural areas to cities, changed our relationship to language. Regional accents lost their promi-nence and the much-celebrated *joual* that Michel Tremblay had dared to put on stage became outdated. *Joual* was not something immigrants – even if they were native French-speakers – could easily relate to. And for the "traditional" *Québécois*, it had become associated with the non-educated lower class and was something we were trying to distance ourselves from. In fact, one of the outcomes of the Quiet Revolution was to trigger a debate over what should be the correct norm of Québec French. In the late 60s and early 70s, two groups held widely opposing views. One group (notably left-wing intellectuals) reject-ed the idea that Québec French should be aligned with International Standard French and demanded instead that *joual* be recognized as an "official" lan-guage. The other group (notably officials from the *Office québécois de la langue française* (Québec Board of the French language)) held the view that *Québécois* French should almost completely conform to International Standard French, except when it lacked terms to refer to specific aspects of the Canadian environ-ment or culture. For the next decade, this debate continued to be a hot topic and created one of the most interesting challenges *Québécois* playwrights have had to contend with.

Prior to the referendum, we produced an abundance of plays – most of them written in *joual* – that were nearly impossible to understand for any non-*Québécois*. (Some of these plays, notably by Michel Tremblay, were translated successfully but the original versions were incomprehensible for other French-speaking countries.) Although this body of work established the foundations of contemporary *Québécois* theatre, it also kept us isolated from the rest of the world. After the referendum, playwrights who were eager to take the cultural discourse beyond the nationalist question began to move away from *joual*. Searching for a new language, they wrote in a slightly heightened, more educated French that leaned toward International Standard French – and therefore could be exported – but retained more or less, depending on the writer, *Québécois* flavor. This departure from realistic dialogue, in turn, allowed formal and aesthetic explorations to replace the realism of the previous decade and freed writers to integrate foreign characters and situations set outside Québec into their work. The playwrights who defined the 80s – among them, Michel Marc Bouchard, Normand Chaurette, René-Daniel Dubois and Marie Laberge – are celebrated for their startling break with the dramaturgy then current in Québec and, in keeping with the province's growing multiculturalism, for their claim for the right to an individual identity that transcended nationality.

But this move away from *joual* was not without its problems. Since *joual* had been the flagship of nationalist theatre, whether to use it or not was a choice that had direct political implications. Given that the referendum vote had been split almost in the middle, playwrights had to walk a fine line or risk alienating half of their audience. In addition, Québec had just emerged from what had been a very insular way of life. Its hunger for the world was real but breaking away from the provincialism of the past was not always easy. People who dreamt big (like artists who had their sights set on France) were often regarded with suspicion, accused of having *des idées de grandeur* (grandiose ideas) and, if they were perceived as trying to change to appeal to the outside world, simply discounted. Equally problematic were audiences' perceptions of language and playwrights' and actors' ability to create believable characters. It was not uncommon at that time for *Québécois* characters to speak a French that sounded either European (had they gone overseas and been infected with the accent?) or like it did not belong to any identifiable culture (had they been raised by non-native speakers?). But to the artists' credit, major societal changes had taken place over a relatively short time so just as people were trying to catch up in real life, playwrights and actors were struggling to find a sound that was representative of modern Québec. With the working-class *joual* accent at one end of the spectrum, the sophisticated European French accent at the other, and the bland *Québécois* news anchorman inflexions somewhere in between, they had to go through every single variation before finally hitting on a sound that was both understandable to foreigners and true to the *Québécois* ear. Still, it took very skilled writers and very skilled actors to handle a language that constantly threatened to reveal hidden political alliances or secret elitism. As the perceived threat of assimilation grew and the enforcement of language laws became more oppressive, the use of French was increasingly coded.

The PQ was re-elected in 1981 and, changing tactic, set out to negotiate with the federal government and propose amendments to the Canadian constitution that would recognize Québec as a "distinct society." In practical terms, this meant that because of its unique position within Canada, Québec demanded rights (which included a constitutional veto and increased powers with respect to immigration) not available to other provinces. A year later, the federal government managed to patriate the Canadian Constitution, outmaneuvering Premier René Lévesque. (Canada, as a British Dominion, was governed by a constitution that was a British law and could be changed only by an Act of the British Parliament. Patriation thus specifically refers to making the constitution amendable by Canada only.) Then in 1984, after Progressive Conservative Brian Mulroney became Prime Minister of Canada with the backing of many PQ supporters, tensions erupted between the so-called radical supporters of the PQ and the more moderate ones. The dispute over Lévesque's decisions to shift toward a more conciliatory approach over constitutional issues and to officially put sovereignty on the back burner resulted in his resignation. The following year, the PQ lost the elections to the Parti Libéral du Québec (Québec Liberal Party).

In his first year in power, Robert Bourassa's Liberal Party successfully persuaded the federal government to recognize Québec as a distinct society. This resulted in two constitutional accords that, in the end, were never ratified. The next ten years were devoted to a series of legal battles over language laws that undid much of what the PQ had achieved, tested the tolerance of both French and English Canadians and made Québécois feel constantly under attack. Beginning in 1979, the Supreme Court of Canada declared Chapter III of the Charter of the French Language – which stipulated that French was the only language of legislation and provided for a translation in English at the end of the legislative process – unconstitutional. The Supreme Court judged that the enacting and passing of laws had to be done in both French and English in the parliaments of Québec and Canada. The Québec government responded by re-enacting the Charter in French and English while leaving the contested chapter untouched. Following the patriation of the Canadian Constitution, the Constitution Act, 1982 introduced the notion of "minority language education rights." This novelty opened another door to a constitutional dispute of Québec's Charter. In 1984, the Supreme Court invalidated a section of the Charter, which had recognized the right of children to English language education only if their parents themselves had received education in English in Québec. Canadians who had been educated in English outside of Québec had to send their children to French primary and secondary schools like all other *Québécois*. Judged retroactively unconstitutional, the section had to be modified so that it no longer clashed with the Canadian Charter's definition of a linguistic minority.

Similarly, in 1988 the Supreme Court ruled that the sections of the Québec Charter enforcing the exclusive use of French on outdoor commercial signs were unconstitutional. The Québec government could legitimately require French to have "greater visibility" or "marked predominance" on exterior commercial signs but could not enforce the exclusive use of French. In response, the National Assembly made use of the notwithstanding clause of the Canadian constitution (which allows Parliament or provincial legislatures to override certain portions of the Canadian Charter) to keep the original law unchanged. This led to formal complaints by three Anglophone Québec business owners who, in 1993, brought their case before the Human Rights Committee of the United Nations. They alleged to be victims of violations of certain articles of the International Covenant on Civil and Political Rights by the Federal Government of Canada and the Province of Québec because they were forbidden to use English in advertising or in the name of their firms. The Committee stated that "a State may choose one or more official languages, but it may not exclude, outside the spheres of public life, the freedom to express oneself in a language of one's choice." The National Assembly amended the Charter of the French Language and introduced regulations on the "marked predominance" of French on outdoor commercial signs.

Outside of the courts, where passions were not tempered by the impersonal nature of law, the language issue often flared up to its full emotional potential. French-Canadians were angry and frustrated, felt unrecognized by English Canada and saw signs of oppression everywhere. As an example of the emotionality of that time, in 1990, French-Canadian pop singer Céline Dion, who had recorded several commercially successful albums in French, staged the cultural equivalent of a military coup by recording her first song in English. While any other language would have been acceptable, her choice of English was seen as a painful betrayal and as one more sign that we were losing precious ground. Even though Dion publicly explained her choice, it took many years for people to forgive her and to recognize that her international English career ultimately benefitted Québec.

In the early 90s, following the failure of the two constitutional negotiations, support for the nationalist movement grew once again. In 1994, the provincial elections brought the *PQ*, led by Jacques Parizeau, back to power. A year after being elected, Parizeau presented *Québécois* with a second referendum on sovereignty. The proposal was defeated but this time by a very narrow margin of 50.6% No to 49.4% Yes and a record 94% of registered *Québécois* casting their votes. Addressing a room of Yes supporters live on TV, a bitter, frustrated, and inebriated Jacques Parizeau blamed the result on "money and the ethnic vote," effectively ending his political career. Controversy subsequently arose over the number of rejected No ballots at polling stations. After an inquiry by the *Directeur général des élections du Québec* (Chief Electoral Officer of Québec), it was established that some ballots had indeed been rejected without valid reasons and that the majority of the rejected ballots were No votes. But the conclusion was that the irregularities were isolated. The controversy unleashed a series of attacks and counter-attacks from both French- and English-language media and left the province bruised, cleaved in two and once again, in need to redefine itself.

Over the course of the next few years, support for sovereignty and for any sort of constitutional change declined markedly. With political leaders enjoying less and less popular confidence, the business class imposed itself as the new spokesperson for the interests of *Québécois*. This placed new emphasis on the economic dimension of nationalism and shifted the identity question away from political ideology. Yet the language issue remained. The "language police" from the Québec Board of the French Language continued to investigate businesses and enforce language laws, becoming somewhat infamous for going too far. In 2000, a Montréal restaurant owner was threatened with fines of up to $7,000 for having beer coasters with English rather than French writing. Other examples include web sites created by Montréal businesses and originally posted in English. Since Québec language laws unequivocally stated that all advertising had to be translated into French, the sites had to be changed into French, or else the owners faced large fines. Even computers had to have a

French interface, which, because of the time it took for software to be translated, was highly impractical.

Post referendum, the artistic community – relieved of its nationalist responsibilities – set out to rebuild the province's confidence. Leaving behind language angst and omnipresent feelings of oppression, it resolutely turned its sight outwards, seeing the promotion of a strong *Québécois* culture on the global market as fundamental in preserving Québec's identity. Yet paradoxically, many of the artists who obtained international recognition did so by bypassing the language altogether. Groups like *Cirque du Soleil* created shows entirely based on visuals. Others, like *Carbone 14* and theatre director Robert Lepage's *Théâtre Repère*, still included spoken words but relied more on inventive staging and a metaphorical use of gestures. Theatre became multidisciplinary – often integrating dance, music, painting and sculpture – and occasionally bilingual. The younger generation of playwrights, like Denis Marleau and Daniel Danis, whose concerns were more global than the previous generation, embraced a more literary style, often creating a poetic *langue d'auteur* (author's language) that stayed clear of Québec's linguistic and nationalist issues.

When I left Montréal in 1997, this rebuilding process was still going on. Had I stayed, I would have experienced the province gradually settling into a stronger sense of self. The language issue was not dead but as the world grew increasingly more connected and people were required to be bilingual in their work environment, the clear French/English dichotomy of my childhood became less defined. Also softened were the cultural pressures to conform to an identity that only wanted to expand in specific, regulated ways. The government still aggressively tries to protect the primacy of the French language – in 2003, displeased with France's choice of the word *mail* as the French translation of email, Québec created the term *courriel* and banned the word email from all government-related documents. But while the nationalist fervor of the referendum eras seeped into every aspect of life, the attitude today is a lot more relaxed.

I did not start writing theatre until after I left Québec. How much of that is a function of my own choices and how much it is a function of my environment, I will never know. But the fact remains that I had to step outside of my culture and language to find my voice. At the same time, Québec's cultural identity was so deeply ingrained in me that it took the better part of a decade to overcome my feelings of guilt at having committed this act of betrayal. As a French-Canadian playwright who writes in English and translates in the wrong direction (from French to English instead of from English to my native French), I felt I was failing to do my part to keep *Québécois* culture alive.

Je me souviens. I remember.

The *Québécois* identity is complex and full of contradictions. It involves a delicate and changing balance of dependence and independence. It means being part of a nation that fights for cultural integrity yet aspires to be cosmopolitan, that strives for sovereignty yet wants to be embraced by Canada, that speaks French yet exists in a world dominated by English. And while we are incredibly proud of our culture, our obstinate protectionism can sometimes be alienating to others and paralyzing for us. Yes, we do choose to make life complicated but when asked why, our seven million answers can be summed up in one profound statement: For the right to be who we are. Perhaps it is this concept, in the end, that sent me on the road twelve years ago. Perhaps within my own culture, I also wanted that right for myself.

Postcards from Gaza
and Other Unspeakable Geographies

LISA SCHLESINGER

[Lisa Schlesinger's most recent plays are *Wal-martyrs, Celestial Bodies, Twenty One Positions* (with Naomi Wallace and Abed Abu Srour) and *Harmonicus Mundi.* She has received commissions from the Guthrie Theatre, the BBC, Portland Stage Company and Ensemble Studio Theatre, and fellowships from the NEA/TCG, CEC International, and the Sloan Foundations.]

> Whatever is unnamed, undepicted in images, whatever is omitted from biography, censored in collections of letters, whatever is misnamed as something else, made difficult-to-come-by, whatever is buried in the memory by the collapse of meaning under an inadequate or lying language -- this will become not merely unspoken, but unspeakable.
>
> —Adrienne Rich

Zachariah is already waiting in the foyer of our hotel in East Jerusalem, the Arab section. He's driven our group all over the occupied territories for the past ten days and now he has left his sister's wedding early to drive me to the airport. At the front desk the night clerk hands me a plastic grocery bag with a box in it. *Waddah left this for you*, he says.

The box is heavy, wrapped in two plastic bags and knotted tightly. *Thank you*, I say, and stuff it in my carry-on. I will look at it later. Now it's 2 am, I'm tired, and it's time to leave.

Driving out of Jerusalem, Zachariah confides that he is in love. The girl is studying to be a doctor but her parents are divorced and his parents don't approve. They have someone else in mind for him. He works so hard, he says, he has already built a house of his own. But now he's a prisoner. His town has been under curfew for 75 days. He hasn't even been able to go home. He can't get a visa to get out of the country. He can't marry the girl he loves. *If he can't work it out,* he insists, *he will find a way out of here.*

Family comes first in Palestinian culture and now that his father is in the hospital, Zachariah is supporting his extended family by driving foreigners like me. A few days ago he'd taken two Chinese journalists into Nablus and while it was a dangerous trip for them it was inconceivably risky for Zachariah. He could have had his ID papers taken away and not returned; he could have been arrested for a *"reason"* no one would need to reveal. We do not talk about these things because, right now, Zachariah is returning from his sisters wedding and he is missing his girl. I ask him if his sister married someone his parents approved of.

Yes, he says, *it was a celebration.*

...

Two weeks earlier I had arrived in Tel Aviv with playwrights Betty Shamieh and Kia Corthron. We would meet Robert O'Hara, Tony Kushner, and Naomi Wallace, the trip's organizer at our hotel. Our purpose was to see how theatre was faring under occupation. Since this meant visiting the occupied territories, the group had been briefed on a strategy for entering Israel. An international human rights attorney confirmed that it is best not to mention Palestinians or Palestine upon entering the country. Betty, Kia and I were to simply say we were tourists visiting the Holy Land. I was aware that there is nothing illegal about visiting theatres and I found this strategy of omission uncomfortable but after talking it over with members of the group, I agreed. I knew that while we were coming to this part of the world to see Palestinian theatre, we would also, inevitably, bear witness to the Israeli occupation.

Why did you come to Israel? The security officer asked me.

Do you have family?

No. I came to see the sights.

It's a bad time here. Why would you want to see the sights? But then without further questions, she let me pass. A moment later, she called me back.

Why didn't you tell me you were traveling with these two?

When the customs official saw Betty's Palestinian surname on her passport, we were put in separate rooms and interviewed in private to see if our stories were consistent: *We are friends, we are tourists, we are visiting the holy land.* The security officials did not ask specific enough questions that it ever became obvious that I'd never even met Betty and Kia before we'd gotten on the plane. It's not illegal to enter Israel. Eventually, they have to let you through, even if they don't want you there.

...

It's the night of the Sabbath and also Rosh Hashanah, the holiday of redemption and forgiveness, the most holy Jewish holiday of the year. We are driving on the rough old highway designated for Palestinians. There aren't many cars on the road. Over the past two weeks, I have become somewhat familiar with these roads. Sometimes they end in checkpoints at the entrances to cities with military personal who check IDs. Sometimes they end in roadblocks of rubble and trash and crumbling cement bulldozed into piles so that cars can't pass and travelers must leave their vehicles and walk around them. Sometimes people unload their belongings and try to find a taxi on the other side so they can continue their journeys. Parallel to us Israelis drive the new transnational highway, slick and black with their freshly painted lines that only Israelis are allowed to drive. Between them is the holy ground they are fighting over, a stark landscape of dusty earth and stone, desert brush and olive trees. The landscape continues endlessly into the hills and darkness. As a Jewish woman and as an American visitor, I am aware I could be driving that clean, fast, Israeli road as we slow down for the last checkpoint before Ben Gurion Airport. Because he is Palestinian, Zachariah can't take that highway, nor can he take a plane from the airport but he can drive me there. He can watch my plane fly away.

...

At Kalandia, the checkpoint between Jerusalem and Ramallah, a soldier asked me why I wanted to "go in there."

I am visiting a theatre, I answered.

This is a war zone. He said and slid his thumb under his bulletproof vest. *I have this*, he said. *You have nothing. You should not go in there.*

Sometimes, while presenting my passport to checkpoint soldiers, I wished I had come to Israel just once as a Jewish tourist and was welcomed here. When I was a child friends and family had visited Israel and returned with photographs of religious sites and holy souvenirs like the little *Chumsah,* a Sephardic Symbol to ward off evil. Israel was often referred to as *home.* I was raised in a non-religious family. We celebrated Jewish holidays as a form of culture, not worship. Yet I was aware of Jewish history. My grandfather immigrated to the US at age 11, after losing his mother in the pogroms of Kiev. Among my family, there was an unspoken support for the state of Israel, perhaps it was thought of as a refuge from the perpetual injury of the past. I first heard the word Palestinian in the context of the Munich massacres at the 1972 Olympics and corresponding photos of Arafat in his kaffiyeh. I was not taught the history of the Palestinian/Israeli conflict, only an instinctual fear. So when it came time to leave for this trip, I decided not to tell my parents where I was going. A friend assuaged me: *You don't want them to worry, of course.* It's true, I did not want them to worry but that is not why I did not tell them.

The checkpoint soldier handed my passport back to me and motioned me on. A few steps farther down the dusty past into the city, a Palestinian man mocked him *I have this. You have nothing. Ha!* Next to his foot, there was a single shoe half buried in the dirt.

...

A soldier halts us. He wears sunglasses, though it is night. He lifts his M-16 and bends his head towards the car window. *Pull over,* he says. We pull to the side of the road where the other Palestinian people wait while their cars are inspected. Zachariah hands him his ID card and motions to me to give him my passport.

Give me your keys and your telephone, the soldier says. *And get out of the car.*

The soldier takes the loot and goes inside. A moment later, he returns, looks at me suspiciously, asks for my airline ticket, takes it, and goes back inside. Then we wait. For a long time.

On the other road, the Israeli cars pass and pass, a way of keeping time.

...

We took a taxi to Ashtar Theatre. A Theatre of the Oppressed based company. The theatre office was modern and tidy and resembled a small theatre office in any part of the world. Over tea at Ashtar, as well as at every other theatre we visited, the artists were kind and warm people, and I couldn't help thinking that theatre artists are a breed of their own. Ashtar was founded in Jerusalem in 1991 and opened their Ramallah theatre in 1994.

Their mission states: *"At Ashtar, we aim for theatre to be a tool for change to serve cultural and social development, and to promote and deepen the creativity of the Palestinian Theatre."*

Yearly, the company creates a new experimental theatre piece that tours internationally, but at home they spend a lot of their time training young people and performing forum theatre based on the techniques of Augusto Boal's Theatre of the Oppressed. Ashtar's forum theatre regularly tours the refugee camps around Ramallah and in other cities in the West Bank addressing topical cultural issues such as honor killing, rape, and domestic abuse. Theatre as a tool for change was a common concern among all the theatres and cultural centres we visited including the Theatre of the Deaf in Al Maghar, the Al Rowwad Cultural Center in Aida refugee camp in Bethlehem, and Theater Day in Hebron and Gaza. It is also almost entirely geared toward young people. And because almost every family has lost someone in the conflict, it serves to heal. Theatre in Palestine, it seems, serves as a form of therapy as well as a format for cultural discussion and understanding. It also brings people together, when possible. Iman Aoun of Ashtar explains that the theatres focus on issues they can actually impact, issues that need to be discussed and that have a cultural significance within their own communities. Suspiciously absent was theatre about the occupation. It was not like one could forget that Ramallah or any other city was under occupation. One is constantly reminded. At 3 o'clock we were told that an unexpected curfew was just imposed and we had to leave the city as soon as possible or we would not be able to leave.

Something about authority figures in uniform always makes me feel I have done something wrong. And the truth is I do all kinds of things wrong and even the things I do wrong are barely even illegal. But on this trip I have been to Gaza. And while it's not illegal to go there, it feels like it is. There is a saying in Arabic, *Go Drink from the Sea in Gaza*. It means something like *go to hell*.

You've got to see it to believe it. Raw sewage spills through the streets into the Mediterranean; the spaces between houses no wider than a man's shoulders; the bombed buildings where the supposed "terrorist" lived but so did children, babies, pregnant women; the graffiti that says THIS IS THE AMERICAN WEAPON. Maybe this is starting to sound like politics but it is also about fear and the distortion of language. Sometimes waiting in silence is a rest note. A long pause. The space between inhalation and exhalation. Sometimes it is a hold. An arrest.

Jackie Lucbeck of Theatre Day in Gaza says: *Because words are more powerful than concepts in our part of the world, we just have to be careful with our words. We have definite no no subjects and these are sex, politics, and religion. But we can talk about all this with secret language, the language of the street that everyone understands. In the West Bank, things are opening up and a lot of new stuff can now happen. In Gaza, self-censorship is the only way to continue work. But there is something fascinating and creative in knowing that you have to be careful what you say and how you say it. We work for teenagers and these kids know everything so any little hint, any little metaphor gets understood. And because so many people are so desperate to talk, to hear, and be heard, our performances always end in talks, and discussions like: who has experienced what one of the characters has experienced? Which character and tell us your story.*

...

When the soldier returns he has his finger on the trigger of his M-16 and this makes me nervous. Where I am going, he asks me fingering that trigger, but he has my ticket so he must know where I am going. What is my middle name, he should know this from my passport. Each time he takes his finger off the trigger and puts it back, I think of the sensitivity of that finger and all the things it touches in just that way he is now touching the gun and how easily the finger could make a mistake.

A feeling comes up from inside me, that suddenly makes me question my-self: *is my passport really mine; did I pick up someone else's ticket by accident?* I know what a ghost is: *the self fainting inside the self.*

On the bottom of the automatic weapon it says MADE IN USA. *We should go home,* I think.

Then, the soldier asks me one last question: *Did anyone give you anything.* Before I even think I say *No.*

...

On the way out of Gaza one of the playwrights asked Jackie whether we should tell the airport security police that we have been there. *Don't lie,* she'd told us, *they already know everything, they already know where you've been.*

...

When the young woman at Ben Gurion airport, who looks like she could be my-cousin-from-the-seventies, sees the Gaza sticker in my passport, she pulls me aside. She has long dark straight hair and two smudges of blue eye shadow on her lids. She looks confused. *What was I doing in Gaza, who was I with, why did I go there, can I prove I went where I say I went and saw who I say I saw and not someone else I am not admitting to?*

How can I prove that? I ask.

Under interrogation, I am told, put the question in a box. Answer only that question. Leave no leads. This is what I try to do. But this seems to annoy her. In turn she rephrases the questions so that the answers are also slightly different and this small discrepancy can sound like a lie. And so far I am not lying even though I've begun to feel like I am. She is much more practiced at this than I am. In David Hare's play, *Via Dolorosa,* he says that it is easy to get into Israel but hard to get out. Still, I was not prepared for this.

Can I show her proof of who I saw? Who I went with? How I went? And did the Arabs drive me? Do I have their business cards? And why did I only see Arab theatre and have Arab business cards?

I can read about Israeli theatre in America, I tell her.

We visited the Arab Israeli theatre in Jaffa where almost everyone wore spectacular shoes and an argument about Ramallah ensued. An Israeli play-wright told us we could not go there –*it's a war zone, he said*- but we already had and someone suggested that he might be interested in going there, too. In fact, it is illegal for Israelis to go to the West Bank so he could not ever know what it is like there except if he was willing to break the law to find out. One of the primary problems caused by the occupation is the fragmentation of space, the inability to cross lines and to "see" the Others' world.

The questioning wearies me so I decide to cheat. *I wanted to stay a few extra days for Rosh Hashana.*

Now, she tests me on my Jewishness.

What holidays do you celebrate? (A few) What Hebrew words do you know? Well, Roshashana! (She's not laughing.) Not many, really. None.

How can I explain to this young lady with the gun that I revere the world and all its gods: the gods of breath, of oak trees, of peace.

She calls her supervisor over. She is meaner and colder and also carries a gun. She assumes I am lying and I really feel I am now, just standing here feels like a lie. And so begins the line of questioning that shuts faith down entirely: what I thought I was I might not be; what I believed, comes to doubt; what I am, who I am, is all called into question. Suddenly, anything could be anything.

We go through everything in my bag to prove that I packed it myself: *these are my socks, yes, this is my skirt, these are my panties,* and as she reads my entire address book, I feel grateful I wrote nothing in my journal at all. She touches everything and now, clearly disgusted with my kind of Jewishness and annoyed she cannot catch me in a lie, she asks her final question: *Did any one give you anything?*

No, I say, and this time, I realize as I say it, I have, just, lied.

There it is, at my side, as I say this word, *no,* in my hand because I have taken everything out and now I must repack it: the plastic bag with the box inside. It's too late to admit *I have made a mistake and actually, yes, there is something that someone gave me, this box, the Palestinian waiter gave it to me, and no, I have no idea what is inside it.*

Have a nice flight, she says.

After I have repacked my suitcase and my carry-on bag, I slide them onto the x-ray machine and walk through the metal detector. If she'd asked me what was in the plastic bag I would not have known and I would not be passing through this metal detector right now because my not knowing means that someone else had to have packed that bag and given it to me without my knowing what is inside it, and the truth is I don't know what is inside it and at this very moment the metal detector could sound, or the plastic bag could detonate and we would, all of us, security police, IDF, New Year's tourists, find out. But it doesn't. And I pass into the duty-free, full of overpriced perfume and Dead Sea salts, unchanged. The plastic bag has not exploded and my lie has not been exposed. I consider slathering myself in all these scents, like a dog rolling in a dead animal for disguise. I don't buy any of it.

...

How is theatre faring under occupation? Perhaps as well as everything else fares under occupation. For one thing it is hard to get to the theatre with all those checkpoints. One night in Ramallah, after a rehearsal one actress found the checkpoint closed and could not go home. Instead, she spent the night in the director's daughter's room. After several years of passing through the Kalandia checkpoint where she and her children were consistently harassed, Iman Aoun decided to leave her family home in Jerusalem and rent a flat in Ramallah so that she could get to work in the morning. It is hard to plan a theatre event anything when sudden curfews are enforced, difficult to gather when large groups of people in one place are perceived by the Israeli military as a threat.

I take Waddah's plastic bag with the box in it out of my carry-on bag. I shake it. Something shifts, something heavy. If objects could laugh, this box would fall down, the bag's sides would split laughing. It has gotten through Israeli security.

...

What would turn an ordinary man, a waiter, say, or a van driver, into a freedom fighter, a revolutionary, even a suicide bomber?

What I saw at the Gaza checkpoint made me consider this question.

At the border of Gaza there is a half mile long - cement tunnel above ground. There is no way to see in, no way to see out. It is surrounded by razor- wire and a watchtower. I've seen something similar at the entrance to the slaughterhouse.

This is not the tunnel to a prison. It is the tunnel the workers must pass through each day on their way to and from work in Israel proper. For months the driver told us there has been no work, but yesterday they reopened the tunnel.

Today the workers are lined up as far as I can see, for miles, to return home. The lines are so long, the driver explains, that people will get home late in the evening, eat dinner, shower, and then return to sleep in the line so that when they open the tunnel in the middle of the night they can get through in time to get to work. If they don't, they are fired, and as you can see, there are many hungry people willing to take their places. Sometimes, women have their babies in that line, sometimes people die trying to get to the hospital, sometimes the soldiers just don't open the tunnel, as a cruel humiliating joke.

...

I unknot the plastic bag and unwrap the box. If I were Palestinian man, a freedom loving man, a weary man, might I use an American, who is going to the airport to transport a desperate message?

I take the box into the ladies room and when no one is looking, open it. Inside there is a sandwich, chocolate, and an orange and a pear. It is the most perfect pear I have ever seen. I scrutinize each thing in this box because by now, my doubt, my fear and my ability to lie have rendered me unsure of everything. Then I throw it all in the trash.

...

Gaza sits on the Mediterranean. It was once a resort site. There are even sun umbrellas still standing in the sand by the sea, but there are no postcards from Gaza. No one says. I wish you were here.

...

When I return to the gate, I try not to think of Zachariah or Waddah, or the lines of people in Gaza. Instead I sit down with the ones who weren't pulled to the side, the ones whose innocence went unquestioned.

Afterward

December 27, 2009

Today is the one year anniversary of Operation Cast Lead, the Israeli siege of Gaza in which 1400 Palestinians and 13 Israeli soldiers were killed. For 21 days, Israeli bombed Gaza from the sky, with conventional weapons but also with white phosphorus, a chemical that keeps burning, that burns straight through skin and flesh to the bone. It was barely on the news. Even in the hopeful days before Obama's inauguration, he said nothing. On the internet Israeli soldiers posted bombings on YouTUBE like video games, the view finder showed the bomber lining up the target and dropping the little flash in the bull's eye. A well-known doctor in Israel called an Israeli television station and a news anchor picked up the phone on the air. The doctor sobbed, they had just bombed his house and killed his daughters. The news anchor sat stunned. The doctor wept. The news anchor said he could not hang up on him. He did not know what to do. For a moment, the news stalled. Then the news anchor excused himself from the set. An extended family was directed into their house for safety by soldiers. The Israeli military bombed the house. 29 people died. 45 family members were wounded. A t-shirt from one battalion showed a pregnant Palestinian woman with a bull's-eye superimposed on her belly, with the slogan, in English, "1 shot, 2 kills."

Now, a year later, Gaza needs medical staff, construction workers, and psychologists. The needy for food, medical supplies, and building materials is imperative and art is a mere luxury. Still thanks to the die hards and dreamers, and workers like Jackie Lubeck and Iman Aoun, Gaza still has theatre. A theatre, for telling the stories the media refuses to publish, for acknowledging the point of view that we in the West may find more and more difficult to comprehend, for healing. Theatre may serve to let those who have been silenced across the world, be heard, by each other, by outside communities, and by that same world that silences it. Perhaps their theatre is not unlike that of the Greeks at the end of one era and the beginning of another who used theatre as a form of ritual, prayer, and healing, as well as social change. I say perhaps, but I mean, I hope.

I hope their theatre is part of calling to the greatest and humblest of gods to bring them freedom and peace, instead of continued cycles of violence and treatment of trauma, again and again. If this were a prayer, a postcard to the gods, this is where I would write *amen*.

Some Thoughts on the Quality of Attention

DIJANA MILOŠEVIC

[Dijana Miloševic is an internationally acclaimed stage director and one of the founders of the Belgrade-based theatre laboratory Dah Teatar, which was one of the first independent theatre companies in the Balkans following the fall of communism. 'Dah' translates into English as 'breath.']

When I think about the word silence I think about different kinds of silence: the silence that opens mind and space and the silence that closes it; the silence that is the opposite of the absence of sound –the sound of noise that covers the truth. When we speak from the point of theatre practice we encounter something that is known to skillful practitioners/artists: in executing theatre actions on the stage or while we write we have to get rid of everything that is not necessary - all the noise that obscures real theatrical action. A performer, writer or director has to 'purify' all actions from the 'garbage' present in everyday life in order to make a theatre piece truly alive and therefore allow silence to have a place to speak. If we apply this idea to the world around us we can say that very often it is not that what we don't write or speak that matters, but rather the attention paid to the glut of information and noise that hides what it is that we do, write and speak that does. We are so overloaded with information from the mass media assaulting our consciousness and our souls every day that is has become extraordinarily difficult to simply stop for a moment and absorb silence itself – in effect, absorb a quality of silence that would allow us to confront and fight censorship alive within us as artists and human beings as well as the censorship that exists outside of us.

In my language, Serbian, the word for theatre is POZORISTE. The root of the word, POZOR, means attention. Theatre is a place, therefore, of attention, where attention is paid. To do theatre is to be awakened, to be alert: to be attentive.

Theatre allows us, even when we are not able to use words, to use physical actions, and thus to speak. When I was a young student, I will always remember my fascination with the character of Antigone, a young woman that opposed the State and its Law without the power of her action: a symbolic gesture of throwing a handful of sand over the dead body of her brother. And with that 'useless' action, she went beyond silence, fear, and censorship. Her action resonates through the centuries.

I founded my theatre Dah Teatar out of the need to identify that kind of personal necessity, to find my equivalent gesture of throwing a handful of sand over the historical, cultural and political memories of death and darkness in my country. In 1991 when Dah was initially formed with Jadrenka Andjelic and Maja Mitic (and later with Sanja Krsmanovic Tasic), my country was undergoing a period of darkness, a time of destruction and violence. To found a theatre group that consisted of a handful of people in fact was the action that I had been searching for to oppose this darkness. This theatre group was useless, impossible but nevertheless necessary. In the beginning we needed to make a place and space for healing our souls through the work; later, as we began to get reactions from the public, we realised it was our entire society that needed healing through facing truths about themselves and the world. And so, that became our task: to go out of silence, to speak in the name of all of us who felt censored during the long time. The healing process of our society started in that very moment.

*

A few statistics about the world's languages based on information provided by UNESCO statistics in 2006:

90% of languages are not found on the Internet.

80% of African languages have no formal written form.

75% of Brazil's languages (540) have died since Portuguese colonisation in 1530.

90% of Australian languages (250) died since English colonisation in 1800.

Of the 6000-odd languages in the world, one is said to disappear every fortnight. Should the English speaking world care? The point is that it's not just picturesque details that are lost if a language dies out, it's also a whole way of understanding human experience.

Some 200 years ago the German explorer Alexander von Humboldt stumbled upon the village of Maypures, near Orinoco River, in what is now Venezuela. While there he heard a parrot speaking and asked the villagers what he was saying. None knew since the parrot spoke Altures and was its last native speaker.

Will our different languages slowly fade out and transform into a special form of silence, like in the case of the above mentioned parrot? While we communicate through the Internet in our different English languages do we slowly become that bird? And what can we do about that? Does theatre have this role of keeping memory of the language alive?

The most recent performance I created with my theatre was a performance on the ruins of the library in Belgrade. It was called *In Search of the City*. The story of the bombed library is the story of how a nation's memory can be erased and how spiritual values are destroyed when you demolish a country's relationship to the archive of memory, to literature and a recorded understanding of human life and behaviour.

In Wim Wenders' film *Wings of Desire* (1987) angels used a human form, but were invisible to human eyes; they listened to the thoughts of people reading books in Berlin's central library. Through angels we heard the sound of human thoughts mixed with the words from the books, in different languages.

While creating our performance on the ruins of the library, I imagined that the audience could hear the books, the books that had been burned and destroyed, through the actors/angels. They spoke about ten different languages. The audience was in front of a protective fence that surrounded the library; the actors would come from inside the ruins, and whisper in the audience's ears the texts from different books in different languages. For me as director this simple physical and aural gesture signified a link to re-awakening lost cultural memory.

*

What is it that we remember and are we more attentive to certain memo-ries rather than others? How to treat harsh memories? Or truth that is horrible? How not to be silenced by the horror of truth?

*

A few years ago I heard the story about the last public execution in the US in 1936. An African American man (Rainey Bethea) had been accused of raping and killing an older white woman. The sheriff who was to perform the hanging was a woman. At the last moment she decided to pass this terrible duty on to a man, who voluntarily performed the hanging. The national press became furi-ous when they did not get the story they expected and instead attacked the very idea of public execution, saying that it was barbarous act. From then on, executions in the US were not open to the public but were for invited audiences only. It is still not clear today in the Bethea case if the accused man committed the crime for which he was executed.

I started to be extremely intrigued. This story posed so many important questions: of justice and race, of duty and the law, of capital punishment, of rituals that are created around executions, and the need to make them theatri-cal and so on. I knew that I was entering "the twilight zone." In today's world, who needs another performance about such a tough subject such as this one? Instead, some of my theatre friends suggested that maybe we should think of doing something light, maybe a comedy, maybe something for children. While I was listening to their words I knew that at the end that the choice was not mine: the story had to be told. My friends and colleagues from Dah Teatar and 7 Stages Theatre from Atlanta accepted the challenge. They agreed with me – there is so much in this story.

Over the course of two years we developed this production, back and forth in Atlanta and Belgrade. Two years of life is a lot. Many events happened in our lives — good ones and hard ones. I slowly started to understand that we were dealing with a subject that is fundamental for understanding our respective societies. Something that sounds like a very 'American' story reflects heavily on my own country. Even though officially the European Union banned capital punishment there is 'unofficial' capital punishment all the time: political assassinations (i.e. one in 2003 when the Serbian prime minister was assassinated), murderers on the streets of the cities all around the world, and crimes in and against families, to mention a few from an endless list. I realised that whoever commits the act of murder officially or unofficially actually believes in capital punishment and is 'taking the court onto the street.'

While working on this production we posed lots of questions to each other. None of us had clear answers. We started the journey together with no clear destination. What we thought we believed in was challenged all the time. All these questions still echo when we perform the piece, as it continues to develop in process. 'Who would you hang?' is a question that actress Faye Allen from 7 Stages asks in the production of her colleagues and of the audience. An automatic response from another actress is 'Nobody – but...' During two years of working on this production I started to be aware of this automatic response that we all have in relation to crucial questions. It is not finding a clear answer to this question that interests me any longer but rather the gap between 'Nobody' and 'but' that we tried to explore through this work.

If we managed to transmit a very simple truth through our performance – it is terrible to kill any human being - then these years of our lives that we devoted to this piece of theatre were fruitful. The space where different voices could be heard had been created. Attention was paid.

The power of the theatre lies in its power to cast light on dark truths and allow a process of mourning to occur in a society. Theatre can create indeed a necessary space for collective mourning, for collective witnessing, for remembrance and action. It is important to ask the question: how to create space where we can meet and be together, a place to mourn, and not be in opposition with one another?

Issues of Representation in Contemporary South African Theatre

CRAIG HIGGINSON

[Craig Higginson grew up and was educated in South Africa. After studying at the University of the Witwatersrand (Wits) in Johannesburg for a BA (Hons) degree in English and European Literature, he worked as Barney Simon's assistant at the Market Theatre for a year before moving to London in 1996. There he wrote for *Time Out* magazine and worked as a director, dramaturge and assistant director for theatre companies including the Royal Shakespeare Company (RSC), the Young Vic, the Hampstead Theatre, the Almeida and the Oxford School of Drama. In 2004, he returned to live and work in Johannesburg, where he works as Literary Manager at the Market Theatre. This reflection was written in 2006, and references players in the political scene, such as Thabo Mbeki, who are no longer in power in South Africa.]

We in South Africa are living in a strange in-between phase. We have one of the most advanced constitutions in the world, endorsing democratic values and protecting the rights of all, and yet the issues of redress and the need for affirmative action dictate that we cannot live according to that constitution.

Not long ago in our past (1948), the predominantly Afrikaans Nationalist government came into power at last (as they saw it). They had suffered under British rule during and after the Anglo-Boer War (a third of their population, mainly women and children, had died in the British concentration camps), and they believed it was time for redress – time to advance their own nation through various forms of affirmative action, which secured the prosperity of white Afrikaners and ensured that black South Africans in particular would not be able to threaten these jobs. The Afrikaner renaissance led to one of the most brutal and oppressive regimes the world has known.

Those familiar with this history – and those familiar with the rise of nationalism in Germany in the 1930s, for example, or in Zimbabwe in the 1990s – may have learned to be wary of the need for a nationalism that is based on race, on notions of some sort of essential identity that can be drawn from religion or ethnic identity. Yet those familiar with the abuses in the past in a country like South Africa are also sensitive to the need for redress – especially when, thirteen years into our democracy, there is still massive unemployment and crime, and white South Africans still own much of the land and control much of the economy.

So what to do? I suppose there has to be a cut-off point. A point at which one feels that redress has gone far enough and one places less emphasis on a race-based nationalism and strives for a more inclusive democracy. In South Africa, this point is far from being realised. In government, business and the academic institutions, the "African renaissance" is only just beginning to develop its momentum. In certain corners of activity – in government, academia and business – it has even become permissible to talk about whites in a way the emerging Nazis were permitted to talk about Jews: they are settlers, not *of here*; they are parasitic; they are growing fatter while we continue to suffer; we need to squeeze them out of the economy, academic institutions and political power; we will sit back while we watch the populace commit increasingly horrendous acts of violence on them because, deep down, we know that they deserve it. Even Thabo Mbeki, leader of the second most violent country in the world after Columbia, recently said that whites must stop complaining about the violence. Recent stories that concern white people include an elderly woman dying from having boiling water poured over her repeatedly by young tsotsis and a five-year-old girl being brutally beaten up by people who broke into her parents' house. But in spite of what Mbeki says, it is actually all South Africans who are suffering from the violence. Every single day, people of all races are being shot, tortured and raped. It is no exaggeration to say that the country is in a state of war.

This may seem an oversimplified and rather brutal summary of the current situation in South Africa, especially when there are also a great many good people doing a great deal of good, but these issues are certainly in the air at present

– as thick and pervasive as flies. Were you to spend any time in the country, you would find these concerns being voiced almost daily by most people, black and white.

So how does this affect our theatre? During apartheid, much of the best theatre that came out of the country was essentially 'monologic' in its approach. By 'theatre' I mean what has come to be known as 'protest theatre' – the work of Athol Fugard, John Kani and Winston Ntshona; and Barney Simon, Percy Mtwa and Mbongeni Ngema – as well as many others. The enemy was apartheid – which provided a long and rather dreary monologue of its own – and theatre responded with a clear sense of its ethical and political role. It was there to provide a counter monologue to the status quo, a monologue that either endorsed a kind of liberal humanism (celebrating our common humanity, our equality) or a kind of Black Consciousness nationalism (celebrating African-ness and telling white people that they were not needed in the struggle for liberation). The dominant trend, and the most sellable abroad, was the first kind of theatre. And it had enormous power in communicating the realities that all South Africans (but most of all black South Africans) lived within apartheid. Plays like *The Island* (1973) and *Woza Albert!* (1979) can, with some justice, be credited with changing the world – or at least with having a very significant impact wherever they went, and they went pretty much everywhere. The US sanctions that finally threatened the apartheid government's economy were imposed thanks to a greater awareness of the injustices of apartheid, and that awareness was, without question, advanced by touring plays like *The Island* and *Woza Albert!*

Many people have been wondering since 1994 (the date of our first democratic elections) what will happen in South African theatre now that there is no coherent "enemy" to defy. We have passed through a ten year period of rather muddy water, but seem to be emerging robustly. Certainly, the audience figures at the Market Theatre, as well as the general standard of work, have risen very significantly in the past couple of years.

But it is generally acknowledged that our common project – our sense of a unified theatre community – ended with the end of apartheid. As a society and in the theatre, what has followed has been a fundamental fragmentation, a season of selfishness you may call it (if you are inclined to be mean-spirited about it) or a season of opportunity and individual growth (if you don't mind about the majority of people in the country, who have been rather left behind by the process). In theatre, we have seen the growth of strong individual "voices" – not so much in writing as in directing – and we have seen a range of new work developing. Community theatre is thriving; there is a great deal of celebratory work, which tends to contain a lot of "traditional" singing and dancing, celebrating the country's rich cultural heritage (this work exports well as it is unfamiliar to many outside the country, even if it often isn't really 'drama'); and there has been a great deal of new work that is influenced by television, and soap operas in particular. This last kind of work is seen in great profusion at events like the Grahamstown Festival. It tends to be hastily written, with thin characterisation, plot-driven relationships and a certain melodramatic style. Amongst all this, there have been fine pieces of theatre that have travelled the world to great critical acclaim – work that combines what we might call 'Western' values of what constitutes good theatre with elements of 'African' culture – whether it be styles of storytelling, or mythical tropes, or approaches to ritual, or modes of representation, etc. A recent example of this syncretic kind of work is *The Suitcase* (2006), which ran at the Market recently and was based on the short story of the same title by Es'kia Mphahlele, adapted and directed by James Ngcobo. Yael Farber's *Molora* (2007), which is currently running at the Barney Simon Theatre (one of our three venues), is another example. Both of these productions have been, or are about to go, on to tour internationally.

So, in spite of this 'season of selfishness,' there is also a sense in which the most developed and advanced members of our theatre community are pulling together in a way that the government, and the country at large, is not always managing to do. This is as it should be. I always felt that the Market Theatre was a few steps ahead of the rest of the country during apartheid – so why should that be any different now? One of the challenges we have faced has been how to find a language and a form that captures the complexity of our new democracy. This means that we need to draw from all our cultural and ethnic roots, as well as giving more space to new works in a wider range of languages. But it also means that there needs to be a shift in our view of things: a less essentialist, more inclusive and internally dialogic attitude towards each other. At the Market, Malcolm Purkey, myself, and the rest of the artistic team, are trying to promote more dialogic work, work that dramatises genuine conflict and tries to find new unities and new ways forward. Malcolm (the Artistic Director) also wants the works we put on to dialogue against each other too – so that our audience are compelled to empathise with a range of realities and perspectives.

To this day (in the year 2006), however, few of our plays manage to be genuinely dialogic. It seems we are still locked in the categories and divisions we inherited from apartheid. Perhaps this is not surprising, as most people working in the theatre grew up during the violent 1970s and 1980s. The new generation who were born after 1994 are still at school – still too young to make their different perspectives (and most of them have very different attitudes regarding their identities) felt. In the meantime, we are trying to give space to people who are often lacking the skills to produce the level of work we are demanding from them. Some, inevitably, have to be excluded – and this has, occasionally, led to feelings of great bitterness and frustration.

At the heart of all our work, time and again, the issue of representation raises its head. The black intellectuals who have emerged out of a Black Consciousness past and continue an essentially Africanist agenda can be fiercely critical of white writers and directors, for instance, who often represent black South Africans in their work. Well known writers like Athol Fugard and Nadine Gordimer have received strong criticism from such quarters recently. White directors who collaborate with black actors in order to create new work predominantly about black realities are also criticised. But actually the criticism goes in every conceivable direction. Zulus are often criticised for their representations of Xhosas, and vice versa, and one often finds accusations of racist attitudes towards any number of groups: mixed race people ('coloureds' in South African lingo), Indians, whites, Zulus, but, especially, the foreigners. Nigerians, Mozambiquans, Malawians, Zimbabweans and others are often said to be represented, predominantly by black practitioners, in a way that is derisive and belittling.

The sad fact is that a lot of these representations *are* deeply problematic. But this is not the issue. The issue should not be who you represent but how you represent it. I actually see this automatic criticism of anyone who represents what is ostensibly 'other' as a dangerous development and an attempt at censorship.

Anyone who makes art knows that whenever we represent anything that is outside of ourselves we are representing what is other. To be a creative person, you need the gift of empathy. The question we ask, as I have suggested, is not so much what we are representing as how we are representing it. However, because we have been so misrepresented in the past, people are naturally suspicious of who will be allowed to speak for them. Also, because we have grown up in a system that has encouraged ethnic divisions, few people seem able to free themselves from still thinking of these divisions in essentialist ethnic terms. This means that those who are suspicious of how we represent each other are often justified – often they really are misrepresented because the writer or director or actor are representing a cliché, a 'received idea' as Flaubert might have said.

One of my tasks as the Literary Manager at the Market Theatre, as I see it, is to explode this notion that there is more dividing us than what unites us, while also ensuring that our writers (and others) are sensitive to difference. We should be free to write about what is 'other.' If we wrote only 'about what we know' (a phrase you hear always – usually coming from people who have never written much at all), we would be engaged in a self-reflective, narcissistic activity that would do little to challenge anyone's ideas about anything. No – we must write about what draws us; we must write about something that is at stake for us – which is very different from writing about what you know. Yet, on the other hand, you need to proceed with great caution, great tact, because when you write about what you do not know you are in danger of falsifying what you represent. The writer (and director and actor) needs to be armed with great rigour and empathy, dexterity and adaptability. These are some of the virtues all good writers share. I don't know of one writer who is generally highly regarded who does not, in some way, possess these qualities.

We have a great deal of work ahead of us. We have work to do on our writers (and other makers of theatre) and on our audience. We have yet to free ourselves from the strictures of apartheid – and, as I mentioned at the outset, we are living in a society that still endorses forms of ethnic nationalism and discrimination – in spite of 'democracy' and our hard-won constitution.

I believe we can look to our audiences to understand better what we are really doing and saying in the work we are making. People from outside of South Africa are often surprised at the audience response to plays here. Black South Africans often laugh when they feel discomfort or pain. Perhaps this is how many people survived the dark years of apartheid. Barney Simon called it ; 'the laughter of recognition.' But in fact there are many different kinds of laughter in the theatre. Some laughter comes from a deep place and some comes from a superficial place. There is, I would maintain, a good kind and a bad kind of both deep and superficial laughter. The good laughter that comes from a deep place is the kind of laughter that comes out of a necessity, but a necessity that advances openness towards one another, empathy, care, a greater awareness. The not so good laughter that comes from a deep place would be the kind of laughter certain of our plays have encouraged: the laughter of deep derision; the mockery of those who sit in judgement of the characters or events. Of course, someone like Brecht would argue exactly against this position. He would say that sometimes there are things to deride, that it is good to laugh at fools and oppressors. But this is the very opposite of what I'm talking about. I am talking about the laughter of the man in power to the foreigner, the homosexual, the prostitute, the aged, the alcoholic, the beggar. And that laughter comes from a deep place: a place deep enough, in history, to pave the way to the Holocaust or the genocide in Rwanda. The more "shallow" kind of laughter is not so serious. Here we laugh at a harmless joke or, when it's not so justifiable, a harmful joke where the victim is dismissed because they are beneath consideration.

There's still a very clear battleground in South Africa, and those who represent the true forces of democracy are still fighting a long fight. We at the Market Theatre want to make work that brings out the best impulses in our people, not work that affirms the worst, that perpetuates the old patterns that we have come to know so well.

On Chicano Theatre and Self-Censorship: What Were We Thinking?

JORGE HUERTA

[Prof. Jorge Huerta holds the Chancellor's Associates Endowed Chair III as Professor of Theatre at the University of California, San Diego. He is also a professional director and a leading authority on contemporary Chicano and US Latino theatre. Huerta published the first book about Chicano theatre, *Chicano Theatre: Themes and Forms* (1982) now in its second edition. Huerta's latest book, *Chicano Drama: Society, Performance and Myth*, was published by Cambridge University Press in the year 2000.]

Prologue: On terminology: What is a Chicana/o?

It is important from the onset to define what I mean when I refer to Chicanas (female) and Chicanos (male), Mexicans and even Mechicana/os. Quite simply, Mexicans residing in the United States legally or illegally, were born and raised in Mexico and self-identify as Mexicans. They grew up in a society in which they were not a minority. I define the Chicanos as the children of Mexicans, either born in the U.S. or brought to the U.S. as infants. Like all immigrant groups, second-generation Chicanos are caught between two cultures, their parents' and the varied cultures of the U.S. Not all descendants of Mexican parents or grandparents call themselves Chicano. Self-identified Chicans/os are making a political statement, cognizant of the many injustices their brethren undergo in the U.S. In contradistinction, those who call themselves Mexican-

American are generally more conservative and harbor the attitude that "I made it, why can't they (the Chicana/os)? This "culture clash" between the Mexican who wants to "blend-in" and the Chicano who challenges the hegemony has been a common theme in Chicano performance and literature for generations. To the Chicanos, a Mexican-American is a "sellout," someone who would rather "pass" for non-Latino, or "Anglo," a common term erroneously referring to all white-skinned Euro-Americans, regardless of their cultural roots.

On the use of the term, Mechicana/o

I will distinguish between the Chicana/o and the Mexican when the differences are important and refer to a conflation of the two as Mechicana/o, when the conditions pertain to both groups equally or similarly. In other words, there are plays in which the characters who are U.S.-born confront situations that someone raised in Mexico might not have to deal with, and vice versa. The Chicana that does not speak Spanish, for example, may not suffer the same alienation a non-English-speaker might. Conversely, that same Chicana might suffer discrimination in an all Spanish-speaking situation. However, language is only one of many factors that distinguish the native-born from the immigrant. With few exceptions, the plays I label "Chicana/o" are ostensibly about Chicana/os living in the U.S. but by their very definition, Chicana/os recognise and celebrate their Mexican cultural roots. And although these plays take place in the U.S., Mexico is always in the background, contributing to the characters' fractured identities.

The Mechicanos should not be confused with the other US Latinos. In terms of population, Mechicana/os make up the largest group. The second-largest group is comprised of the (mainland) Puerto Ricans, U.S. citizens since 1952 when the island became a U.S. commonwealth. The third-largest group is the Cuban-American, either Cuban-born or born in the U.S. All three groups have active theatre communities, often with distinct agendas, but all with the common goal of bringing to the stages of their communities (and beyond) the lives of their compatriots. Members of other Latino groups have also emerged on the stages of this country; Colombian-born John Leguizamo is perhaps the best-known.

Preliminary question: What is Censorship?

When I think of censorship I always think of being censored by someone else, not self-censorship. Those of us who create art, who write scholarly articles and books about marginalised communities, have always had to deal with a variety of forms of censorship. The most insidious form of censorship is simply being ignored by the dominant culture, thus rendered invisible; what some have termed "The Invisible Mexican." In 1970, when I began researching Chicano theatre, it was clear that few scholars and critics had given any attention to the theatre in the Mexican and Chicano communities of the Southwest. Were we ignored by the scholars because our initial theatrical expression was Spanish religious folk drama *en español?*

The earliest theatre in the Spanish-speaking communities of the Southwest was twice marginalised; first as religious *folk* theatre and secondly because it was in a foreign tongue. In the 1920s, when secular Spanish-language professional theatre was prominent in cities with large Spanish-speaking populations (such as Los Angeles, California and San Antonio, Texas), this activity, too, was ignored by non-Spanish-speaking critics and scholars. Thus, the Mexicans and Chicanos suffered the first and most virulent form of censorship, elision.

In California the avoidance of anything Mexican or Chicano by the dominant society began soon after the arrival of the Anglos and the inevitable Mexican-American War which resulted in the citizens of a Mexican territory abruptly becoming "strangers in their own land" in 1848.[1] Suddenly, the *Californios,* as they were called, became second-class citizens. For some scholars such as Frederic Jameson, this was a form of "internal colonisation," being colonised from within one's own land. Jameson states, "...in the United States itself we have come to think and to speak of the emergence of *internal* Third World voices, as in black women's literature and Chicano literature...."[2]

---

1 I refer to California because the history of the Spanish-speaking populations varies from state-to-state. In both New Mexico and Texas, for example, the Mexicans have long been recognised, albeit marginalised, by the dominant culture. Further, in New Mexico many people claim lineage all the way back to the early 17th century. California history books taught in the first half of the 20th century basically ignored the contributions of the Mexicans to the culture of California.

2 Fredric Jameson, "Modernisms and Imperialism," in Terry Eagleton, Fredric Jameson and Edward W. Said *Nationalism, Colonialism and Literature* (Minneapolis: Minnesota, 1990), 49.

As history has shown, the coloniser must eradicate all that he can of the colonised subjects' cultural identity and self-worth. Language is the first to be challenged with erasure, along with spiritual (non-Christian) beliefs and historical memory. Thus, the history of the Spanish-speaking Californians was effectively censored from the books for over a century until revisionist historians began to set the record straight in the latter part of the 20th century. It was this climate of erasure that late 20th century artists and scholars performing and investigating Mexican and Chicano theatre faced, especially in California. Perhaps their dedication to revealing and celebrating the Chicana/os' socio-political and cultural artifacts initially preceded any form of self-censorship for there were many truths to be revealed.

I think we would all like to believe that we do not self-censor but that would be dishonest. We do it all the time in our daily interactions with other people, why not in our artistic and scholarly lives? As I thought about how I would contribute to this collection I realised that the theme demands an assessment of what the term, censorship, means. So I turned to my Word Thesaurus, a simple act of inquiry that led to the following synonyms: restriction, suppression, control, cutting, editing, expurgation and bowdlerisation. Curiously, these are all applicable to any artistic and/or scholarly effort. We restrict what we're saying and suppress ideas, themes or words that would not enhance our vision, be it aesthetic, cultural or socio-political. We control, cut and edit ourselves with abandon, and we expurgate. What I didn't understand at first blush was the verb, *bowdlerise*. What is that? Here's what I learned from Miriam-Webster online:

'Bowdlerise' is a transitive verb that comes from the name of an English editor, Thomas Bowdler, who died in 1825. It means "to expurgate (as a book) by omitting or modifying parts considered vulgar." Also, "to modify by abridging, simplifying, or distorting in style or content." In the first definition, what catches my eye is the adjective, vulgar, because in many ways, censorship has had to do with getting rid of the vulgar. But now I have to ask: whose definition of *that* adjective? Here's what our trusty Miriam-Webster on-line has to say about the adjective, vulgar: 'of the mob, of or relating to the common people.' It can also refer to plebian, 'lacking in cultivation, perception, or taste, morally crude, undeveloped, or unregenerate; offensive in language; lewdly or profanely indecent.'

156

Chusma and/or Rasquachi:

'Plebian' could be a polite way of saying *chusma* or *rasquachi*, two wonderful terms in Spanish that have historically been used to describe and denigrate the poorer classes. The adjective, *chusma*, is one of those delicious terms, an insult, really, that places the observer (who is making the reference) above the person or persons to whom he is referring as '*chusma.*' The Latinas and Latinos reading this will all have their own translations of *Chusma* and they will all be correct. *Chusma*, like beauty, is in the eye of the beholder. It is also a value-judgment. In her biting satire, *Chicas 2000* (1998), Alina Troyano, under her nom-du-Teatro, Carmelita Tropicana, defines *chusmería* as 'shameless, loud, gross, tacky behavior, in short, tasteless with attitude.'[3] In the glossary of the same script she defines chusma as 'people of color trash.' The irony in Troyano's performance is that she, as a Cuban-born lesbian living in the United States, is *chusma* in the eyes of her (homophobic) community as well as the conservative members of the dominant society. So in response she embraces the term and throws it right back in their faces.

In a similar manner, although they did not use the term, *chusma* or *chusmería*, the early Teatro Campesino celebrated the Mexican notion of the *rasquachi*, an adjective that does not refer to a person or persons but to their socio-economic condition of working-class poverty. In Tomás Ybarra-Frausto's words, 'Rasquachismo is brash and hybrid, sending shudders through the ranks of the elite. In an environment always on the edge of coming apart (the car, the job, the toilet), things are held together with spit, grit, and movidas. Movidas are the coping strategies you use to gain time, to make options, to retain hope.'[4] Thus *chusma* and *rasquachi* can be used to condemn and to distinguish, as in Tropicana's 'tasteless with attitude.' For some, this is a post-colonial condition caused by the coloniser's suppression of the subaltern subject in order to maintain a capitalistic 'cheap pool of labor.'[5]

---

3   Alina Troyano, *Chicas 2000*, in *I, Carmelita Tropicana: PeRforMing Between CultuRes* (Boston: Beacon Press, 2000) p. 72.

4   Tomás Ybarra-Frausto, "Rasquachismo: A Chicano Sensibility," in Teresa McKenna and Yvonne Yarbo-Bejarano, eds. *Chicano Art: Resistance and Affirmation, 1965-1985* (Los Angeles: Wight Gallery, 1991), 156.

5   Of course, globalisation has changed the economic condition of the working class in the U.S. as skilled and unskilled jobs become more and more scarce because of outsourcing to Third World countries.

So why am I riffing on the terms, *rasquachi* and *chusma*? Because it started out as 'vulgar.' The unwashed poor, the dirty little scum, those people-who-are-not-like-us. Because it has to do with social class or pretensions of superiority. The other definitions of 'vulgar' in Miriam-Webster are also apt and all conjure distinct types in each of our imaginaries. Here is what I am wondering. What is the relationship between the so-called *chusma* and the artist? More important-ly, *is* there a relationship between the scholar and her/his *chusma*? Do we, as artists and/or scholars try to get rid of the rasquachi or the chusma in ourselves, thus self-censoring? The following questions arose as I considered this issue: How do we self-censor? Why do we self-censor? Who or what are we protect-ing? What happens when we do not self-censor?

Trampa sin salida, a vulgar acto?

Returning to the adjective, vulgar, I am reminded of an experience I had as the director of El Teatro de la Esperanza in 1972, an opportunity missed because we did not self-censor our art. Our university-based Chicano theatre group, un-dergraduates under my (graduate student) direction were producing an acto[6] written by one of my students, Jaime Verdugo. Titled *Trampa sin salida,* or *Trap Without Exit,* this acto was inspired by the actual killing of a young incarcerated *pachuco,* or street youth, by Los Angeles County Sheriff's officers who reported the death a suicide.[7] The dialogue was quite real, full of 'fucks' and other vul-garities, reflecting the way these young men communicate with one another and the world around them. In short, the *pachucos* maintain a 'Fuck you!' atti-tude to those outside their circle.

When we were invited to perform at a local high school we knew that the vulgar language would be considered unacceptable in such a setting by teach-

6   The term, "acto," was given by Luis Valdez to the short, farcical sketches he and his fellow striking farm workers developed in the mid-1960s. The ideal acto attempts to educate and entertain an audience about social injustices. The acto is usually satirical, ending with the triumph of Good over Evil. For more on the Chicano's actos, see Jorge Huerta, *Chicano Theatre: Themes and Forms* (Bilingual Press, 1982), Ch. One. See also Luis Valdez, *Luis Valdez, Early Works* (Arte Público, 1990), pp. 1-133.

7   *Trampa sin salida* is published in Jorge A. Huerta, ed. *El Teatro de la Esperanza: An Anthology of Chicano Drama* (Santa Barbara: Teatro de la Esperanza, 1973), pp. 12-27. I also discuss this acto more fully in *Chicano Theater: Themes and Forms,* pp. 161-167.

ers and administrators. But thinking of ourselves as radicals eager to challenge any authority and with the concurrence of the Chicano high school students who had invited us to perform we decided not to censor the play by cutting the vulgar language. We expected this would be problematic and actually welcomed the opportunity to confront the conservative high school establishment. The reader might be asking: "What the hell were you thinking!"

The acto began and after seven minutes and an equal number of 'fucks,' the principal ran onto the stage in front of the actors who kept on playing while he shouted 'This assembly is cancelled!' We had decided beforehand that if anyone attempted to stop the acto the actors would move downstage of the curtain and continue. Luckily, a riot did not ensue when the actors continued the acto as the curtain fell behind them. What surprised us the most was that many in the audience cheered when the principal stopped the acto. Further, more than half of the students in the auditorium marched right out. About three hundred mostly Chicanas and Chicanos stayed, demanding that we be allowed to continue. The principal was forced to acquiesce and permitted the troupe to perform its other actos, which we assured him were free of vulgarities. We did not tell him that the characters sometimes used vulgar words *in Spanish*.

Chicano theatre has always been bilingual (Spanish-English) and even trilingual, when one considers the patois of the youth, termed "caló," which is neither English nor Spanish but a language of their own devising. Because of this linguistic distinction we had the option of not censoring ourselves in Spanish or caló. We sensed that the non-Latino principal would not understand the non-English vulgarities and did not delete these while we did censor the vulgar words or phrases in English. It could be said that we enjoyed a linguistic superiority to the principal, reducing him to *our chusma* for lack of education. We and the students in the audience were no longer the 'culturally deprived,' he was, as they laughed at words he did not know and thus could not censor.

I relate this incident of long ago because it is an example of when self-censorship would have been more productive than not. The moral of the prohibited acto, the political lesson, is not that pachucos use vulgar language, but to demonstrate the duplicity of the Sheriff's Department labeling the deaths suicides when it is common knowledge that these tough youths do not take their own lives. The language lent a kind of authenticity to the acto, but what good was it if we could not get to the heart of the acto's main objective? We wanted to 'speak truth to power,' as they say, but never got the opportunity.

The irony in that situation is that the acto's message was not one that school officials would have nor could have promoted publicly. Certainly, poor people of all backgrounds have always known that the police and sheriff's officers are not necessarily their friends. But in 1972 the general population still harbored delusions of kind-hearted 'officers of the peace,' out there to 'protect and to serve,' as the Los Angeles Police Department motto goes. Not in Watts. Not in East Los Angeles. Therefore, *Trampa sin salida* would have upset the principal, regardless of the vulgarities being said. But by challenging him to censor us we missed the opportunity to point-out a social injustice that few people outside ethnic and working-class neighborhoods recognise. Perhaps those students that cheered when the acto was stopped and then left the auditorium so obediently saw the *pachucos* on stage as their *chusma*, mere punks who did not deserve their time, much less their sympathy. Undoubtedly, the Mechicano students would have called themselves Mexican-American, attempting to distance themselves from such 'low lifes.'

Battle Hymn of the Republic: a Chicano Verfremdungseffekt

On the opposite side of the issue, the early members of the Teatro de la Esperanza did not self-censor when we hosted an on-site reporter for a federal agency that was funding our summer program to work with at-risk youths in a community center in Santa Barbara's barrio. We were much influenced by Bertolt Brecht's theories and determined that we would attempt a kind of verfremdungseffekt, or estrangement by changing the familiar lyrics of the "Battle Hymn of the Republic" to reflect an anti-hegemonic argument *in Spanish*. The music remained the same but the new lyrics called for social justice rather than the status-quo. When the reporter arrived and we learned that she did not speak Spanish we knew that we could sing our revisionist "hymn" without fear of losing our federal funding. Had the reporter been Spanish-speaking we would not have sung that song, basically censoring ourselves for the right reason, economic survival.

Unlike the vulgar language in *Trampa sin salida*, the language in the revised "Battle Hymn" was not vulgar, per se, but it could have been construed as such by purists. Instead of praising "the coming of the Lord," we were singing of the coming of Social Justice and the Spanish-speaking audiences would listen with extra care to see how we had altered the lyrics. To the reviewer, we were a nice, non-threatening student group, singing familiar hymns with passion and commitment. So censorship cuts both ways, I believe. There are times when self-censorship is about self-preservation and there are times when self-censorship is superseded by a more urgent and necessary cause.

I believe one persons' *chusma* is another person's hero. By producing an acto about the *pachucos* at Santa Barbara High School we were embracing those misunderstood youths as victims of a racist, insensitive society. From the educational system to the justice apparatus, the playwright and the rest of the production team all thought that the truth behind the killing of a young Chicano at the hands of the authorities must be exposed. We did not think about what the charges against him were, nor why he was incarcerated, because we believed that he was inherently innocent. To us, he was not *chusma*. But to the students who cheered when the curtain was dropped and to many people in the Mexican-American community, *pachucos* were their *chusma*. The conservative Mexican-Americans do not care how or why the *pachucos* get into trouble with the law.[8] Further, the Mexican-American worries that he will be seen as a *pachuco* by the dominant society, categorised or stereotyped as a low-life because of the color of his skin.

As noted earlier (footnote 6), the acto form was an early example of what Yolanda Broyles-González later termed the 'rasquachi aesthetic,' in her analysis of the humble roots of the Teatro Campesino's early actos.[9] We consider the actos rasquachi because they could (and can) be produced anywhere, from the fields to union halls to the streets, with minimal costumes, props or design elements and very little technical support. The actors wore signs around their necks with the name of their character such "El Patrón" ("The Boss"), "Campesino ("Farm Worker"), etc. To add to the satire the villain usually wore a pig-faced

8   As I write this, California's governor, Arnold Schwarzenegger, has called for the building of more prisons. Where are the classrooms? What about paying the teachers a decent salary?

9   Yolanda Broyles-González, *El Teatro Campesino: Theater in the Chicano Movement* (Texas, 1994), pp. 35-58.

mask. The acto form is simple but not simplistic, didactic as well as entertaining. Above all, the early actos pointed towards a clear solution to the conditions of the farm workers: join the Union, as they ridiculed the greedy growers and their henchmen. Indeed, as Freud and others have shown, laughter is a weapon, a form of empowerment, if only for a moment, giving the oppressed a feeling of superiority over their oppressors. By turning the boss, the teacher, the policeman into *their chusma,* the actors were giving their humble audiences a sense of superiority and hope for better wages as well as improved working and living conditions. Most importantly, these performers were not professionally trained, adding to the *rasquachi* quality of it all.

La gran carpa de los rasquachis: celebrating the common man

Of the many collective creations Luis Valdez and members of the Teatro Campesino produced, I believe their opus magnus was *La gran carpa de los Rasquachis (The Great Tent of the Underdogs)*, created between 1972 and 1973.[10] This raucous, physical and farcical piece was the logical culmination of the Teatro's investigation of the early 20th century Mexican performance style as evidenced in carpas, or tent shows. The carpa companies would tour to working-class neighborhoods on both sides of the US-Mexican border, setting-up their tents and charging a modest ticket price to humble people eager for a little entertainment. The shows included singers, musicians, dancers, acrobats and other popular entertainments. A highlight would be the sketches in which the actors would perform farcical, slapstick recreations of the humble Mexican's daily experiences. Popular targets on the northern side of the border were the Mechicana/os who denied their Mexican heritage and attempted to 'pass' for Anglo, as discussed earlier. Most importantly for our discussion here, the *carpas* were *rasquachi.*

The Teatro Campesino's *Gran carpa de los Rasquachis* celebrates the *rasquachi* as it follows the travels and travails of one, Jesús Pelado Rasquachi, who

---

10 For more on the Teatro Campesino's *La gran carpa de los Rasqusachis* see Jorge Huerta, *Chicano Theater: Themes and Forms* (Bilingual Press, 1982), pp. 199-207 and Françoise Kourilski, "Approaching Quetzalcóatl: The Evolution of El Teatro Campesino," *Performance*, 2 (fall 1973), 37-46.

162

crosses the border into the United States, follows the crops, falls in love, mar-
ries and raises confused Chicano children and eventually dies, a broken man, in
the welfare office. Jesús is a Mexican Everyman, of course, symbolic of the
struggles of the Mexicans who come to the United States with grand hopes of
economic success, only to be defeated by low-paying jobs and a system that
virtually kills them. In the production the actors moved from scene-to-scene in
a choreographed, stylised fashion with an almost constant musical undertone,
such that the play, like a dance and *commedia dell'arte*, is really impossible to
publish. I mention this piece here, because it signals for the Teatro Campesino
and its director, a move to what I call '*rasquachi* with class.'

La gran carpa de los Rasquachis was performed in front of a backdrop of
burlap bags, potatoes sacks, rice sacks, and the like, sewn together, reminding
the audience of the farm labor many poor Mexicans encounter when they cross
the border. The costumes, too, were basic khaki pants for both the men and the
women, over which they placed accessories to distinguish their station and
even gender, as the actors (except the actor playing Jesús) played multiple
roles. What made this piece an example of *rasquachi* with class were the carefully designed and executed costumes, masks and props as well as the ensemble work of the actors/musicians/singers. The Teatro Campesino members had
moved beyond the simple acto style, with signs across their chests, to a genre
that required physical, mental and spiritual training. The piece was so popular it
earned critical and audience acclaim throughout the U. S. and abroad. Having
achieved a production that reached the highest levels of *rasquachi* performance, Mr. Valdez was ready to leave *rasquachi* behind.

Leaving the *rasquachi* behind: Valdez goes to Broadway

With the success of *La gran carpa de los Rasquachis*, Luis Valdez was inspired to write his most successful play to date, *Zoot Suit*, first produced in 1978
in Los Angeles, California and subsequently on Broadway the following year. [11]

Valdez's odyssey from the fields of California as a union activist to what has
been known as "The Great White Way" marked a turning point for the play-

---

11   Luis Valdez, *Zoot Suit and other plays* (Houston: Arte Público, 1992, pp. 21-94.

wright/director that could be termed a rejection of the *rasquachi*. By partnering with a major regional theatre, the Center Theatre Group of Los Angeles and then with the Broadway producers, Valdez had to make artistic compromises, which for some critics would be considered self-censoring.[12] While the Teatro Campesino ensemble had reached a zenith with the extremely stylised and performative *Carpa*, it was clear to Valdez that he needed to work with professionally trained actor, singers and dancers who could most effectively bring his docu-drama to life. This was not an easy decision, to be certain, but Valdez knew that if his artistry was to develop, his cast and the entire production team would have to come from the mainstream.[13] There is no room for the *rasquachi* on Broadway.

Where are we now: Is the Mexican still invisible?

This discussion began with an explication of the term, censorship and its various permutations, followed by my observations on various forms of the term, 'vulgar.' This led me to focus on *chusma* and *rasquachi* as terms that aptly describe the form of theatre being produced in the early days of Chicana/o theatre. Having been born out of a socio-political struggle, the early Chicano theatre workers did not self-censor. Instead, these activists exposed the many injustices Mechicana/os were encountering daily. The problem was that they usually found themselves 'preaching to the choir' instead of reaching those audiences with some political capital: the politicians, school board members and others who could possibly change conditions for the better. Early Chicano theatre was *rasquachi* and the Mexican-American elites wanted nothing to do with those so-called radicals. By not self-censoring, these early performers were lim-

---

12 For some of the Chicana/o criticisms of Valdez's decision to produce his play on Broadway see: Broyles-Gonzales, 208-234; and Yvonne Yarbro-Bejarano, "From 'acto' to 'mito': A Critical Appraisal of the Teatro Campesino, *Modern Chicano Writers*, ed. Joseph Sommers and Tomás Ybarra-Frausto (Englewood Cliffs, NJ: Prentice-Hall 1979, pp. 160-66. pp. 176-85.

13 In the period leading up to the production of *Zoot Suit* I remember Luis Valdez telling me that when he auditioned Hollywood actors he discovered a wealth of talent he had not known with his own company. Was he rejecting, thus censoring **is** own actors by replacing them with professional actors? Were the Teatro Campesino actors, most of whom had not studied acting formally, "too *rasquachi*" for him? Have I self-censored by never having revealed this discussion in print before? See also Yolanda Broyles-Gonzalez (1994), in her critique of Valdez's decision to cast non-Teatro Campesino ensemble members in *Zoot Suit*, pp. 177-80.

iting the scope of their impact while also performing a very vital function in the education and socialisation of their communities. Recall that it was more about politics than Art: the Message was much more important than the medium.

Following the 1974 Broadway success of Miguel Piñero's *Short Eyes* and the record-breaking run of Valdez's *Zoot Suit* in Los Angeles (despite its critical failure on Broadway), regional theatres across the country began to court Chicano/a and Latino/a playwrights in the 1980s. For some producers the motives were strictly monetary (hoping to tap into those 'Latino Dollars'), but several important 'projects' helped launch the next generation of Latina and Latino playwrights, playwrights who continue to write and get their plays produced across the country, but not on The Great White Way. [14] However, my contention is that many of these playwrights, like Luis Valdez a generation before them, continue to mediate their plays to appeal to non-Latino artistic directors, a form of self-censorship.

A milestone of sorts was reached when Nilo Cruz's fine play, *Anna in the Tropics*, won a Pulitzer Prize in 2003, the first play written by a US Latino to be so honored. Ironically, this play had not yet been produced on Broadway and when it was, it had a limited run. This play deals with a Cuban-American family of cigar makers in Tampa, Florida, in the late 1920s and is not a critique of the dominant culture (like *Zoot Suit*, for example); thus a very 'safe' play. Indeed, this play was the most produced Latino play in regional theatres and universities all across the country. And yet, like *Zoot Suit*, *Anna in the Tropics* was neither a critical nor financial success on Broadway. To date, the only critical and financially successful play by and about Latinos to succeed in the commercial arena of Broadway is *Short Eyes* in 1974. Whether on Broadway or in the regional theatres of the United States, Chicana and Chicano playwrights continue to be 'the Invisible Mexicans.'

---

14 See my critique of so-called "mainstreaming," "Looking for the Magic: Chicanos in the Mainstream," ed. Diana Taylor and Juan Villegas, *Negotiating Performance: Gender, Sexuality & Theatricality in Latin/o America* (Durham & London: Duke University Press, 1994), pp. 37-48.

Always on the Edge of Being Forgotten: the Victims of the Atomic Bombings

CHIORI MIYAGAWA

[Chiori Miyagawa is a playwright based in New York City. She had the great honor of having three atomic bombing survivors—Ms. Toshiko Tanaka, Mr. Hiro Iso, and Mr. Takeshisa Yamamoto—attend the first preview of her play, *I Have Been to Hiroshima Mon Amour,* in New York City in May 2009. Miyagawa is part of an NGO, Hibakusha Stories (Hibakusha means survivors of atomic bombings), which aims to increase the public and youth awareness of nuclear non-proliferation issues. *Thousand Years Waiting and Other Plays,* a collection of Miyagawa's seven plays, is forthcoming from Seagull Books as part of the international *In Performance* series.]

I have been in a perpetual state of broken-heartedness for months as I approach the opening of my play, *I Have Been to Hiroshima Mon Amour,* in NYC. What I feel inconsolably sad about is that as I learn more and more about the victims of this holocaust, their unimaginable suffering, I realize how unlikely it is that they will ever be granted their rightful place in history as victims of a war crime. Decades of censorship and propaganda by the U.S. government have insured this anonymous population's unending obscurity in the narrative written by the victor. Of course there are many individuals, artists and activists, who have attempted and continue to try to bring them to light, but collectively, humanity has forgotten about them. Why is it that I, a Japanese-born American, can immediately recall representations of the German holocaust as if they are part of my personal memory, yet have to go looking for images of people in

Hiroshima and Nagasaki to educate myself of their true plight? The answer is obvious, and my generation is guilty of maintaining the censorship that was enforced by the government for over thirty years by self-censorship called apathy.

In 2007, we saw some of the images that have been hidden from us for over sixty years: images of people whose teeth and bones are exposed from their mouth up to their nose because their lips were singed off; swelled and severely scarred faces of women who no longer looked human; small orphans crying from the pain of extreme burns and the loss of their parents; and charred, broken human remains. At least audiences who subscribe to HBO saw them in the documentary film by Steven Okazaki, *White Light/Black Rain*. There are many more where images where these came from, most of them have not and will not be seen: naked people of all ages wandering among fire like scarecrows with their arms held away from their bodies because their skin was hanging like shredded ribbons; people trying to push ruptured organs back into their bodies; and the Ota River full of mangled corpses, people who thought jumping into the boiling water would ease their agony. The horror of the aftermath was extensively documented by the U.S. military in color film—Kodachrome and Technicolor—which were still rare even in Hollywood in 1945. These images along with the confiscated black and white film and photographs taken by the Japanese media have been one of our dirtiest secrets.

According to Greg Mitchell—an editor and publisher dedicated to revealing the methods that the government had engaged in to suppress the details of the brutal effects of the atomic bombings—the original color footage of the victims that had been labeled "Top Secret" were quietly declassified in the 1980s without the world knowing about it. Where does the public go to find the truth about an atrocity if it doesn't know that the evidences existed in the first place? How does one know to go to the National Archives in College Park, Maryland, and ask for #342 USAF?

Some residents of Washington, D.C. or people passing through the capital in 1995 could have encountered a tiny fraction of the truth if it weren't for the intervention by the U.S. Congress on the Smithsonian exhibition at the Air and Space Museum, "The Last Act: The Atomic Bomb and the End of World War II." The exhibition planned for the fiftieth anniversary of the end of the war did not happen. Not the way the curator imagined anyway. Congress and the American Legion strongly objected to the fact that the exhibit portrayed the Japanese as victims. Under the political pressure and the threat of cancellation, the curator, Martin O. Harwit, rewrote the script five times, and was finally forced to drop the narrative all together. Even a watch, found in Hiroshima with its hands frozen at 8:15, the time of the detonation, was not allowed to remain because the item somehow gave the Japanese a human face. We have had no idea what human faces really looked like at 8:15 am on August 6, 1945 in Hiroshima, and we have the U.S. Congress to thank for over six decades of ignorance.

Over two hundred thousand people, the great majority civilians, died instantly when the bombs detonated first over Hiroshima, and three days later over Nagasaki. Those who didn't even know what happened were the lucky ones. People who survived long enough to witness the monumental suffering of fellow civilians and experience unimaginable pain, only to die in a matter of minutes, hours or days, were the unlucky. People who survived, deformed or blind, who gave birth in the postwar period to children with leukemia, were ill and haunted by deep sadness for the rest of their lives. But if the U.S. tax dollars were going to be spent for propaganda, there was no way the survivors would be looked upon as victims.

The consequence of the censorship of images of the atomic aftermath is the dangerous state of mind that the American society is in today. Take for example, the words 'weapons of mass destruction.' Most people have no idea what these words actually represent, and it has become a popular phrase, handy for criticisms or jokes. The journalists have even come up with a nickname for them—WMD. We're all afraid that Iran or North Korea will attack us with WMD (which looks like some brand name—BMW, WMD—an average consumer can get confused), but we don't even know what the actual repercussions would be, because the information about what the earlier, much less powerful version had done to human beings has never been fully available to us, not even with this groundbreaking documentary film, because it hasn't aired on a major network. In *White Light/Black Rain*, the facts that the U.S. government personnel studied the effects of the bombs on the surviving injured and ill, deformed, and mortified population; and that they handled the victims as laboratory rats and made notes, but did not give any medical treatment, are briefly mentioned in the testimony of one woman and never investigated further. If the filmmaker had dared to expose this inhumane act on top of the incomparable war violence more prominently in his work, would the film have been seen even on cable? Or would it have been too much for the delicate American corporate nerves?

At the time of the Smithsonian controversy, as the items that 'dwelt to excess on the horrible effects of the atomic bombs' were being omitted from the exhibition, Barton Bernstein, a professor of history at Stanford University commented in *The New York Times* that the revisions of the exhibition left 'Americans impoverished intellectually.' We are the one and only country that has conducted experiments of atomic weapons on cities which were inhabited by civilians who were already starving to death. Not wrestling with this historical demon has left us emotionally numb to the point that we regularly converse about WMD as if they are suicide bombings. Members of the American Legion were emotional and rather irrational in their arguments against the Smithsonian exhibition, yet they had every right to express them. But what was Congress doing? Depriving the general public of knowledge - the crucial tool that would prevent the cruel act from being repeated again. It wasn't enough that the 1995 exhibition was ruined by the time it opened, that it turned into another glorification of the victor, but that Congress actually called for the resignation of the curator for hating his country. I don't imagine the more than eighty Republicans and Democrats who demanded the dismissal of Mr. Harwit had seen the effect of the atomic bombings on humans back in 1995. I hope they all have cable TV and a subscription to HBO today.

We learn to empathize with humanity by handing down memories so that the next generation may contemplate them and revise them if necessary. This is the rational process that will ultimately save us from ourselves. I believe political theatre functions in the same way. Theatre artists are masters of revisiting the past; while the film industry often fabricates the future or recreates the past, we tend to imagine the past, which has a different purpose. We don't teach history, but we correct unjust memories. If the subject matter is the present, we introduce memories to audiences who otherwise would not have them. Memories are fragile—we remember very little, and we remember wrong. Yet, we are dependent on others' memories for our existence. This nature of memory resembles theatre—it is ephemeral and impermanent, and every audience member will remember it differently. This gives us, political theatre makers, an enormous opportunity to inject tiny seeds of memory for audiences to carry out of the theatre and walk down the streets with them. And within a year, ten, twenty, a hundred conversations about this given event may occur, and people who didn't see the show would create memories of the message that the play communicated.

The victims of the atomic bombings are always on the edge of being forgotten. If they are not remembered, they did not exist. It is not only tragic for them, but it is perilous for us, this apathetic forgetting, this self-censorship of the heart. We can remain blind and impoverished and keep the version that says it was necessary to drop two atomic bombs on the country that was already annihilated by fire bombings. This is less painful. Who wants to feel guilty about the previous generation's mistakes? It's easier if we can chant 'it saved American lives' and cite some numbers that the military included in its press releases to justify the use of atomic bombs. Or we can come out of moral lethargy and think about why the two cities where the U.S. dropped the bombs were left intact. All through the terrifying years leading up to the defeat, B-29s passed through the sky over Hiroshima and did not drop a single fire-bomb. These cities were saved as human testing sites to study the magnitude of damage possible by the brand new nuclear weapon. Why do we continue to believe the lie that the U.S. dropped leaflets warning the citizens of Hiroshima to evacuate the city the day before? Why would the military jeopardize such an important and expensive experiment by emptying the city of its subjects? *White Light/Black Rain*—a deeply moving film which finally gives voices to the survivors—does not verge on this treacherous frontier. Perhaps the next generation of filmmakers, theater artists, and museum curators will be encouraged by this film—which paved the way to giving back the survivors their humanity—to achieve an alternative way to understand who the victims were on August 6 and 9, 1945. Perhaps the Smithsonian will be allowed to mount another exhibition that portrays the Japanese as victims on those two days of war, and Congress will think twice about censoring it.

But is it already too late? Government censorship and propaganda have been enormously successful. Most of the American public was manipulated into associating the images of beautiful giant pink mushroom cloud in the sky and a skeletal dome of a building—both void of humanity, both romantic—with the atomic bombings, the U.S. government therefore faced no significant opposition for continuing nuclear proliferation. The world could have looked different today had it not been for this criminal censorship. Why do we continue to be submissive to it? We live in a lethal world today because of our willingness to continue to be ignorant. In Errol Morris' documentary film, *The Fog of War*, Robert McNamara admits that General LeMay and he were behaving as war criminals toward Japan during WWII: "Proportionality should be a guideline in war. Killing 50% to 90% of the people of 67 Japanese cities and then bombing them with two nuclear bombs is not proportional... But what makes it immoral if you lose and not immoral if you win?" Is he not credible? Why is there no demand by the public to issue an apology to Japan about this holocaust? What can we do, as theater artists, up against such disinterest? I have no answer. Unless more stories like those told in *The Fog of War* and uncovered in *White Light/Black Rain* reach a wider public soon, we may approach the brink of destruction in a state of moral deficiency at a critical moment of history. The moment may be closer than we would like to admit.

Silence Echoes with Multiple Meanings

DRAGAN KLAIC

[Dragan Klaic, a Permanent Fellow of Felix Meritis in Amsterdam, taught arts and cultural policies at Leiden University. Initiator of the European Festivals Research Project, writes and lectures on the contemporary performing, arts, cultural memory, and international cultural cooperation. Author of several books, most recently *Europe as a Cultural Project* (Amsterdam: ECF 2005) and of many articles and contributions to over 40 edited books. Dragan Klaic passed away on 25 August 2011 after battling a long illness. This essay was approved for publication by the author prior to his passing. Its publication is dedicated to his memory.]

Artistic silence knows many varieties. The silence of contemplation, preceding early stages of creation. The silence of numbness and exhaustion, marking the creative vacuity. The imposed silence, of artists in exile, cut off from their habitual cultural context, peers, and native language. I am thinking of those numerous German theatre professionals running away from Hitler in 1933 and seeking another territory of their own language, in Austria (until 1938 *Anschluss*), Switzerland and in short-lived émigré companies elsewhere. Those actors who reached the US hoped to get roles with accents in Hollywood as my fellow post-Yugoslav exiles and friends Mira Furlan (extra-terrestrial ambassador in *Babylon 5*, a French woman in *Lost*) and Rade Šerbedžija (in a variety of East European villain roles in dozens of films) have done some generations later in the same Hollywood studios. For the theatre directors emigrating because of Hitler exile meant silence. Leopold Jessner could not do anything in California. Bertolt Brecht could not direct, so he kept writing in his Santa Monica cottage, carefully preparing his post-war career. Max Reinhardt stayed aloof from the triviality of the Broadway *show biz* and ran for a while an acting school, silently supported by a rich admirer. After 1945 German antifascist émigrés had a choice to go back, to one of the two emerging German states, or stay in exile. Soon afterwards, the Cold War produced new columns of exiled performing artists who carried the melodies of their native language as a most precious possession and an unbearable burden, the obstacle to their adjustment and integration elsewhere. Apartheid in South Africa, dictatorships in Latin America, repressive Arab regimes kept the flow. The post-Cold War conflicts instigated new theatre exiles, dispersed and lonely, who were pushed out of their professional lives without hope of return, especially from Africa and Asia.

Is the silence of inner exile much different? I am thinking of my former close friend L, a former theatre director, a maverick and a charismatic leader of an alternative theatre movement and cultural-political project that collapsed with the disintegration of former Yugoslavia in the 1990s. After an enigmatic association with the Milošević regime 1994-2000, L has been staying silent, out of theatre and out of politics, withdrawn from the cultural center he built from a former factory in Belgrade. Now empty, without budget and programs, this edifice is only occasionally rented out for disco parties to pay the electricity and the phone bill. In his self-imposed inner exile and protracted silence L reminds me of the hero of Ibsen's play *John Gabriel Borkman* (1896), a failed tycoon and swindling industrialist, who paces endlessly on the upper floor of his mansion, brooding his demise and his *hubris*. But L, it seems, has no sense of *hubris* and no remorse – only a stoical acceptance of his outcast role, framed as a side effect of some enormous conspiracy to liquidate the former Yugoslavia and punish him for his resistance.

This case stands in contrast to other variants of the inner exile and artistic silence, not self-chosen but imposed by political powers, as on the numerous blacklisted US artists, pursued by media, FBI and courts for their supposed leftist sympathies in 1930s, rephrased as a communist conspiracy in the 1940-50s. On the other side of the Iron Curtain, not much is remembered of the inner exile of artists silenced for their ideological errors and unreliable background, for their reformist sins and stubborn resistance to the political campaigns of the authorities. Pavel Kohout sought to create a living room theatre in the 'normalised' cultural constellation after the defeat of the Prague Spring in 1968, and to keep the actress Vlasta Chamostova, banished from the Czech stage, from going mad by writing plays for her. Tom Stoppard derived from this valiant effort, folded by persistent police interference, his 1979 play *Cahoot's Macbeth* and Kohout himself, once in Western European exile, returned to the experience in his play *Marie Struggling with the Angels* (Marie zápasí s anděly 1978).

I still remember watching Mira Stupica play Vlasta/Marie fighting her nightmares and her secret police shadows in 1984 at the Belgrade Atelje 212. The production greatly displeased the Czech ambassador as did all Atelje 212 productions of dissident plays by Vaclav Havel, then silenced in Prague, but alive and well on the Belgrade stage. Some years later, some of us, loyal spectators of Kohout and Havel productions, slid into our own inner exile in Belgrade under the onslaught of nationalism. When the war started in 1991, many of us were gone for good, dispersed on all continents and connected only by our anger and disappointment. Suddenly we have become a considerable exilic community, in New York, Toronto, Oakland and Sidney, in Amsterdam, Berlin and Paris, and yes, ironically, even in Prague, where the ex-dissident Havel had in the meantime become the head of state.

The dissident muse and the long hand of censorship

Censorial systems, formal and informal, once dominating the theatres of Central and East European communist countries, collapsed in the hot years 1989-90. They were all dismantled as the first deed of the post-communist 'transition' as an early self-liberating *gestus*. Since then, censorship has been re-appearing only incidentally in the transition countries, as an arbitrary imposition of some arrogant politician, a panicky impulse to suppress something that enervates, exposes and unsettles, a bad habit striking back. Religious bigots and nationalist fanatics would occasionally wish to forbid a scene or an entire production that offends or irritates them yet this hardly ever happens. Presumably, censorial interventions take place occasionally behind the scene, as a subtle secret pressure, a threat or blackmail, but they are practically never registered and exposed. What probably survives is self-censorship, a stubborn habit, difficult to overcome and drop for the generation that lived for decades under the censorial threat and thus learned to watch itself in order to keep out of trouble. For younger artists, who joined the theatre profession after 1989, censorship is hardly more than a bad odor of the past, or a collection of anecdotes, of dubious authenticity, retold endlessly by the older colleagues in the theatre buffet. What once was a much felt surveillance, pressure and forceful intervention has in time become part of the fading mythology of dissidence.

In 1995 I initiated a research project in the critical, subversive and dissident theatre in Central and Eastern Europe between 1945 and 1989. Theater Instituut Nederland (www.tin.nl), that I led at the time, and De Balie center for culture and politics in Amsterdam (www.debalie.nl) developed a conceptual framework and commissioned seven researchers in Central-Eastern European countries to examine their dissident performing arts traditions and theatre's clashes with the authorities. On the basis of their reports a symposium of veterans, researchers and a new generation of artists took place in Amsterdam at the end of 1995, followed with a weekend program of public interviews, case presentations, debates, documentaries and specially commissioned performances, all under the title 'The Dissident Muse.' We wanted at the time to salvage incidents, documents and remembrances of dissidence and censorial reprisals before they disappear in the collective amnesia, to reconstruct the role of theatre as a substitute for a non-existing civil society under communism and to explore how theatre could play a critical role in the emerging fragile democracy of the post-communist countries and in the routine, blasé democracy of the EU. We also hoped that our program will prompt more research, further gathering of materials from private archives, vivid discussion, oral history projects, and extended analysis of the capacity of the stage to surpass occasionally the prevailing conformism of the communist epoch.

Not much came out of this expectation after our program was successfully completed. Many veterans in Central and Eastern Europe preferred not to remember, younger colleagues tended to look more to the future than to the past. Some research was conducted and findings published, some memoirs appeared, here and there old photos were found and properly stored in public archives, but the tradition of stage dissidence remained little researched, in contrast to the attention given to the samizdat publications. [15] The secretive mechanisms of theatre censorship stayed hidden or undocumented even when

---

15   Wojciech Orlinski, 'How to Overcome Censorship' in *Post*, the IWM Newsletter, 94 (Fall 2006), 5-6.

the consequences were more or less known... plays banned, production altered, postponed or made to disappear from the repertory, ideological campaigns waged in the media, enforced self-criticism and ritual remorse, and individual artists blacklisted for a while. I was able to engineer some restorative maneuvers in recent years by commissioning some articles for a section on theatre as a literary institution, within a large complex research project on the literary cultures of East Central Europe. 16 Some of the authors involved addressed the issues of dissidence and censorship in a series of specific and emblematic cases, digging out new evidence and details. Even under the supposedly liberal Yugoslav regime, for instance, where there was no formal and continuous censorship, some 70 productions were suppressed between 1945 and 1991. [17] Kazimierz Braun in his *History of Polish Theater, 1939-1989* amply documented the theatre constellation thorn between the 'spheres of captivity and freedom' [18] and confirmed what our 1995 program indicated clearly: that the dissident muse was first of all a Polish dame and that only in Poland theatre was subversive and dissident in its staunch opposition to the regime while in all other countries it merely sought to stretch the range of esthetical freedom and social truth, without challenging the tenets of communism.

Censorial incidents punctuate prevailing indifference

If we can assume that there is practically no real censorship in theatre in Europe today, this is not because of some "end-of-history" triumph of tolerance but rather because theatre does not matter so much. Other media are more influential and important and therefore strictly watched by formal and informal power structures. European governments do not monitor Google and Yahoo as the Chinese authorities do (with the consent of these corporations!) but television is taken seriously, subjected to all sorts of standards and quotas. Public

---

16 Marcel Cornis-Pope & John Neubauer, eds., *History of the Literary Cultures of East Central Europe: Junctures and disjunctures in the 19th and 20th centuries.* Amsterdam: J. Benjamins 2004 (vol. 1) and 2006 (vol. 2)

17 Aleksandra Jovicevic, 'Ingenious Dramatic Strategies Reach Across the Yugoslav Theatre Space,' in *Ibid*, vol. 3, 2007.

18 Kazimierz Braun, *A History of Polish Theater 1939-1989*, Westport, CT & London: Greenwood Press, 1996.

176

television can be hardly insulated from political expectations and informal pressures, especially in the news and documentary programs, despite or rather thanks to supposedly democratic and transparent licensing procedures and formally autonomous boards of supervisors. Berlusconi controls the Italian commercial television channels as a tycoon and the public ones as the Prime Minister. Even theatres that claim that they are driven by an artistic mission increasingly offer sheer entertainment while a growing segment operates clearly and openly as show business, seeks to amuse and distract, putting any potential censor out of business.

There are occasional incidents that are more a matter of cowardice and opportunism within the theatre itself than of censorial pressure from the outside. When the *Intendantin* of the Deutsches Opera in Berlin wants to withdraw the production of Mozart's *Idomeneo* (Fall 2006) because at the end severed heads of Buddha, Jesus and Mohammed are displayed and the wrath of radical Muslims is feared, this is just silly paranoia, countered quickly by the performing arts professionals as well as media and politics and probably some strengthened police presence. When Stephane Lissner, the boss of La Scala, considers not to show in Milan a new version of Leonard Bernstein's *Candide* that he co-produced because in a scene Bush, Blair, Berlusconi and other world leaders play ball in swimming gear, it is the same fear of offense and revenge, a desire to keep theatre proper and nice to everyone, an entrenched bad habit of opera houses. The sentiment is clearly not shared by some regular spectators of La Scala who mercilessly booed away the tenor singing Radames after his first aria in Franco Zeffirelli's new *Aida* in December 2006. He left the stage at once in a temper tantrum but later felt sorry soon afterwards and sung next evening at the piazza in front of the opera house, begging to be allowed back to the stage. Censorship? No, but an individual singer's cowardice against a specific form of cultural bigotry, perpetuated by some opera audience members, convinced they are the keepers of true Verdi and proper *Aida*. At least opera *afficionados* sustain some passion, even if ill placed.

And when the Birmingham Rep suspended in the year 2004 further performance of *Bezhti* after 400 young Sikhs threatened violence because they are outraged by a scene, this is an audience development program gone berserk. The young Sikhs were invited to follow the staging process of a play by Sikh author Gurpreet Kaur Bhatti as an effort to prove the company's serious commitment to community outreach. Yet the youths understood it as a license to exercise censorial prerogative, not just by boycott but by violence. Never mind that 60.000 Sikhs live in the Birmingham area. Instead of developing a young multicultural audience, the Rep created hothead enemies and then capitulated in the face of their anger, without even trying to develop some strategies of deliberation, debate, esthetic and political reasoning. An ominous signal at the time when multiculturalism as a policy of social appeasement displays in the UK and elsewhere in Europe its fractured and fragmentising condition, its inability to prevent radical social frissons and escalating ideological confrontations among religious, cultural, ethnic and linguistic bulwarks. If panic leads to self-censorship instead of a suave program to develop the intercultural competence both of the Rep staff and its audience, the lesson is that theatre people have to fear their own fear more than anything else.

Beyond those incidents, broadly reported and quickly forgotten in the media, censorship seems not to be a European problem but rather a frequent occurrence if not a systemic feature of other cultural constellations, especially in Africa and Asia, where authorities and stirred up angry masses tend to quickly finish off artistic perpetrators of whatever overblown outrage. The USA displays proudly its First Amendment yet remains a hotbed of all sorts of censorial vigilantism, carried out on moral and religious grounds, often followed by the disappearance of the work, sponsors' flight, producers' angst and de-funding threat. But even in Europe, the sense of failure of multiculturalism as a policy that sought to ensure social cohesion prompts emphatic demands for 'respect' of sensitivities of specific groups, especially minorities that may feel discriminated and marginalised in their values and traditions. A step further is a growing inclination to condemn and sidetrack opinions and gestures, expressed within an artistic context, that could be considered by some groups as offensive. The right to offend, however, is not only a necessary feature of a democratic and open society but also an essential capacity of the arts - and not just through satire. If art cannot offend, outrage, provoke, make the public uncomfortable, and criticise society, what is art worth? This maverick, muckraking, iconoclastic characteristic of arts should not be confused with the hate speech that is in many countries legally sanctioned. In a democratic society courts arbitrate the confusion of realms between art as provocation and hate speech occurs.

Silencing by policy

In Europe, the cradle of cultural policy is part of public policy; systemic exclusion and silencing of artistic vision does not occur because of censorial mechanisms, but rather as a consequence of deficient instruments and procedures, deployed in the distribution of public resources for artistic endeavors. Some of the policy provisions, consciously or not, perpetuate inequality, discrimination and marginalisation among the artists and keep some at bay within the zone of silence, despite half a century of rhetorical investment in concepts such as democratisation of culture, cultural democracy, decentralisation, access and participation. Again, this is not a matter of purposeful evil or of a silent conspiracy but instead of policy-making laziness, ideological blindness and delays in adjusting policies to quickly altered circumstances of cultural production.

Emerging artists in Europe are inevitably quite vulnerable. To grow, develop professionally and consolidate their own socio-economic position, they need peers, colleagues and supporters; funders and intermediaries, benevolent critics and commentators, patrons, clients and audiences. Yet cultural policies, in most countries, are geared to benefit established cultural institutions, not the emerging individual artists. Since policies favor producing and distributing institutions, emerging artists jealously seek institutional acceptance and support and at the same time fear and resent their grip, instrumentalisation and dominance. In the performing arts, many beginning professionals reject the established career pattern of yesterday, to seek to join an established company and rise gradually in ranks from supportive roles to major, most prominent and most appreciated tasks. It is not so much that artists impatiently seek a short cut but instead that they prefer to run their own affairs and remain in charge of the artistic process rather than to yield to the prevailing influence of complex and often un-transparent institutional mechanisms that characterise the major rep companies.

The continuous appearance and renewal of autonomous, non-profit groups and temporary production units across Europe in the last 50 years, competing for incidental, project subsidies with the established permanent companies, signals this ambition to concentrate on their own artistic pursuits without cumbersome institutional luggage. Practically everywhere in Europe this type of theatre activity receives crumbs from the public subsidies cake, dished out often in an arbitrary fashion, without proper criteria, transparency and systems. More recently, insistence on efficiency and businesslike modus operandi of cultural institutions again favors big organisations over the small ones and sidelines temporary or starting initiatives. The popularity of one-performer shows, for instance, might indicate not so much an esthetic revival of the narration from a perspective of a unique and specified character as the performer's loss of trust in theatre as a collaborative process, perceived as too bureaucratic in large institutions and as unsustainable in small, impoverished and marginalised groups.

Cultural policies tend to favor institutions over individual cultural operators, to advantage established institutions over new initiatives in a pioneer phase of institutionalisation, and to better endow bigger institutions than smaller ones, especially if the former connote history, tradition and prestige. Through the institutionalisation of the performing arts, competitive, contentious and even querulous environments are fostered that allow policy makers and funders to play the subsidy-dependent applicants against each other. [19] Furthermore, systematic cultural policies and subsidy distribution procedures tend to classify and standardise various types of artistic production and could ultimately lead to a straight jacket in which some artists cannot or do not want to find themselves. [20] As artistic approaches develop rapidly and traditional disciplinary boundaries weaken, much of the subsidy system remains driven by traditional discipline labels. In the early 1990s the Flemish Ministry of Culture could not fit the work of Jan Fabre in any of the existing subsidy categories yet could not ignore it either because of his international success. So the Ministry designed a special category for Jan Fabre. He was lucky, but many of his peers elsewhere feel excluded by the idiosyncratic nature of their work.

While traditionally cultural policy used to be a preeminent prerogative of national governments, with decentralisation numerous regional and municipal authorities now appear as cultural policy players on their own, often with considerable ambitions and means. [21] Consequently, artists tend to move in a calculating fashion to places with richer cultural infrastructure and more generous

19   Simon Mundy, *Cultural policy: a short guide*, Strasbourg: Council of Europe, 2000, 14-20.

20   Paul Kuypers, *In de schaduw van kunst*, Amsterdam: Prometheus 1999, 95-96.

21   *Ibid*, 128-138.

funding of the arts. Much debated artistic *mobility* [22] could be seen as a tentative voyage of individual artists from the zones of silence and marginalisation to greener pastures, whether in the form of migration, temporary relocation or some sort of globalised nomadism. Globalisation discourse tends to play down the importance of place because supposedly with digital communication means one can work from anywhere and reach anyone. And yet, it seems that globalisation makes specific places increasingly competitive with other attractive locations. The patterns of mobility indicate a trend of artists moving to bigger places, with bigger concentration of the creative class, [23] with some cultural metropolises functioning as a strong magnet. In case of London or New York, it is the size of the market with ample work opportunities that matters while the current Berlin boom [24] indicates that the density of artists settled and the availability of affordable living and working place seem to be more of a pull factor than the generosity of the cultural policy provisions.

Old and new patterns of exclusion

Other, more widespread forms of exclusion and effective silencing of artists evolve from the entrenched patterns of discrimination on ethnic, cultural, religious ground of women and of the disabled, taking place in the world of arts and culture, behind the façade of legal equality. [25] Well orchestrated and prolonged efforts to combat this sort of discrimination remain rare: Arts Council England sought to advance the status of Black artists through its Decibel campaign 2003-8 (www.artscouncil.org.uk/decibel) and in the Netherlands the Atana program (www.atana.nl) has provided since late 1990s an original method to recruit, train and engage decision makers and advisors for arts and cultural organisations, selecting participants with at least two different cultural back-

22 *A Study on Cultural Cooperation in Europe* (2003), Report for the European Commission, Brussels: European Forum for the Arts and Heritage and Interarts (www.eu.int/comm/culture/eac/sources_info/pdf.word/summary_report_coop_cult.pdf) and European Cultural Foundation, *On the Road to a Cultural Policy for Europe*, Amsterdam: ECF 2004.

23 Richard Florida, *The Rise of the Creative Class*, New York: Basic Books 2002, 67-82.

24 Richard Benoit, 'Berlin cool comes from the cold,' *Financial Times* 25-26 February 2006.

25 Ria Lavrijsen, *Culturele diversiteit in de kunst*, Den Haag: Elsevier 1999, 12-23.

grounds. [26] In many other countries there are some organised attempts to support women artists, mainly thanks to an infrastructure, political capital and skills borrowed from the feminist movement, but the sidetracking and silencing of artists from other fragile groups goes unaddressed.

For most Roma, almost a 15 million large ethnic minority, dispersed across Europe, the very idea of becoming an artist is a most challenging, highly improbable and hardly attainable goal since so many are excluded from even basic educational opportunities and condemned to perpetuate their socio-economic marginalisation. Only isolated amateur and semi-professional Roma artistic initiatives appear here and there, lacking support, training, capacity development and continuity. It is too early to say whether the current Decade of Roma Inclusion 2005-15 (www.romadecade.com), supported by the European Union, several national governments and private foundations, will make a substantial difference, especially for the cultural participation and expression of Roma since its primary objectives are the improvement of socioeconomic status, educational opportunities and health conditions but not cultural advancement. With amateur and community arts forms among Roma developing erratically and slowly, professional Roma artists are a rarity, by and large unacknowledged, isolated and unconnected with other fellow Roma artists and lacking any local, national or Europe-wide Roma cultural infrastructure. Roma arts festivals appear occasionally but lack networks, information, prominent high-caliber artists and functioning organisational base to achieve a sustainable impact – only Khamoro, the World Roma Festival (www.khamoro.cz) has been held yearly in Prague since 2002. The idea to create at the Venice Biennale 2007 a Roma pavilion, championed by the Roma program of the Open Society Institute (www.osi.hu), was a symbolic breakthrough.

It is uncertain whether the current *cultural diversity* discourse could really alter the patterns of marginalisation. Diversity is such a vague concept that once applied to arts it could encourage tokenism and formal symbolic representation and perhaps not much more. Even the 2005 UNESCO *Convention on cultural diversity* [27] tackles primarily the global dimension of cultural diversity but

---

26   Rob Boonzajer Flaes: 'Questioni globali, soluzioni locali. Lo sviluppo di politiche interculturati come professione,' in Simone Bodo, ed., *Culture in movimiento, Strumenti e risorse per una citta interculturale*, Milano: M & B Publishing, 2006, 72-78.

27   *Convention on the Protection and Promotion of the Diversity of Cultural Expressions*. Approved by

leaves national governments quite free to tolerate the continuation of discriminating practices on their own territory, all previously ratified human rights conventions notwithstanding. Yet when politicians seek to rationalise public subsidies by requiring cultural diversity of the art public, they forget that it cannot be achieved without cultural diversity of cultural producers, that one cannot expect to have cultural diversity in the auditorium without having it first on the stage, backstage and off stage. [28]

The recent emphasis of art and culture *leadership* and some private and public investment in the leadership development programs, especially in the UK (such as the Clore Duffield Foundation, www.cloreleadership.org), and the Treasury funds funneled through the Arts Council England could be understood as a determination to develop arts leaders for today and tomorrow who will be able to cope with the vagaries of the cultural policy, cut through the red tape of the public funds distribution, and successfully engage private means of foundations, patrons and commercial sponsors. The concept of leadership, more habitual in the Anglo-Saxon world than elsewhere, inevitably connotes some elitist expectations and stirs up fantasies of omnipotence. Derived from politics and business, it is being applied to the arts, confirming the advanced institutionalisation of the cultural production despite old romantic myths of lonely artistic practice. And yet, it would go too far to assume that the upcoming generation of cultural leaders, exiting from newly set up incubators, will automatically give voice to the silenced and marginalised artists and appear as their spokespersons and advocates. More probably they will be snatched by the prominent institutions and absorbed by the existing coteries of influence and prestige. [29]

---

the 33rd Session of the General Conference of UNESCO in Paris, 20 October 2005 (http://portal. unesco.org/culture/en.ev.php-URL_ID=29123&URL_DO=DO_TOPIC&URL_SECTION=201.html). See also Nina Obuljen & Joost Smiers, eds., *UNESCO's Convention on the Protection and Promotion of the Diversity of Cultural Expressions: Making it Work*, Zagreb: Institute for International Relations/ Culturelink 2006.

28 Toni Bennett, *Differing diversities: cultural policy and cultural diversity*, Strasbourg: Council of Europe 2001, 17-21, and 'Cultura e differenza: teorie e practice,' in Simona Bodo & Rita Cifarelli, eds., *Quando la cultura fa la differenza*, Roma: Meltemi 2006, 21-37.

29 Charlotte Higgins, 'Form-fillers Need Not Apply, the Crisis of the UK Arts Leadership.' *The Guardian* 18 June 2004.

It is exactly the censorial, exclusivist character of many artistic informal networks, clans and cabals, permeated with prestige, common history and much influence peddling, that also should be mentioned here in the footsteps of Pierre Bourdieu, as a sociological factor that both facilitates the integration of some and reinforces the isolation and professional distance of other emerging artists. [30] For a frustrated beginner, this disadvantageous condition is to be overcome more likely by the intervention of a mentor, patron or intermediary than by frenetic networking, thus by some investment of *intergenerational solidarity* - a topic rarely discussed in artistic circles.

It is a fashionable commonplace to say that with internet, no artist could be alone, isolated and silent. But are 50 million weblogs in the world an indicator of the enhanced e-sociability and e-creativity or rather a signal of pervasive patterns of loneliness, pathetic efforts to come out of silence and reconnect with others, communicating ... what actually? Some arts and much more gibberish and ego-trip rhetoric. And while internet pages increasingly present art works and artists, new multiple divides and exclusions have become obvious. One third of all internet pages are in English, 50% encompass a group of 9 languages, such as Chinese (13.3), Japanese, Spanish, German, French, Portuguese, Korean, Italian and Russian (2.2.), and the remaining 20% are shared by all other world languages. Europe with 12.4% world population has 38.6% internet users among its inhabitants and Africa with 14.1% world population only 3.6%. Real-word zones of silence and marginalisation have acquired their cyber-counterparts. [31]

The prevalence of economic perspective

These disparities are further reinforced by the explosion of the cultural industry, capable of producing and marketing in enormous series a great array of products of high, steady quality and low price. Under their influence and economic strength public authorities are increasingly appreciating the arts for its potential economic value and not any longer primarily for its traditional expres-

---

30 Pierre Bourdieu: *La distinction* (1979), engl. *Distinction: A Social Critique of the Judgment of Taste*, Cambridge, MA: Harvard University Press 1987.

31 Source: www.internetworldstats.com

sive or representational role. This shift of expectations puts the artists in a rather awkward position. While they used to look for public patronage in form of a subsidy in order to be sheltered from the commercial pressures of the market and enabled to create rather freely, they are now being directed to the market by the same public funders. If they grant the artists a subsidy, it is primarily in order to enable them to break into the market as soon as possible. Non-commercial artistic pursuits are increasingly seen as a prelude, as a warming up act for the commercially viable work that almost inevitably requires involvement of the corporate world, of the manufacturers and distributors of the cultural industry products and of intermediaries, banks, agents, lawyers and consultants. Many artists do not want such a working context, resent the dependencies it imposes and see them as alienating and even dangerous for the integrity of their art. [32]

Going commercial usually implies specific aesthetic choices and compromises, narrows the range of experimentation, brings about the loss of artistic autonomy and shifts motivations and primary concerns. Those artists who switch from the non-profit to the for-profit artistic production - as is common in music, architecture, design, fashion and film, and less in the performing arts – discover that they need specific competences in order to act as entrepreneurs and grasp the complexities of art as business or risk losing control and ending up exploited by the corporate interest and intermediaries.

Two extreme versions of artistic silence take shape on the stage overshadowed by the powerful processes of economic globalisation and their cultural consequences: one, of the artist marginalised by the lack of support and recognition, discouraged and despairing, frustrated and on the edge to give away their own artistic aspiration in order to reach some socio-economic stability; and of a more successful artist, struggling with the corporate encroachment and silenced by subservience to commercial interests that escape comprehension and influence. Between public subsidy, given as a temporary provision, meant to prompt commercialisation, and the cultural industry that turns artifact into a serial merchandise, the artist has not that many options left: the passing, accidental support of the private foundations; teaching or some other

32 Joost Smiers, *Arts under Pressure: promoting cultural diversity in the age of globalization*, London: Zed Books, 2003, 137-38.

job as a way to make a living while pursuing their own artistic vocation with the remaining leftover hours; hard artistic work with little means and exposure in somewhat autonomous conditions; and finally immersion in the community, and investment of artistic energy in community art projects. Silence looms steadily above those options: a frustration, despair, insecurity or disorientation and many artists would admit that they shift regularly, almost daily, among these options and pursuing them all simultaneously, juggling roles, discourses, attitudes and postures.[33]

The value of a niche

In the performing arts, many actors, directors, designers, technicians and other professionals frequently transgress those boundaries, working in a commercial and a non-profit setting; restructure their relations with colleagues, partners and employers accordingly; adjust to the prevailing ethos, implicit values system and organisational culture as needed. Others stick to one realm, putting up with its restrictions and shortcomings, seeking to benefit maximally from the advantages it is supposed to offer. Visibly, across Europe publicly supported theatre companies struggle to make ends meet against the steadily rising costs and fledging subsidies, fighting the toughened competition of commercial theatre and other forms of entertainment industry. Small innovative artistic initiatives, poor, fragile, only occasionally and gingerly supported, struggle even more and face marginalisation, anonymity, exhaustion and extinction. The greatest danger for the performing arts today is not the censorial scrutiny of political powers nor the grass root vigilantism of ideological fanatics but the indifference of the spoiled consumers, overwhelmed with aggressive marketing of entertaining options for their scarce free time. Clearly, commercial theatre has an upper hand in this competition for audience loyalty, offering an easy, amusing content, packaged in steady, recognizable templates, embellished with popular stars and much glitz, and propped up with hefty advertising budgets.

---

33 Ann Markusen, Sam Gilmore, Amanda Johnson, Titus Levi and Andrea Martinez, *How Artists Build Careers across commercial, nonprofit and community work*, Minneapolis: Humphrey Institute of Public Affairs, University of Minnesota 2006.

Even if performing arts are seen chiefly as a public form of art practice, one that is intrinsically framed as a public event, taking place in a defined social context, many performances occur today in a shrunken, delineated public sphere, in the pockets and reservations of specific public interest, in the niches of special affiliation, in the less visible corners of social life. Not the spectacles of commercial theatre with mass audience and glittering neon advertising, not performances in the prestigious, highly institutional public theatres, of course, but occasional and rarely repeated performances in small arts centers, in galleries, studios and private apartments, in odd, appropriated places, in village festivity halls, in rural churches, on the urban periphery, in schools, clubs, associations and micro communities. Those strictly socially embedded performative practices have given up on a presumed general audience and seek to define and reach an encoded, homogeneous and specific public of shared experiences, values and interests: local dwellers, émigrés, children, senior citizens, some professions, students, linguistic and ethnic communities, homemakers, patients, prisoners...

Around those performative events there is a circle of silence, partly imposed, partly self-chosen and pre-arranged, as a safety buffer to keep away the buzz of commercialism and the politics of public funding with its red tape, to allow concentrated work, intensive communication with the public (10 people or perhaps 100 but not 500 and not 2000) and a build up of social capital on a small scale. Such a *niche theatre* could be seen as a localised practice, articulated in answer to globalisation and commercial uniformity of the cultural industry products and the consumption impulses of an increasingly blasé general public. The niche theatre brings also the dangers of self-referentiality, of shrunken ground to stand on, of disappearance and oblivion - but could reinforce the artistic energy and support it with peers and audience trust and loyalty until it can reach out to broader audience, not only local specific constituencies. Zones of silence are thus not only imposed regimes of restrictions and not only realms to abandon quickly in the pursuit of success and fame but possibly self-built shelters to grow, mature and develop.

3

'Our story is strange. Somebody help us': Censorship and Self-Censorship in *The Silent Twins*

BRIDGET BENNETT

[Bridget Bennett is Professor of American Literature and Culture in the school of English, University of Leeds, UK. Her most recent book is *Transatlantic Spiritualism and Nineteenth-Century American Literature*, (Palgrave Macmillan: New York, 2007). She is currently working on a book on ideas of danger within United States culture, and their relationship to constructions of home.]

J. and I are like lovers. A love-hate relationship. She thinks I am weak. She knows not how I fear her. This makes me feel more weak. I want to be strong enough to split from her. Oh Lord help me, I am in despair. Can J. and I get back together? I really aim to be alone. Yet, even as I say this, I am deceiving myself. Can I stand being alone? I need someone to talk to, a friend. J.'s bed is empty...I wonder if she will ring her bell to come back to me? My heart does not beat so fast now. It only beats fast when J. is around, always with J. [1]

---

1   Extract from the diary of June Gibbons, written in Broadmoor hospital, April 1982. Reproduced in Marjorie Wallace, *The Silent Twins* (London: Vintage, 1996), p. 171.

This poignant and anguished piece of prose is an extract from the diary June Gibbons wrote in Broadmoor special hospital in April 1982. It details her despair at being forcibly separated (for only a day, as it turned out) from her identical twin Jennifer. The pair were put in separate rooms after they had attacked each other violently. The desire to be alone and the immediate sense of the impossibility of being apart from her sister, is at the centre of this piece as it is in the larger story of these tormented siblings. The relationship between censorship and self-censorship, indeed the issue of the boundaries between the two, is particularly contested in the case of Jennifer and June Gibbons, the so-called 'silent twins' of the title of this brief essay. Here, issues of self and other, of silence and volubility, strain at the borders, showing their shortcomings or limitations when they are invoked as oppositional terms. The distinction between censorship and self-censorship becomes less clear in an instance in what is at stake, indeed what becomes quite literally a question of life and death, is the very concept of the self. This essay will complicate the ways in which it is possible to make such a distinction by taking as its subject the case of Jennifer and June Gibbons.

On 11 April 1963 twin girls, Jennifer and June, were born in Aden to Aubrey and Gloria Gibbons. [2] The couple had moved from Barbados to Britain in 1960. There, Aubrey joined the RAF and the growing family moved to follow his job as a meteorological assistant. Within Britain they lived in Yorkshire, Devon and then in Haverfordwest in Wales, the town associated with the start of the most documented parts of the existences of Jennifer and June. From the earliest period of their lives the two operated within a world in which they were each other's main protagonists and interlocutors. Their mutuality was reproduced and reinforced in a number of ways. They spent a great deal of time together which was reinforced by the family's frequent moves; their mother regularly called them 'Twinnies' rather than using their individual names; several extant photographs show them dressed identically and posed in precisely the same way. Later in their lives, they would perform as an uncanny double act moving simultaneously in carefully synchronised ways and functioning in a disturbingly symbiotic manner that seemed to suggest they shared a single identity with one set of desires. Yet in the first few years the main worry of their parents was the girls' relative silence. The fact of coming into language late is frequently associated

---

2   The information about their biographies comes from Wallace, *The Silent Twins*.

with twins, especially identical twins, so initially this was something that was noted but not considered especially problematic. In other ways they were developing well: they were happy at home and enjoyed each other's company. But increasingly their teachers were discovering that they were withdrawn from their peers and were extremely reliant upon each other. They did not interact well with other people, even close family members. They were marked out by a combination of difference and sameness. As black children in rural England in the 1960s and 1970s they were easily distinguishable from their white counterparts. Yet as children who were virtually indistinguishable from each other they merged together troublingly. In this manner, both their differences and their similarities seemed perversely exaggerated. The sense of separation that came from being obviously and visually marked out from their schoolmates may well have been a profound influence upon them, making them into allies against a world that they clearly had enormous difficulties engaging with in any fruitful way. As black children in an overwhelmingly white environment they were statistically insignificant, virtually invisible. By choosing to submerge themselves within each other they further augmented and deepened that invisibility, retreating into the private world governed by a secret language that separated them from everyone else. This process was not straightforward though. By operating as a unit comprised of two individuals who behaved as if they were just a single one, they became both less and more invisible. They reduced their individuality: the qualities that might have been attributed separately to Jennifer or to June were impossible to distinguish. Since many found telling the pair apart beyond them in any case, this simply compounded the sense of them being one, not two. By increasing their oddness, their difference and distance from others, they increased their joint visibility. As twins, as black twins, and most particularly as identical twins who were black in an almost exclusively white school and community, they were prominent. Individually they were increasingly insignificant. As they behaved in a way that censored their own interactions with others and resulted in their exclusion from the worlds of others they were increasingly thrown upon their own companionship and rivalry.

The pattern of exclusion and exclusiveness that characterised their school lives gradually permeated the home too. They had three other siblings: an older brother and sister, David and Greta, and Rosie who was four years younger.

They scarcely spoke to their older siblings or to their father, but they frequently played with Rosie for several years until she, too, found herself on the edge of their powerful two-ness, unable to get through the barrier that separated them from others. Their mother was not as shut out as their father or older siblings, nor was she invited into their closed fantasy world of dolls and rituals of play, as Rosie initially was. Their refusal to speak to others except on their own terms, combined with the creation of a private shared language, made creativity, censorship and self-censorship crucial aspects of their joint mode of existing in the world. The language that they spoke together shut others out and bound the two of them together. Their lack of engagement – even within the family home – was carefully regulated or choreographed by a series of looks or glances that were profoundly meaningful to each other but virtually undetectable to others. These could operate as modes of checking or censoring behaviour, of making sure that the pair acted in unison or as one. Such behaviour might then manifest itself as a form of self-censorship. Yet was it? What was the self that was being effaced in the case of Jennifer and June Gibbons? Were they censoring themselves, or was one of them censoring the other? How much of their destructive behaviour was chosen, how much born out of a compulsion regulated by repeated acts of coercion that inhibited any kind of individuality and subsumed it within joint performances? What appeared to some to be a mutual decision arrived at by the workings of a single set of desires appeared to others to be an epic battle waged between two individuals about the very nature of self and other. While it might initially seem that they chose to act as one, or indeed could only act together, Jennifer had perfected an almost indiscernible glance at her sister that controlled her movements and speech. This act, repeated over years, and combined with other signals, was a brilliantly and destructively effective mode of censorship that produced oneness from twoness, and turned the pair into a formidable combination.

The Freudian concept of the uncanny provides a fruitful way of reflecting on the ways in which twins, especially identical twins whose behaviour mirrors each other like these two, can be considered. In Freud's formulation, the double has a particular uncanny power. His examples of the double come largely from the work of E.T.A. Hoffman, but his 'themes of uncanniness which are most prominent' have significant resonances for the case of Jennifer and June Gibbons and for the complex identifications they felt for each other. He writes:

Thus we have characters who are to be considered identical because they look alike. This relation is accentuated by mental processes leaping from one of these characters to another – by what we should call telepathy – so that the one possesses the knowledge, feelings and experience in common with the other. Or it is marked by the fact that the subject identifies himself with someone else, so that he is in doubt as to which his self is, or substitutes the extraneous self for his own. In other words, there is a doubling, dividing and interchanging of the self. [3]

Certainly this description describes much of what others saw in the pair, and undoubtedly too they were seen as being uncanny, odd, sometimes even chilling. Yet it is in the last part of Freud's claim here, in the account of a form of identification in which the self comes into question, are the crucial issues to the current volume.

Just under two decades after their birth, Jennifer and June found fame, or infamy, after a series of incidents involving theft, arson and attempted arson, in West Wales. The story of their lives up until their 1982 trial and the sudden and wholly unexpected death of Jennifer in March 1993, is detailed in a remarkable work by Marjorie Wallace called The Silent Twins (1996). She recounts her initial engagement with their story when, working for The Sunday Times she followed their trial and found it an 'extraordinary occasion.' As she writes:

The twins, tiny and vulnerable, said not a word apart from a few grunts which the court interpreted as pleas of guilty. The unemotional legal pantomime went on around them without touching them. A doctor gave evidence; the lawyers made their submissions; the judge pronounced sentence. It seemed simple, unthreatening, but the calm tones of authority sentenced the frightened children to be detained in Broadmoor special hospital for an indefinite period. [4]

The harsh sentencing was prompted by the claim that they were both psychopaths, whose condition could not be treated anywhere but a hospital such as Broadmoor. It is a diagnosis that Wallace eloquently refutes. Part of what underlies her argument that the diagnosis was mistaken is that she had access to a powerful series of documents written by the two: diaries, stories, novels.

---

3   Sigmund Freud, "The 'Uncanny'" pp.339-76 in Albert Dickinson (ed.) and James Strachey (general ed.) Art and Literature The Penguin Freud Library volume 14 (London, New York, Victoria, Toronto, New Delhi, Auckland, Johannesburg: Penguin Books, 1990), p.356.

4   Wallace, The Silent Twins, p.3.

The substantial volume of written work they produced shows that the two were far from 'silent' — indeed that they were remarkably articulate and voluble, when they chose to be. What it also shows is that they adopted self-censorship as an elaborate and ritualistic form of engagement/non-engagement with a world that they frequently found highly problematic and unsatisfactory. They were not psychopaths, but were trapped within a destructive and inescapable pattern of behaviour which had emerged at a very early age and had developed and stagnated over the years. Despite considerable research and extensive communications with both Jennifer and June, Wallace concludes that,

> No one knows when it began, whether it started in infancy, or in their first school, or at Braunton, but by the time they were eleven the battle lines had been firmly drawn both against the outside world and internally, between twin and twin. [5]

Wallace's summative statement neatly suggests the crisis of individuality and of identity that seems to have been experienced by both girls from this period onwards. While on the one hand they each withdrew from everything that constituted what was outside of themselves into the apparent safety of their pairing, on the other hand that very withdrawal forced them into ineluctable encounters with each other and with themselves. The gradual movement towards themselves, as outsiders were steadily shut out from them, made the vicissitudes of their relationship very clear to them. At the heart of the destructive dynamic that characterised this was their twinship.

The story of Jennifer and June Gibbons has become more generally familiar to an audience within and beyond Britain where it had received press coverage, through a television documentary, directed by Jon Amiel (with a screenplay by Wallace) which was first screened in 1985, three years after they were sent to Broadmoor. [6] Wallace's book has also recently been the basis of a French opera *Jumelles* in 1990 and also new opera (in English), called *The Silent Twins*, which premiered at the Almeida Theatre in Islington in July 2007. [7] When I went to see this production it was clear, in the conversations that could be heard (or over-

---

5   Wallace, *The Silent Twins*, p.14.

6   When I talked to various friends and acquaintances about writing this piece, I was surprised how many had heard of the case and found that it was mainly through the documentary.

7   The music of *Jumelles* was composed by James Giroundon and Pierre Alain Jaffrennou and the libretto written by Michel Rostain.

heard) at the interval that the audience knew something of the real circum-stances behind the opera. Even those that did not already know of Jennifer and June Gibbons would have been able to find out key details of their lives from the programme. This (like the publicity still) included photographs of the girls. In two instances it chose images in which they were dressed identically, emphasis-ing their uncanny resemblance to each other. Extracts from their diaries were reproduced in the programme in bold type, larger than that of the main text, and set out separately from it, making it clear that their so-called "silence" was factitious.

The libretto was compiled by April De Angelis, largely from the words of Jennifer and June themselves. De Angelis described her methodology in the programme, commenting that 'The glorious and sad paradox of the silent twins is that they weren't really silent at all; they were adventurous and passionate communicators who in novels, journals and poetry recorded their responses to the world with perception, articulacy and originality. It's just a shame there was no one there to hear them.' The Almeida production seemed motivated to be as true as it could be to Wallace's account and to her careful deciphering of the closely-written diaries that both girls had kept since they were sixteen years old. Since the production details specified this fact, the words they speak on-stage, and the words of their journals that are projected onto white screens at one point, take on even more powerful significance than might ordinarily be the case with a libretto.

These words break through and efface the self-imposed silence with which the pair faced the rest of the world. Their humour, sadness and violence are extremely compelling. The visual detail of their tiny handwriting, magnified so that it could even be read on the screens onto which it was projected, is also moving. The words onstage seemed to represent nothing less than a torrent of emotions, reflections and thoughts on the impossibilities and the possibilities of being a twin, written by two women who were inescapably caught within that very experience. It seems likely, then, that many audience members had at least some familiarity with the story of the Gibbons twins before attending the opera. Those that did not would have read key facts about their tale in the pro-gramme. The fascination that such a gripping story might have for them would only add to a more general, cultural and societal attitude towards twins. Watch-ing the opera leads to an engagement with profound questions about self and others which are at the basis of many of our most powerful fantasies and fears about twins, particularly identical twins. The neurologist Oliver Sacks makes this point particularly well in his review of Wallace's book, when he opens by writing:

> We assume we are all individuals, autonomous, unique - and this assumption is suddenly tested, even shattered, when we meet twins. It is not just the biological rarity and extraordinariness of identical twins that so impress the imagination. It is the exact, the uncanny, doubling of a human being, a doubling (we may see, or imagine, or fear) which may extend to the innermost, most secret depths of the soul. There is always a shock of interest, surprise, pleasure...and consternation on encountering twins. We gaze from one to the other: identical faces, expressions, voices, movements, mannerisms and feel a mixed sense, a double sense, of both marvel and outrage (this is reflected in some cultures, which sometimes revere twins and sometimes destroy them). [8]

The cultural construction and representation of twins within Western culture is highly complex and has led to the production of many cultural works that play upon the contradictions, confusions and (often) the comedy of such pairings. [9] The visual aspect of representing identical twins is particularly problematic and has led to numerous strategies in films or television (a single actor playing both roles, for instance). Representing identical twins on a stage, especially when – as in this opera – they are both always together and not wearing disguising costumes, is very demanding. The Almedia production cast two singers, Alison Crookendale (Jennifer) and Talise Trevigne (June) who both looked like each other as well as resembling the women they were playing.

This singular achievement built upon the publicity photographs of the real twins that were used to advertise the production. One part of its effect was convincingly to reinforce the primary conflict between the pair: the question of the constitution and separation of the self. This was further augmented by the score. It was composed by the black, Belize-born singer/composer Errollyn

---

8   Oliver Sacks, "Bound Together in Fantasy and Crime," http://query.nytimes.com/gst/fullpage.htm l?res=9A0DE1DC1E3AF93AA25753C1A960948260 accessed 3 September 2007.

9   For a fascinating and comprehensive account of such representations see Juliana de Nooy, *Twins in Contemporary Literature and Culture: Look Twice* (Basingstoke and New York: Palgrave Macmillan, 2005).

Wallen, herself just five years older than her two subjects. [10] She aimed to capture an array of silent or secret movements and gestures in her orchestration to suggest the ways in which Jennifer's control of June, in particular, an important part of the opera and the story of the pair, was represented. As Sarah Unwin Jones outlined in *The Times*:

> Wallen is orchestrating the cacophony of oddities – the secret signals, mute moments and speeded-up birdsong language – with a view to drawing the maximum sound possible from her small ensemble. The notorious "secret signal," an almost imperceptible movement of the eyes that Jennifer used to control and silence June for more than 20 years, has been orchestrated by a trill on the clarinet. [11]

The 'trill on the clarinet' is accompanied visually onstage by one of the most eerie sideways glances it is possible to imagine. "Jennifer" slowly looks over at her sister without moving any part of her body except her eyes. As she does this, "June," without even seeming to notice the movement, freezes. Jennifer of course freezes simultaneously. Described in this manner it sounds clumsy. Yet the incredibly intense power that the mere flicker of Jennifer's eyes has on a figure who in every other way appears identical reveals the dramatic surrender of individual self to a collective or joint self. One of the ways in which this secret signal gains its power is through the fact that it was captured in one of the photographs of Jennifer and June that was used inside the programme. For those who, like me, read this before the performance, seeing this look reproduced onstage was truly uncanny. The manner in which it was dramatised, and the effect it had on June, was chilling. The way in which it acted as a double of the photograph in the programme again emphasised its powerful effect. As an audience member I found myself repeatedly glancing at that photograph in order to recollect the experience I had when seeing it reproduced onstage. The effect of this was to encounter the same uncanny feeling repeatedly, which multiplied it and made it still stronger, even though (indeed probably because) the photo-

---

10 On the night I attended the performance I noticed that the audience contained more black women in their thirties and forties than I had ever seen at a London theatre. This included Wallen herself, who was mixing with the crowd.

11 http://entertainment.timesonline.co.uk/tol/arts_and_entertainment/stage/opera/article2000468.ece accessed 8 August 2008.

graph was of Jennifer and June themselves, not the women playing them onstage. A further sense of its power came from the fact that the singers were
dressed identically and at many points in the opera moved in precisely the same
way, much as Jennifer and June had. When the eye movement showed that
Jennifer was imposing her will upon her sister, who was unable to resist it except at violent moments, the elaborate creation of sameness was radically un-
dermined. This was one of the ways in which the performance allowed the issue
of power between the two to complicate the visual display of sameness which
initially provides the obvious way of reading the pair.

One of the most profound examples of Jennifer's control over June, and
June's compliant response to it, comes right at the end of the opera and closely
follows biographical fact. After eleven years in Broadmoor hospital the pair
were told that they would be released to a unit in Wales. In the final meeting
she held with them in Broadmoor, Marjorie Wallace was 'disturbed' by their different demeanours and also by the way that they made a gesture that she had
not encountered for some time which meant that they had made some kind of
pact together. While June exhibited 'calmness,' Jennifer exhibited 'restless-
ness.' Then, in an exchange in which their speech reflected the manner in which
they could both mimic and speak for each other, a dramatic revelation was
made. Wallace describes it in this way:

> In the same inconsequential tone she uses to ask for a cigarette, Jennifer said:
> "I'm going to die." "What makes you think that?" I asked. "I just know. I just
> know," said June. [12]

She was right. Or they were. On 9th March, as the bus taking them out of
Broadmoor to Wales passed through Crowthorne on its way to the motorway,
Jennifer uttered her last coherent words. "'Oh June...at last we're out.'" By 6.15
that evening she was dead of myocarditis which had destroyed her heart muscle. [13] It was a death that surprised and shocked everybody except, it seems, the
two women. While the details of Jennifer's death were not reproduced onstage
in this manner, the impossibility of both of them leaving Broadmoor successfully is compellingly evoked. Identically dressed, and carrying a suitcase each in

---

12 Wallace, *The Silent Twins*, p.266.
13 Wallace, *The Silent Twins*, p. 267.

exactly the same way, Jennifer and June move towards the edge of the raised area that represents their incarceration. Carefully synchronised they seem to be on the verge of leaving, but as they move their legs in order to step over an invisible barrier that keeps them from integrating with a world beyond themselves, Jennifer glances at June in the manner already described. The pair stop. This is repeated. It is only once Jennifer collapses and dies, almost immediately, that June is free to cross that invisible barrier very slowly and deliberately, and, alone for the first time in her life, leave behind her now silent twin. This miniature of a profound act of resistance brings with it little celebration due to the immense loss accompanying it in the form of Jennifer's death. The end of the opera, like Wallace's book, brings with it several important and unresolved questions. Chief of those, and hauntingly, is 'What will happen to June?' [14] This final question strains against issues of censorship and self-censorship. At what point should this story remain untold? When should June be allowed to become genuinely silent should she choose to do so? What are the limits at which such a private tale, made public through appalling circumstances, be allowed to become private once again?

---

[14] Wallace, *The Silent Twins*, p.274.

Drag Queens, Freaks, Queers, Mermaids, Shaman, Humanity, and the Art of Heterogeneity: A View of Taylor Mac'

NINA MANKIN

[Nina Mankin is a performer, writer and dramaturg. She was the dramaturg for Taylor Mac's *Red Tide Blooming,* performed at PS122 in New York City in the spring of the year 2006, as well as *The Young Ladies Of,* performed at Here Arts Center in the year 2007. She is currently working (as dramaturg and muse-wrangler) with Ricky Ian Gordon on his upcoming musical, *Sycamore Trees.* Nina has recorded two albums of original songs and is currently working on her third album. She has worked with numerous theatre artists and musicians as a performer and as a dramaturg. Nina has an M.A. in Performance Studies from NYU.]

'My job as a theatre artist is to remind the audience of their humanity'

—Taylor Mac

Censorship, Taylor Mac will tell you, is everywhere: 'We censor ourselves constantly, everywhere we go in life. Censorship is group-think (and group-think is censorship) – it's about homogenization. To stand out, to express yourself, is to stand up against that force that wants to make everything the same.'

Taylor Mac doesn't stand out when you see him walking down the street. This performer who has made a career decorating his often naked body with a creative assortment of found materials, giving his passionate (and sometimes shocking) insights into the workings of love and politics while wearing six inch stilettos, is, offstage, a soft spoken white guy in a t-shirt and jeans. 'My performance is about turning myself inside out and putting my inside on the outside' he said recently. 'It's very common for someone to come up to me after a show, when I'm out of costume, and tell me that I'm actually good enough to perform without the trappings. I know then that I've made them uncomfortable, that they don't want their understanding of what is 'normal' to be challenged. Because what they're really saying is 'you don't have to be a drag queen! You're good enough to just perform in your jeans and t-shirt because drag is cheap and you could be highbrow.' And they're right: I choose to be lowbrow and cheap and outrageous and shocking in order to surprise them into feeling and thinking - to get them to stop censoring themselves and their emotions, if just for right now.'

Taylor Mac grew up in suburban California in the 1980s. Not the California of organic food and the Internet boom, but the lower middle class and working class California; 'Tract houses blending into nothing' he writes, lining endless expanses of malls and auto supply stores. Taylor's mom started an art school for kids out of his childhood home. Taylor traces his own theatrical aesthetic, in which such crafty materials as thumb tacks, rubber gloves, soda cans, envelopes and rubber bands adorn his body in costumes that he calls 'drag,' back to these days, as he says in the interview in this volume, 'there was always a lot of collage going on.'

Taylor Mac is a drag artist who never dresses in what most people think of as drag. There are no fake breasts or traditional make-up or women's clothing. And while his expressionistic costuming is at times extremely sexual, it isn't about the traditional trappings of gender so much as it's about the beauty (and ugliness) of disguise itself. Because, as Taylor is fond of saying, whatever role you play, 'it's all drag.' It would be a mistake to call Taylor a transvestite. The 2000 American College dictionary defines a transvestite as: 'A person who dresses and acts in a style or manner traditionally associated with the opposite sex.' Revealing some indication of cultural change, my 1987 edition defines transvestite as 'A person who exhibits an *abnormal desire* to dress and act...' (emphasis mine). While Taylor's work pays homage to a history of cross-dressing that, in Taylor's personal history, goes back to drag clubs in San Francisco and Provincetown in the '90s, Taylor never 'cross' dresses. Still, Taylor Mac claims such drag queen/transvestite icons as Mother Flawless Sabrina and Ethyl Eichelberger as personal heroes and mentors. Along with Sam Shepard and Shakespeare.

In his plays and his solo performance work, (a differentiation that Taylor Mac himself has recently decided to reject, calling all his work 'plays'), Taylor never plays the part of men or women so much as he *plays* with his audience's insecurities (and pleasures) – about their own gender identification, sexuality and disguises -- by revealing his own (or those of the character that is Taylor Mac.) It's sometimes discomforting, but 'comfort' is one of the things Taylor Mac has made it his life's work to challenge:

> If you express yourself really for who you are, it can make people really uncom-fortable, which can be risky. You risk annihilation – literally, as physical violence, as well as emotionally as shame and rejection. And of course there's the fear that if I say something truthful onstage no one will want to book me. Talking about the boyfriend who stuck crystal meth up my ass while I was sleeping is probably not going to get me booked at Lincoln Center! But that's the role of the artist (or artists I admire). I have to choose to do that or not - not because I just want to say shocking things – and believe me I have no illusions that I am in the least 'avant garde' in that way -- but because I believe that is what a play needs at that particular juncture in order to do what I want it to do which is, yes, push those boundaries that try to keep us all comfortable. ...While also being very entertain-ing!

Including Taylor Mac in a volume about resisting censorship, makes sense. His work often contains graphic descriptions of gay sex, told as personal stories in his solo work. There is usually nudity: in his apocalyptic high-jinx musical about the imminent revitalisation (real estate euphemism for obliteration) of Coney Island, *Red Tide Blooming* (or *R.T.B*, which premiered at PS122 in 2006) everyone gets naked at one point or another. All of his work challenges conven-tional norms of gender: Taylor's phantasmagorical characters largely identify both as masculine and feminine (the hero of *R.T.B.* is a hermaphrodite sea crea-ture) and even his more "conventional" heroes, like the central character in his yet-to-be-produced play *Blue Grotto*, struggle with issues of gender identifica-tion. And Taylor's main political bête noire – already alluded to in this piece: the homogenisation of culture, (or dwindling down to same) is often represented in his work by the evils of the religious and political right. So, rich subject matter for any hungry arbiter of culture and taste.

Long before Charles Ludlum's Theatre of the Ridiculous and Alan Ginsberg's *Howl* (1957), and further back even than 19th century drag salons and cabarets, this kind of radical content has been associated with what many queer studies scholars have called 'world making.' This is what Shane Vogel, writing about drag cabaret performers Kiki and Herb, calls 'the mapping of commonly accessible [queer] worlds that allow for the creation of counter-publics[15]' – alternate norms that can exist independent of (oppressive) societal norms. This kind of performance, then, is as much about the creation of an insider outsider community as it is about the material itself. But while Kiki and Herb, and the writer/performer Charles Busch before them, have taken this kind of queer community building all the way to Broadway, Taylor Mac is very consciously not trying to project this sort of insider culture onto his work and his audience: 'I'm not interested in all these distinctions: who's inside, who's outside,' Taylor said to me recently noting his desire to play to all variety of audiences. 'Having people want to book me in gay venues only – assuming that only a certain kind of person is going to get what I do or, more importantly, will get something from what I do—that's a kind of censorship that happens to me all the time. I don't think of what I do as gay theatre .'

Taylor Mac realized he would be an actor about the same time he became a political activist. In high school he snuck off to the San Francisco AIDS Walk, to the horror of his teachers who asked him to remove his ACT UP! button on his return (he didn't). And he was very involved in the environmental movement. Taylor left San Francisco State after one year of actor training to walk across the country in protest of nuclear energy. He credits that year of communal living (and dumpster diving) as the basis for much of his artistic ethic. Taylor eventually continued his actor training at the American Academy of Dramatic Arts (AADA) in New York City and worked off and off-off Broadway, acting in other people's plays, throughout the late '90s and into the '00s.

Even while Taylor was performing in other writers' work, he was developing his own writing and performance in the world of Downtown clubs and im-

---

15 Shane Vogel: "WHERE ARE WE NOW?: Queer World Making and Cabaret Performance," GLQ: *A Journal of Lesbian and Gay Studies* 6(1): 29-59 (2000)

promptu performance spaces where new vaudeville and burlesque flourished from the late 1980s. Five years ago, Taylor Mac was presenting his drag performance and plays almost exclusively at these downtown parties and burlesque/ vaudeville clubs. Though this is still very much Taylor Mac's world, something has been changing. Now he's invoked by theatre and performance curators as one of the leading lights of a new generation of theatre artists. In 2007 he received the James Hammerstein award for playwriting and he recently received very competitive (and highly prestigious) grants from both the Rockefeller Map Fund (2008) and Creative Capital (2009). He was named one of New York's Best by *The Village Voice*, *Time Out NY*, and *The New York Press* and was one of *Out* Magazine's One Hundred People of the Year in 2008. And, in a testament to Taylor's success at blurring the boundaries between performance and playwriting, he was recently elected into the exclusive theatre community of New York's New Dramatists.

I first met Taylor in 2004 while working on the HERE Arts Center adaptation of the Orpheus myth (directed and co-conceived by Kristin Marting.) I started working with him as a dramaturg, and also as a singer/performer, shortly thereafter. In *Orpheus*, Taylor played the (very straight) pop rock star title role. Halfway into the run, Taylor brought in a publicity postcard for his show *Live Patriot Acts* (2003, PS122). The piece, a cabaret-styled performance of Downtown artists responding to the current political climate, was a follow-up to his *The Face of Liberalism* (2004, The Marquee), which was Taylor's solo response to the War On Terror. Taylor had been doing performance pieces at bars and clubs while also pursuing a career as an actor. It was in *Liberalism* that Taylor first put together the mish-mash of rants, original songs, stories and wild costuming that would become his signature: theatre in which Taylor 'brings the party' to his audience, while doing fundamentally political work. *The Face of Liberalism* featured such songs as the raucous 'The Revolution will not be Masculized' and the beautifully poignant a cappella 'Fear Itself' ('We've nothing to fear but fear itself/I'm afraid of fear itself.' which Mandy Patinkin, one of Taylor's increasingly diverse array of collaborators has recently been adding to his own solo show). This solo-performance piece ran for six-months, once a week, to sold-out audiences in a basement bar on the Bowery.

The postcard for Live Patriot Acts shows Taylor standing, back toward the camera, wearing only a g-string and stilettos, his red white and blue painted face turned provocatively back toward us. I was stunned: Taylor Mac never hides; he's just completely unassuming. And his salt-of-the-earth, poised and unobtrusive persona hardly suggests the political and aesthetic extremes of his performance credo and idiom.

Toward the beginning of his solo show *The Be(a)st of Taylor Mac* (2007, The Public Theatre) Taylor goes into a characteristic rant. Theatre artists, he complains, want their work to be seen as *universal*, not gay or political or black, Latino, feminist, Filipino, Asian. It's a dizzying explosion of labels that ends with Taylor taking a deep breath and declaring that he is, in fact, a *homosexual* theatre artist and, if you're straight, you can just, well...listen (big audience laugh). He then proceeds to go into a very moving, very funny, story-song (of his own – most of the songs Taylor performs are original) in which he juxtaposes his own empty attempts at sexual connection with the birth of a (heterosexual) friend's baby. The piece ends quietly, the audience too moved to applaud. These pieces perform a *humanism* that is at the heart of Taylor's concept of heterogeneity. Humanism: a belief in the potential for human goodness and transformation through the search for truth, morality and human commonality. Secular Humanism, a philosophy that was declared super un-cool by the post-sixties generation of academics steeped in post-structuralism and identity politics.... My partner, who has never seen Taylor Mac before, and whose discomfort I could sense during the earlier rant, turns to me at the end of this pair of theatrical pieces and whispers, 'He's a shaman!'

I've heard Taylor use the word shaman to talk about what artists do, particularly queer artists who he says (admittedly citing one of his friends and mentors Penny Arcade) are 'not gay or straight: *queer* is a person who was ostracized by society to such a degree that they could never ostracize anyone else.' He adds, 'For Joseph Campbell that's the definition of a shaman: someone who had a profound experience at a young age that separated him/her from society and so they are in a unique position to help society heal.'

I do think Taylor communicates with the spirit world in his theatrical flights of human transformation. At times he is most certainly channeling the seminal performance artist/writer/filmmaker Jack Smith (or maybe Smith is just whispering into his ear saying things like 'use what you've got,' 'dirtier,' 'get angry here,' 'now talk straight at them'). The night of the first PS122 Ethyl Eichelberger awards I was stunned when I realised that Taylor was dressed in a costume

(Taylor makes most of his own) that was almost identical to one of the self-styled outfits the writer/performer wore in the documentary screened that night. Taylor, who was awarded the first ever 'Ethyl,' had never seen Ethyl before. Taylor now says that his work is perhaps closest to Ethyl's amalgamation of classical story-telling and wild revelry (interestingly, they both studied at AADA). If Jack Smith is whispering in one of his ears, I do believe Ethyl now whispers in his other. I think, at times, like all good shaman, Taylor is able to cure human suffering. And, like all good trickster/shaman, sometimes he cures folks by *making* them suffer – following one of his rants can be as exhausting as it is exhilarating.

Taylor embraces his role as societal clown. He has recently taken to referring to himself as a Shakespearean fool – a highbrow shaman. Even his most naturalistic writing contains extremes of corporality and theatricality that make one feel like the drama could blow apart into comedic insanity at any moment. Or go someplace emotionally devastating – both of which are true.

Taylor mostly acts in his own plays and he is always IN the audience. At times he demands audience complicity through direct participation. In the workshop production of *The Young Ladies Of*, Taylor's epistolary exploration into desire, loss and cultural obsession with fathers, (which premiered at Taylor's artistic home, HERE, in the Fall of 2007 and is now touring extensively), the audience wrote letters that were used in the piece. For a while he played with the idea of having audience members act as assistants throughout. In *R.T.B.* he wanted the audience to have flash cameras so that they become creative soul-snatchers. Taylor believes in audience participation (in whatever form it takes.) He sees participation as part of his own duty, both as a theatre artist, and as a citizen.

Taylor Mac's clownish corporeality is often confrontational, as when his actors do naked gymnastics down center stage, under the noses of a stunned front row. It is sometimes arresting, like when he talks about the dried semen flaking off his chest following a vacuous sexual encounter. And sometimes it's terrifying, like when he wrenches off the duct tape that has been securing his penis to his butt in *R.T.B.* ('It really doesn't hurt that much" he'll tell anyone who asks afterward 'it depends on how well I shave.') But, once again, Taylor doesn't see this as characteristically avant-garde (and he's not interested in shock value) so much as it's his way of giving his audience a good time – bringing them together, finding collective human commonality, in the wildness of the event.

Taylor moves between theatrical genres with an excessive disregard for continuity but that doesn't ever mean that his work disregards theatrical structure. Structurally, Taylor Mac's work has embraced the conventions and principles of classical western narrative – whether Aristotle or Joseph Campbell (with whom he has an ongoing obsession).

When we first got together to work on *R.T.B.*, the script was a bunch of half-written scenes and possible songs with a few strong characters. I asked Taylor what he thought it was about and he said, 'It's about one lonely freak looking for other freaks in a world that rejects difference,' and he added, revealingly, 'Actually, I think it's 'The Last Unicorn.' And so, a story that features Lynne Cheney as a cut-throat lesbian pulp fiction writer in love with Saddam Hussein; a has-been performance artist desperate not to grow old; and a hermaphrodite sea creature who finally has the bravery to stand up to the Collective Conscious, is actually structured very much like a traditional fairy tale.

'God is in the detail' – a Taylorism (he says it's an expression but the only version I've ever heard invokes the devil, not god....) I've come to understand this phrase to mean that the challenge, *the radicalness*, of a thing is in its specificity (the more uniquely individual you can make a dramatic experience, the more universal, the more *humanist*, it becomes). I think this is one of the reasons Taylor categorically rejects using any brand names or references to celebrities in his work: branding is cultural whitewash. It's part of the *homogeneity*, the 'dwindling down to same,' that Taylor has taken on as his global antagonist. Brand names obliterate details and it's in the details that Taylor finds *heterogeneity*, what Taylor says he strives to achieve in his art. To continue with this logic, then, *God* (and Taylor Mac does not refer to himself as a religious person) is in the inherent variety of human existence.

Much of the work Taylor Mac does with a dramaturg is very traditional: breaking work down into a classical three act structure, delineating arcs, beats and turning points (some of which may not yet be written). Taylor is not afraid of re-writing and he often comes back with a completely rewritten play. The biggest challenge, working dramaturgically with Taylor, is to not pull him back. Taylor's style is to overwrite and there are inevitably moments in his work when words spill out in an excess of meaning and emotion that cries out for revision because it just *doesn't* work. But allowing himself to fail is part of Taylor's methodology. It's a slippery line, but when he hits it just right, I do believe it's that failure that allows for a kind of numinous opening in his audience, maybe because of their giddy surrender or exhaustion or some other kind of ineffable alchemy; you can feel the audience move in toward him in the potential train wreck, and the next moment pays off like crazy.

'My dramaturg says...', Taylor declared to my infinite discomfort (even though I'm obviously pleased to be invoked!) at the 2007 No Passport 'Dreaming the Americas' conference at the Martin E. Segal Center at CUNY Graduate Center in New York City, 'that I am an artist working in the genre of pastiche.' The term came up over one of Taylor's and my marathon breakfast meetings when he was struggling with how to label himself. 'You embrace discontinuity,' I suggested, 'You enjoy stylistic collisions; your work is excessive; you don't care if you're cool and, in fact, you would rather be kitsch than cool; you're a *pastiche* artist.' Taylor now says that he is a theatre artist working in the genre of pastiche.

I recently turned to that bastion of contemporary culture, Wikipedia, and was delighted to find the advisement that, in architecture, the mere invocation of the word pastiche can be enough to condemn a piece as 'unworthy of further consideration' and that writers should 'use the term with caution.' In fact, one of the coolest things about pastiche is just how historically *un*cool it is. The modernist idea of pastiche (Rococo being the most recognised *genre*) infers that the artist doesn't know what he is doing – that he's just arbitrarily taking things (ornament, iconography, historical and structural components) out of context and throwing them together: collision for effect, not for meaning.

But postmodernists know that there is no such thing as content without meaning. Which brings us back to this ineffable open place Taylor Mac sometimes manages to win from his audience. Pastiche, to postmodernists, infers a void; before the pastiche, there was a place that desired filling. The interesting question then becomes, not so much what is the pastiche, but rather what is the void that this excess (because *pastiche* implies excess) reveals?

Taylor's work does seem to be filling a void, at least for many of the audience members and theatre artists with whom I talk about his work. He says that it's the *pastiche*, the *heterogeneity* and *variation* he presents that opens up his audience to feel they are in the presence of something new. The audience has space to experience the void because the work doesn't reinforce the easy labeling that is inherent to homogeneity (which is what makes something insider art). So Taylor's pastiche is a kind of *anti-genre* (or perhaps it is a *post*-genre in which the exclusivity of genre itself is criticised). 'I believe people are trained to think of themselves and art, politics, feelings, etc. as being one thing.' Taylor emails me, 'I'm trying to show that we are more than just one thing (which of course includes being one thing at the same time as we are many). I'm using [pastiche] as a way to emphasis the various things that we are.'

Inviting his audience to experience the variety of being human is Taylor Mac's theatrical mission. Taylor sees himself, and his cohort of 'freaks' (an accolade he gives to anyone who consciously lives outside the homogeneous world of same – public nudity being a shoe-in for nomination) as emissaries of heterogeneity. And this work takes place wherever they choose to don their drag – whether it's in a theatre, on the street, or at a cultural event like the Coney Island Mermaid Parade.

The Mermaid Parade: Taylor Mac is dressed (or *not* depending on your point of view) in a hoola-skirt of multi-colored hand-painted six-pack plastic rings (that do actually look something like seaweed). His shaved head is half covered by a fraying blond wig. His large sand-covered feet sport six-inch pumps. Sky blue grease paint covers his entire face. His green-painted cheekbones float like tropical islands in the blue, while the glued-on seashells arcing above his eyebrows create the effect of some kind of weird African mask. Taylor is also sporting a long strand of pretty white seashells that descends down from the blond wig all the way across his bare torso to his gold-emblazoned nipples. He looks like some androgynously lusty Neptune who has been dressed up by a group of nine-year-old girls at a birthday party. We're on the boardwalk at Coney Island just after the Mermaid Parade. This is one of the most important yearly performances for Taylor and his community of freaks, missionaries, as Taylor sees it, of all that is good in the world: missionaries of heterogeneity.

Taylor and his post-parade cohort (most of whom also work in the club and new vaudeville circuit) are on the boardwalk in a Fellini-esque mélange. Most of the others are dressed more conventionally 'mermaid' than Taylor. 'Tigger' (James) Ferguson has on a long shimmering white fishtail cut so low it exposes his red pubic hair. He drops the tail to reveal a large plastic octopus covering his sex. Taylor's friend Darrell is all pink and pastel blue with a luxurious tetra head-fin and enormous fake eyelashes. His gorgeous airbrushed tail is poised, impossibly, half way down his butt. Dirty Martini, the definition of voluptuous, her gorgeously large bare belly and breasts defying any contemporary notion of 'fit,' has her mouth stretched wide in a happy guffaw. It is, as Taylor writes in *Red Tide Blooming* (which, not coincidentally, ends at the mermaid parade), a 'freaky conglomeration...a divine picture.'

Taylor Mac likes classical act structure. This time on the boardwalk is the second act in a three- act day that will end in a tranquil post-parade languor on the beach (the bitter-sweet ending of *R.T.B.*) The first act in the day has been the parade. All the freaks (straight, gay, transsexual, kids, grown-ups, families) danced down the middle of Coney Island's Surf Avenue between throngs of gawking onlookers. They danced past the judges and out, in a glorious "messy mass of divergence" (also from *R.T.B.*), onto the boardwalk. This is when the second act begins: when the freaks seminally mingle with the onlookers who take millions of picture while the freaks accommodate by smiling and posing with mom.

In *R.T.B.* the Collective Conscious (the villain, represented by a bright green Gap-like sweater puppet) wants to eradicate all things that make it uncomfortable. Hermaphrodite sea creatures, and freaks generally, make the C.C. particularly uncomfortable because they challenge the rationality of the 'Collective Conscious visualisation of the Armageddon' that has all the cool kids and other posers mesmerised into a state of passive homogeneity. At the climax of *R.T.B.*, The Collective Conscious finally taunts the otherwise timid hermaphrodite sea creature (Olokun, played by Taylor Mac) into taking heroic action. It is a moment that makes the Collective Conscious (and the audience) genuinely, climactically, and sublimely, uncomfortable.

On the boardwalk, this moment of sublime uncomfortability happens when a group of young Hispanic men stumble into the mayhem. The young men strut up to the now tail-less and almost naked Tigger (remember the plastic octopus...) and stop dead in collective amazement. They are at once horrified, furious, disgusted and completely intrigued. They stammer and chortle words like 'gross!' and 'faggot,' and make exclamations to Jesus as they skirt around the freaks who smile congenially, seemingly without fear. It's unclear what the young men will do. They could beat someone up or strip off their own clothes and join in; it looks like they don't quite know themselves. What is totally clear is that this is a moment they won't quickly forget; maybe it's even changed their lives.

There is a section in *The Young Ladies Of* when Taylor writes a letter to his Vietnam War lieutenant dad who died when he was still very young. He asks his father about the nature of bravery and pride and then he tells him about himself: 'I have learned that bravery comes in all kinds of forms, as does fear. I like to think I'm a brave person although sometimes I falter.' And he continues, 'Bravery comes from overcoming fear in the need to make a change.' This is the bravery Taylor Mac is celebrating when Olokun stands up to the Collective Conscious, it is this bravery he is celebrating when Taylor crows 'Work!' to the transvestite strutting proudly down Second Avenue. And it is this bravery that is exhibited as one of the mermaid comrades drops her tail, smiles, and puts her arm around a confused looking young Hispanic man.

This is the good that freaks – queers, shaman, artists (as defined earlier in this essay) – do for society; they create discomfort, they shake things up. They bring joy and anxiety and sheer "what the fuck!" amazement at what Taylor Mac sees as the best of humanity: our continual variation, our homogeneity; our humanity. These moments, these interventions, (my word), are what Taylor Mac relishes in his work. In a group email Taylor sent out from a recent tour of the U.K., he recounted an interaction he had with 'a three-toothed old macho man in the audience for one of the shows.' 'He kept talking back to me all through – he was either drunk or crazy or a little bit of both. At one point I called him 'darling' and he said, in an offended way, 'You call me darling!' I'm not sure what brought him to the show, but by the end of it I had him up on stage dressed up in mylar and posing feminine with me. When I bowed, he came up on stage and shook my hand saying 'Well done.' And Taylor concludes, 'Some of you do this on a daily basis, and I am in awe.' Indeed.

"A Great Ox is Standing On My Tongue."[16]
Fighting the Fear of the Christian Right: The Aquila Theatre Company Touring America

PETER W. MEINECK

[Peter W. Meineck is the artistic director of the Aquila Theatre Company and Clinical Assistant Professor of Classics and Ancient Studies at New York University.]

The Aquila Theatre Company has been touring the United States since 1991, visiting sixty-seventy venues a year on a schedule that takes them from Southern California to Maine; Florida to Alaska; and nearly all fifty states in between (Hawaii, disappointingly still eludes). The New York based Aquila, originally a London company, has gained quite an insight into the cultural diversity and geographic span of America by taking contemporary productions of classical drama and an educational program to an audience of around 120,000 a year. This is a cultural landscape hardly trodden by most theatre companies; in America touring theatre groups are a dying breed. There's a reason for this, and its only partially economic; the early twenty-first century in American arts has become one of the front lines in a war between conservative and liberal forces - and more recently between a new strain of Christian fundamentalism and artistic freedom of expression. While these 'culture wars' are nothing new, the tactics have grown more insidious and are so far proving much more effective.

---

16 Meineck, P.W. (trans.) *Aeschylus: Oresteia – Agamemnon* 36. Indianapolis and Cambridge: Hackett Publishing 1998.

Most of Aquila's venues are large performing arts centers, funded by the local authority, corporate sponsorship, individual donors and a combination of foundation and government contributions. A typical arts center serves a middle-sized community often far away from a major urban center where the population is served by local repertory companies and Broadway touring shows. According to the most recent census information[17] over 50% of Americans live in either rural (21%) or non-centralised (29.4%) communities. That means over 140 million Americans have little or no access to a resident theatre. Many American towns have sought to attract visiting arts into their communities and since the 1980's there has been a boom in arts center construction and venue conversion often fuelled by private and corporate funds. Most of these venues tend to have between 1000-2000 seats and present a host of events to a subscription based audience ranging from dance companies, classical and folk music, small operas, lectures and some musical theatre. "Straight" plays are rare and classical drama even rarer. Only Aquila and the Acting Company, also based out of New York, have managed to carve out viable tour circuits from these kinds of venues. By taking its work to so many communities across America Aquila has experienced first a rise in arts censorship that has less to do with the nature of the plays themselves, but everything about community control and who gets to make the rules on moral codes of behavior.

In 2001 *New York Times* foreign correspondent, Chris Hedges followed Aquila for a few days while the company was touring a new production of Rostand's *Cyrano DeBegerac* through the South. Hedges was interested in how communities famed for their religious conservatism would respond to a modern production of a classic play. He had his own particular interest in this subject having recently retired from overseas assignments covering conflicts in Bosnia, Serbia, the Middle East and the Gulf. Hedges' view was that intolerance for artistic freedom of expression is the first step towards a kind of totalitarianism that appeals to the basest instincts of class-ism, racism, misogyny and prejudice. For Hedges, the hijacking of popular morality by religious fundamentalist demagogues led to the kind of brutal conflict he had witnessed first hand. In March of 2001 Hedges joined Aquila in Texarkana, Texas, actually two cities that straddle the Arkansas/Texas border with a combined population of around

---

17   U.S. Census Bureau, Census 2000, Summary 1.

55,000. The Perot Theatre, named for Texarkana's most famous billionaire son and one-time presidential candidate, Ross Perot, sits in a desolate downtown next to a vast parking lot and an abandoned warehouse. The 1600 seat art deco auditorium opened in 1924 as the Saenger Amusement Company's Gateway to the West Theatre and is now operated by the local humanities council as a performing arts center.

The performance of Cyrano, Hedges attended seemed very well received by the audience, but midway through the first half when Robert Richmond's new translation had Cyrano compare his famous large nose to a 'penis' a teacher suddenly leapt up and removed her entire class from the auditorium. This leader of a group of Christian home-schooled children was quoted in *The New York Times* as stating, 'I cannot condone the use of vulgar and sexually suggestive language.' When Hedges questioned the students who were aged around 13, one replied, 'I don't think they had the license to do that, to pervert it like that.'[18] Hedges had captured something that had been growing in America, a basic intolerance to any art form that seemed to contain sexual material. This fear of simple words that describe the sexual organs produced another incident of censorship in 2007. This time a Newbery Medal winning Children's book by Susan Patron *The Higher Power of Lucky* was removed from some libraries for containing the word 'scrotum' in a description of the body part that had no reference to sexuality.

Aquila's Cyrano was far from a smutty version and the 'penis' gag was certainly in keeping with the spirit of the original, but the resulting complaints set off a firestorm. The local home school organisation rallied their evangelical leaders to complain vehemently to the arts center, the local newspaper reported entered the fray with an inflammatory report and many subsequent presenters at later venues requested that the word be removed from the production. It wasn't, except for specific school shows, which the Texarkana's evening performance was not. Fundamentalist Christian leader Bob Jones III publicly fuelled the fire by writing an open letter to his community from his office on the campus of Bob Jones University - an evangelical college where at that time interracial dating was banned and all students had to maintain a 'good Christian moral character.' Jones had not seen the performance of Cyrano that has played at the

18   Hedges, Chris. "Troupers on a Never Ending Tour," *The New York Times* April 1st 2001.

Peace Center in Greenville, South Carolina, but that did not prevent him from asserting that this production 'was not fit fare for Christian people' and was 'raunchy and vile - corrupted and perverted.'

In one respect it all seems laughable, a bunch of conservative prudes getting far too hot under the collar because of a 'willy' gag. Hedges pointed out the cultural dichotomy in noting that as the home-schooled students left the Perot Theatre the door that slammed behind them held a sign asking the audience to refrain from bringing firearms into the theatre. But what could once be brushed off as the moral quirks of a splinter movement or the ranting of a religious extremist have started to have a real effect on censorship and the theatre in America. It is worth noting that in May 1999, presidential candidate, George W. Bush chose to speak at Bob Jones University, thereby establishing his credentials with the Christian right. Bush's focus on Faith-Based charities to provide welfare and social services has also permeated the arts. Recently Hedges has taken on what he sees as an open assault on American cultural freedom from the Christian Right in his book *American Fascists*.[19] He has noted that the Christian right is becoming ever more extremist and coined the term 'Dominionism' for a movement 'that seeks to cloak itself in the mantle of Christian faith and American patriotism.' This new movement is well organised and determined to stamp its mark on all facets of American cultural life.

The tactics have certainly changed and Aquila has noticed. In the 2006/07 national tour the company performed a new adaptation of Shakespeare's *Romeo and Juliet*. There was a simple concept at the heart of the production: Just six actors would learn every part in the play and before each performance the audience would randomly pick the roles they would play that night from a bag. Directorially, the idea was to break down the notion that *Romeo and Juliet* was a pretty love story and ask audiences to see the play anew and be engaged right from the top of the show. This casting by the hand of fate certainly caused a reaction and after the initial surprise, it was overwhelmingly positive. Then something strange started to happen. At a performance in Omaha an audience of around 1000 watched a performance with two men playing opposite each other. The role of Juliet was taken by Kenn Sabberton, a British actor in his mid-

---

19 Hedges, Chris. American Fascists: *The Christian Right and the War on America*. New York: Simon & Schuster, 2006.

fifties. As this was announced four people walked out before the show had begun, but the next day the company was informed that 150-200 people left in disgust and were bombarding the venue with complaints.

Here was the disconnect: the audience had clearly enjoyed the show; there was no marked attrition after the intermission, but the four that walked out after the casting lottery must have been very well organised. They never saw the performance, but the next day the arts center received a flurry of angry calls apparently from audience members appalled at what was going on in downtown Omaha. Could this be the same audience who stood and cheered the night before? What about the 150-200 people who left? This would have been 20% of the entire audience. One would imagine someone would have noticed! The arts presenter was mortified, and this was someone who knew Aquila's work very well indeed. Of course the vast majority of the audience had not had a problem, but a very vocal minority who had not seen the work made their objections known. The next day, a presenter who had booked Aquila for the past ten years made it clear that the company would never be able to return to Omaha. The religious censors had won.

Running a large performing arts center is a balancing act, there are a lot of seats to fill in communities lacking a theatre-going tradition and on any given night they must compete with Must See TV, The X-Box, bars and restaurants and the most popular of all live entertainment in America - WWF Wrestling (with 'Monster Trucks' running a close second). Art must be balanced with donations and ticket sales, most often to subscribers who have not made an investment in choosing to see any one particular show. The Arts presenter is the unsung hero of the performing arts world and it's a slippery tight-rope to walk. Like *Cyrano* several years earlier, Aquila received worried calls from future presenters and requests not to present the male/male version of *Romeo and Juliet*. Female/female was apparently fine which threw up all sorts of questions about the nature of the debate. Was this out and out homophobia? The gay marriage debate had been raging, so why not object to two women? Was it all about Juliet? Was it OK for Romeo to be cross-gendered but not Juliet? Was her role somehow sacred? Aquila's casting conundrum seemed to provoke, misogyny, patriarchal attitudes and complete fear. How could a 400 year-old play be quite so powerful?

Perhaps because *Romeo and Juliet* is a 'classic' it is therefore presumed 'untouchable,' but Shakespeare staged the play with a young man or a boy playing Juliet and all male versions of Shakespeare are very common. What Aquila experienced with *Romeo and Juliet* was something different. It seemed as if what was provoking so much reaction was the idea that chance decided the roles. Had a New York company come into town with the male/male show it might have been easy to reject as the concept of outsiders wanting to make some kind of political or cultural point. But here the audience was not only subject to the hand of fate, they were also complicit in the decision. This was what seemed so dangerous and created such a barrage of noisy protests.

Hedges is right, up to a point, the Christian Right has organised and is vocal in a new way. Their voice can be clearly heard on school boards, town councils and now in arts centers and it's becoming more and more difficult to dismiss what they are saying as only the ideas of a few fundamentalists on the fringes of American society. They are actively and publicly censoring the arts and in much of America they are succeeding.

In October 2006 it was widely reported in the American media that Sydney McGee, an elementary school art teacher, had been suspended by the Frisco School Board in Dallas, Texas, after a parent of one of her fifth graders complained that her child had been exposed to nudity on a trip to the Dallas Museum of Art.[20] This became a national story and the media was outraged. But the effects of the story proved beneficial to those who would seek to censor art. In this way the media played a role in reinforcing the power of the voice of the Christian Right. While some saw this story as yet another example of ridiculous Southern conservatism, it viewed very differently by arts educators and presenters. It was very clear to them that Sydney McGee was suspended because of one complaint and this was further proof of the precarious nature of their positions. This story helped further paralyze the presenters about to receive Aquila's *Romeo and Juliet.* The company was even told by two separate presenters, neither of them in the South, that they would loose their jobs if a male/male version of the play were presented at their venues. One wonders if the Christian

---

20 Ayers, Karen. "Frisco Teacher Told to Take Deal of Face Firing." *Dallas Morning News* October 17th 2006.

Right has become far more adept and using the media to promote their message.

When we think of censorship we imagine a form of state control; Winston Smith purging texts on behalf of the state in Orwell's *1984* (1949) or even Yossarian in Joseph Heller's *Catch-22* (1961) comically deleting nonsensical phrases in the letters of the enlisted men and signing them all 'Washington Irving.' This new form of censorship is far more insidious and induces a form of self-censorship borne out of institutional fear. The Arts presenters who pleaded not to receive a male/male *Romeo and Juliet* had no problem with the idea themselves and knew that the vast majority of their audience, if not all of them, would enjoy a thoroughly rewarding evening of theatre. They feared the vocal extremist voice that had taken root in their society and was organised, active, incredibly energetic and above all *noisy.*

Artistic expression is under threat; must we all listen to the same music, appreciate the same art and enjoy the same plays? And should these be judges by the standards of the extreme form of one religion? The western idea of the theatre was invented in the sanctuary of Dionysos *eleutherio-* Dionysos *the free -* and was a place where the societal borders were crossed and taboos explored. In the theatre we can experience what lies beyond the bounds of our experience and return safely having learned something more about what it means to be human. The Christian Right views theatre, either as a historical exercise that proves the value of western Christian values, or a radical forum for liberal extremists. If they accept the genius of Shakespeare, it is a canonical paragon of their adopted Anglo-Saxon cultural heritage and they certainly have no interest in actually engaging with the controversial and thorny themes that still electrify his plays.

The vocal complaint is not the only way the religious fundamentalists are exerting powerful control over the theatre in America. Arts funding has also changed and there has been a marked shift away from supporting the actual creation of theatre into theatre as education. This is particularly clear when considering federal funding. In 2003 Dana Gioia was appointed Chair of the National Endowment for the Arts. He immediately set about organising a national initiative called *Shakespeare in American Communities* which was to help pay for six companies including The Guthrie, The Acting Company and Aquila to visit all fifty states with a Shakespearean production. Gioia had a gift for persuading

Republicans to increase arts funding. At that time they controlled both houses and the Presidency. He put out a persuasive message of how America was founded by men owning just a bible and the complete works of Shakespeare. It suited both the Bush agenda by decentralising attention form the large urban artistic centers on the East and West coasts, and provided much-needed funds for performing arts centers to book Shakespeare.

The first year of *Shakespeare in American Communities* was quite successful, with an additional $1 million given by the Pentagon to finance a tour by the Alabama Shakespeare Company of military bases. But the following year the program underwent a major change. The funding was not earmarked for productions of touring Shakespeare but for Shakespearean educational performances aimed at schools. As the Dallas incident shows, performances aimed at schools operate under completely different sets of artistic guidelines than a show created with a regular paying audience in mind. The school student has been asked or ordered to attend the performance as part of his or her education. The school is held responsible for what the student is exposed to and both teachers and arts educators are constantly being hauled over the coals for all manner of infractions, including too revealing tights in classical ballet, suggestive gestures on stage, explicit lyrics in music and for one performance of Aquila's *Much Ado About Nothing* in 2001 – Italian masks with elongated noses that were considered far too phallic.

Many foundation funders have followed suit, placing an emphasis on arts education rather than art *as education.* The school daytime performance becomes a sanitised version of the evening show. This would not be alarming, but for the fact that presenters and funders are backing away from more provocative theatre completely and the art form is being increasingly viewed as either mass entertainment *or* education – the Broadway show providing the safe distraction (although in Texarkansas, *Chicago* caused a costume stir after it was revealed that the actors were performing in their 'underwear'), and the classic play, serving the high school syllabus. Inspired arts educational funding would provide resources to help students understand the play and bring them to the theatre empowered and better informed. There they might well experience stories that challenge their view of the world and have their minds opened to a different perspective. An effective theatre education program could help provide a bulwark against censorship by teaching that art is about exploration. Sometimes it can be uncomfortable and sometimes exhilarating.

Aquila decided that the best way to deal with this issue for *Romeo and Juliet* was to include the presenters in the process. In empowering the audience Aquila had not equally included the person responsible for booking the company. A letter was written to each venue outlining some of the issues surrounding the show and the company's own opinion about their nature. It was made quite clear from Aquila's perspective that the company regarded them as homophobic and motivated by a vocal minority who in most cases had not even seen the performance. It was acknowledged that when the presenters booked the show two years earlier they did not know the concept (neither did the company at that time) and so a compromise was offered. The presenters could choose either a gender specific production or the full version with the casting lottery. They could not have any other say in the casting or artistic nature of the show. Aquila tried to inspire the presenters to accept the second choice and most did. Some chose to let the local press know in advance and it made for a good pre-publicity story (controversy sells), others chose to place the performance in context by hosting pre-show talks. The few that selected the conservative option received an excellent show regardless and there was still cross-gendering in some of the other roles.

When visiting someone else's house, a certain sensitivity to one's hosts is no bad thing. Compromise is not a term that comes easily to most artists, and Aquila learned that tolerance cuts both ways. To the Christian Right, the Aquila Theatre Company represents a group of liberal extremists from afar, proselytising their view of Shakespeare and advancing a left wing agenda to a local audience. The company learned that in some houses it was better to be gentle. When the show was not performed that way the company would have preferred, the Aquila artists ensured that the audience knew they had missed something special. In pre and post show talks, workshops and social gatherings people were told about the casting lottery and in turn they asked their local presenter why they considered them not able to 'handle' the company's original production. One presenter even admitted to having underestimated his audience.

Aquila learned that a stand against this new form of intimidation to create arts censorship should not be viewed as a polarising zero-sum game, it's an ongoing battle and it can only be won with dialogue and respect. The members of the company and most who work in the arts may not personally agree with the views of the Christian fundamentalist, but we do need to respect their right to voice that opinion and to organise and protest. But we must not be afraid. We too have a voice and it's a powerful one. We can also organise and protest. We should seek dialogue via our art and the discussion it provokes with those who hold totally opposing views. It would make for an invigorating debate and allow the views of those who would censor to be publicly aired and challenged.

No teacher needed to be suspended in Dallas for showing her students a Rodin, and no arts presenter need lose their job for hosting a radical performance of Shakespeare. Audiences should be free to express their opinions and presenters must accept that innovative art will never please all. A complaint is nothing to be feared but could be viewed as part of an artistic dialogue. When we operate from a basis of fear we censor ourselves and allow the oppressor to flourish, like the frightened watchman on the roof of the house of Atreus in Aeschylus' *Agamemnon* "a great ox is standing on our tongues." His silence enabled violence, murder, tyranny and despair; ours will only empower intolerance, bigotry, homophobia and misogyny. Chris Hedges concluded his book on the Christian Right, *American Fascists,* by writing 'Tolerance is a virtue, but tolerance coupled with passivity is a vice.'

Fomenting a Denim Revolution:
Post-Soviet Censorship and the Necessary Role of an Underground Theatre in Belarus

RANDY GENER

[Randy Gener is a writer, editor, critic, playwright, and visual artist based in New York City. He is the 2007-08 winner of the George Jean Nathan Award, the highest accolade for dramatic criticism in the United States, for his essays in *American Theatre* magazine, published by Theatre Communications Group, where he is the senior editor. An earlier version of this essay first appeared in the May/June 2009 issue of *American Theatre* magazine, published by Theatre Communications Group.]

72 % of Belarusians find it difficult to define the word "democracy."

Belarus holds 186th place out of 195 in the degree of freedom of press.

And is in the list of 13 countries—enemies of the Internet.

About 20,000 young women in Belarus are in need of employment.

13 model agencies, in cooperation with the Ministry of Culture, sold Belarusian young women into sexual slavery.

2,842 criminal cases were instituted in Belarus in 2007 for human trafficking.

About 1,000–1,200 people disappear in Belarus annually.

70% of radioactive waste after Chernobyl disaster fell on the territory of Belarus.

2,800 settlements are located in the areas contaminated with radioactive cesium.

After the Chernobyl disaster, the number of chickens suffering from thyroid gland cancer has increased by 200 times.

70% of those who experienced the disaster refuse to talk on this topic.

—excerpts from a series of projected subtitles from *Numbers*, the third part of *Zone of Silence*, by the Belarus Free Theatre.[21]

The search for the truth can never stop. It cannot be adjourned, it cannot be postponed. It has to be faced, right there, on the spot. Political theatre presents an entirely different set of problems.

—from 'Art, Truth & Politics' by Harold Pinter.[22]

Belarusians today live in a Russified independent state called Belarus. If your GPS brain-unit simply draws a blank or if you feign recognition but dismiss the place as yet another inconsequential, archaic, East-European Slavonic post-Soviet satellite, then you have just demonstrated that Communism is having the last laugh.

You have also unintentionally revealed that the West lacks a clear-cut ethical stance vis-à-vis the repression of young people, counterculture artists, rock musicians, conscientious liberals and independent intellectuals struggling to survive in the undemocratic regimes of the post-Cold War world. The question has been asked too many times before: Why should the government of a modern European nation-state be afraid of a play, a performance, an audience—and a small theatre collective?

Step inside the cold oblivion into which Belarus condescendingly gets assigned. Americans and Western Europeans picture Belarus as a black hole, a negative space hermetically sealed from the rest of the continent, lacking a distinct national identity, and ruled by an authoritarian who has clung firmly to power since 1994. The country's economy and information technology, especially its media, is almost entirely under state control. Its state-owned artistic institutions, we are told, remain frozen in the Soviet past. Anecdotal proof: Its security service is still called the KGB. Its central boulevards, reconstructed by

---

21 Belarus Free Theatre, Subtitles and songs for the production of *Numbers*, unpublished manuscript.

22 Harold Pinter, "The Nobel Lecture: Art, Truth and Politics," http://nobelprize.org/nobel_prizes/literature/laureates/2005/pinter-lecture-e.html (December 7, 2005).

Moscow architects following the Great Patriotic War of 1941–1945, remains a showcase for classical Stalinist architecture. Vladimir Lenin's monument, adorned with fresh red carnations, still stands proudly in central Minsk in front of the House of Government. Down the block, a Soviet-style grocery is called, simply, Bread Store.

Unlike its European kin, many of whom have emerged as feisty democracies, Belarus failed to develop independently from Russia after formally becoming a republic in 1991. Because of its recent Soviet past and its complicated earlier history (World War II laid Minsk to waste), Belarus never made a sharp break with the past. The removal of the Communist Party from its political scene may have deprived the country of its driving force, but instead of building new state institutions based on the rule of law, democratic procedures and a market economy, Belarus (along with Moldova and Ukraine, after a brief perestroika) inherited the dysfunctional essence, the corrupt practices (only mildly reformed) and ideological resilience of the Leninist mindset. (In Belarus, that brief flowering of openness and competition lasted from 1991 to 1994.) Although its 9.9 million inhabitants have attained the basic prerequisites to pursue their own destiny, in the understanding of those who advocate for political and social change in the government, Belarusians remain meek and obedient and, from a Western standpoint, delegitimized—stuck in a Communist-era time warp. Orphaned by the collapse of the U.S.S.R, the country lacks geopolitical weight and has actually lobbied for state reintegration with Russia in some form. Its current regime and centrally planned economy are commonly described as 'Soviet lite.' Although it is not immediately apparent to a foreigner, the Belarusian language and specifically Belarusian aspects of history are shunted aside and discredited from official settings and public life.[23] Under the regime of President Alexander Lukashenko, the country bends to the will of what the international media like to call 'the last dictatorship in Europe.'

---

23 In a controversial 1995 referendum, President Lukashenko reintroduced the old Soviet symbols of Belarusian identity, including the flag, national crest and the bilingual status of Russian. As a result, Russian is more widely used in education and public life than Belarusian. The Belarusian opposition has stated that this intense Russification was achieved at the expense of the teaching and development of Belarusian. Moreover, linguistic divisions that were cultivated during Soviet times have been reinforced under Lukashenko. Speaking in Russian is associated with high-ranking officials and urban sophisticates, whereas speaking in Belarusian belongs to simple, rural folks—and never the twain shall meet, except in highly controlled, official settings and in the realms of oppositional culture and banned publications.

This last epithet (foisted first by the former U.S. Secretary of State Condoleezza Rice[24]) is sadly true. On the map of Europe, Lukashenko's Belarus remains one of the last few places where freedom of speech and assembly are considered criminal acts, even though the constitution legally conforms to many international standards on human rights, access to information and freedom of expression. Opposition activities and counterculture forces are frequently harassed, repressed and detained. There have also been instances of politically motivated killings, kidnappings and disappearances.[25] With a few exceptions, the names of relevant artists, cultural producers and independent journalists both at home and abroad have more or less been eliminated from the public discourse—in a figurative sense, they have disappeared. Given this distorted state of affairs—which includes a policy of limited contact even with Europe's other so-called pariah states (the border between Belarus and Ukraine, for example, has been the site of numerous arrests of artists, students and journalists)—the small amount of information we do get to hear about Belarus is mostly dismal and negative. For Westerners, particularly bleeding-heart liberals, free-speech activists and neoconservative critics, the cries for help are heartbreaking and alarming.

'It is awful,' Nikolai Khalezin and his wife Natalia Koliada, co-founders of the renegade ensemble Belarus Free Theatre,[26] wrote to Brooklyn-based writer and actor Aaron Landsman in the first of many emails seeking international support. 'More than 500 people are arrested for the last five days in Minsk, 300

---

24 In her confirmation statement to the Senate Foreign Relations Committee, Condoleezza Rice used the term "outposts of tyranny" to refer to countries she felt threatened world peace and human rights. She identified six such "outposts" in which she said the United States has a duty to foster freedom: Cuba, Zimbabwe, Myanmar, Iran, North Korea and Belarus. She added, "The world should apply what Natan Sharansky calls the 'town square test': if a person cannot walk into the middle of the town square and express his or her views without fear of arrest, imprisonment or physical harm, then that person is living in a fear society, not a free society." See http://foreign.senate.gov/testimony/2005/RiceTestimony050118.pdf (January 18, 2005).

25 The 2005 report by United Nations Special Rapporteur on Belarus, Adrian Severin, is highly critical of President Lukasheno's regime, stating that "it is the general conclusion of Special Rapporteur that Belarus is now turning rapidly into a real dictatorship, with clear totalitarian inclinations. The report also cited a number of violations of international human rights standards, including the disappearance of four opponent of the regime in 1999/2000 and the continuing failure of the authorities to properly investigate them, as well as continuing harassment and closures of NGOs, independent media, some religious and ethnic minority organizations, educational institutions and trade unions. For full report see http://www.unhcr.org/cgi-bin/texis/vtx/rsd/rsddocview.pdf?tbl=RSDCOI&id=441182040 .

26 The troupe is also known as Free Theatre of Minsk or MFT to its followers.

more in the regions. During the night, the camp was destroyed. People are arrested. They stayed in different jails along the walls, and nobody allowed them to go the toilet. We stayed there every night. Yesterday, when we were stayed for already eight hours and got absolutely freezed, we went home and in one hour I got a call that the camp is destroyed and all people are arrested. I cannot read news anymore because it is just awful.'[27]

Landsman received this e-missive, dated March 24, 2006, not long after the large-scale protests in Minsk's Oktyabrskaya Ploshchad (October Square) were clamped down. On March 19, Lukashenko had been voted back to office in a landslide re-election widely criticized in the West as having been rigged and marred by fraud. Subsequently, at least 10,000 to 40,000 protestors (estimates vary) gathered around the clock in the square and set up tents despite subzero temperatures at night. The main opposition leaders had called for protests to keep up until Saturday (March 25), when a major rally was expected, coinciding with the anniversary of the creation of the first independent Belarusian republic in 1918. The protestors defied the authorities, who had repeatedly issued threats and even resorted to sending text-messages to reiterate warnings to classify demonstrators as "terrorists" (an offense punishable by eight years' imprisonment or even the death penalty). On Friday night, riot police were dispatched to the Square to dismantle the demonstration, which culminated on Saturday. Among the 377 to 460 activists, participants and journalists who were arrested (estimates vary) at the square were the 60-year-old Belarusian theatre director Valeri Mazinski; Pavel Harlanchuk, an actor/director of the National Academic Drama Theater (the national Russian theatre, named after Maxim Gorky), and Svetlana Sugako, a 19-year-old musician and assistant director, who was detained for attempting to bring blankets and warm clothes to her Free Theatre colleagues.[28] The protests, which were documented in the movie *Ploschcha (Kalinovski Square)* by documentary filmmaker Yuri Khaschevatsky[29], continued after the square was closed off, but the numbers dwindled to a few

27 Natalia Koliada. Email correspondence to Aaron Landsman, March 24, 2006.

28 The violent dispersal of peaceful demonstrations in Minsk on March 2006 included arbitrary arrests of political activists, journalists and youth organization leaders, including two of the presidential candidates Alexander Milinkevich and Alexander Kozulin.

29 Because of transliteration issues, he is also known as Juri Chatschewatski, Yury Khashchavatski or Yury Khashchavatsk. The 2007 film, whose English title is *Kalinovski Square*, can be viewed on http://feathersblog.blogspot.com/2007/09/square-by-yury-khashchavatski.html.

hundred. More than 1,000 people were sentenced to 15–30 days in prison or were fined. Many activists were subsequently fired from their workplaces or barred from universities.

In the email, Khalezin and Koliada continue: 'But EU [European Union] and the States [U.S.] make just statement, but no real sanctions. I think, the sanctions will come into force only if we are killed right in the street. It is absolutely terrible. Two our assistants to director of the Free Theatre are arrested. People are severely beaten up. Most of the people who are arrested in the previous three days are people who were trying to bring blankets, tents and warm clothes. Your support really help us to continue our fight, but we are not sure for how long time we will have our strengths.'[30]

Let it be noted, for the sake of analyzing the deep paradoxes and strange peculiarities confronted on a daily basis by writers, artists and musicians in Belarus, that Lukashenko has been elected into office three times—and that however harsh or repugnant his regime may be to his multiple opponents, he seems to enjoy an extraordinarily high level of support among ordinary Belarusians who have mainly been concerned with their economic stability and material well-being, especially outside the cities. Based on many conversations I've had, many Belarusians seem to prefer the status quo to the possible alternative, the kind of political and social and market-forces-driven anarchy they have seen befall other former Soviet states, who recently joined the European Union. Products in Belarus are affordable, the official unemployment rate is low, and the government pays pensions regularly and relatively amply (in line with price inflation). For the most part, Lukashenko protects his loyal and law-abiding Belarusian citizens from such ravages as crime infestation, absence of social security and beggars on the streets. Lukashenko's brand of materialist populism, a kitsch aesthetic shot through with patriarchal folksiness (one popular song, 'Listen to Bat'ka,' refers directly to his nickname, which in Belarusian means 'Daddy'[31]), has successfully defeated the recent attempt to incite 'a col-

---

30 Koliada. Email correspondence, March 24, 2006.

31 In addition to Bat'ka, Lukashenko also likes to use, in reference to himself, the term khozyain. Although Belarusians feel that this term is notoriously difficult to translate, in English khozyain could mean "boss," "leader," "owner," "master" or "ruler" but with its affirmative associations of power, goodness, reliability, masculinity and superiority. Before independent Belarus held its first presidential elections, he made his reputation as a KGB border guard and a leader khozyain of a large collective farm.

ored revolution,' styled after the Velvet one in the Czech Republic in the late 1980s and bearing idealistic similarities to the recent revolutions in the Georgia (Rose in 2003), the Ukraine (Orange in 2004) and the Central Asian republic of Kyrgyzstan (Tulip in 2005).

The Belarusian opposition dyed its protest blue—a Denim Revolution. The label was coined after a militia officer, in September 2005, seized the forbidden national flag (a white-red-white banner) in a public demonstration in the central square of Minsk. As Khalezin memorializes the event in his solo play *Generation Jeans*—the first Belarus Free Theatre production to be presented in the U.S., thanks to the Under the Radar Festival at the Joseph Papp Public Theater in New York in January 2008—a member of the youth resistance movement Zubr, named Nikita, 'took his jeans shirt off and fixed it to a stick. As soon as the jeans shirt rose over the crowd, it was already not a shirt but a flag: the flag of the jeans generation, the generation of free people.'[32]

In 2006, at the height of the protest actions of the Belarusian democratic opposition, Landsman became one of the first American artists to extend a helping hand to the Free Theatre. (In the same year of *Generation Jeans*'s arrival in New York, Free Theatre participated in the Arts in One World gathering at California Institute of the Arts, thanks to the Trust for Mutual Understanding's support. The hotINK International Play Reading Festival, curated by New York University Tisch School of the Arts professor Catherine Coray, also presented a staged reading of Khalezin's earlier effort *Here I Am*.) Landsman says he found 'the broken English' in that above-quoted email 'really affecting, strangely,' explaining 'When I got the original email from them, my heart went out to them in a way that it does not normally do. I can't rationally make sense of. Sitting in a café in Austin, I was blown away by that email. It put everything in focus. I wanted to help these people.'[33]

'My thought,' Landsman wrote back to Khalezin and Koliada, 'is that a reading of your work would raise awareness here about what you do and perhaps galvanize some of the New York theatre community to get off their asses and help their fellow artists in a country where things are obviously much more dif-

---

32 Nikolai Khalezin, *Generation Jeans,* unpublished manuscript.

33 Aaron Landsman. Phone Interview, February 2009.

ficult than they are here.'[34] Soon Landsman was engineering an October 2006 reading of four new Belarusian dramas with the help of actors from the LAByrinth Theater Company, Naked Angels and Tinderbox Theater as part of the Culture Project's Impact Festival in New York. This international day of solidarity was presided over by the British playwright Tom Stoppard, making a personal appearance. 'I decided that this is something I will do strictly as a charitable act,' Landsman says.[35]

> In addition to *Generations Jeans*, the scripts presented at Impact were *We Belliwood*, a collage of short works and verbatim dialogues based on real life by young Belarusian playwrights Pavel Priazhko, Konstantin Steshik and Pavel Vassilievich Rassolko, all of which elaborate on the theme of young people struggling for Belarusian self-identification; Koliada's *They Saw Dreams*, about women whose husbands experienced forced disappearances; and Andrei Kureichik's *The Sky*, about six friends who decide to win back a degree of personal freedom by opening a night club in Minsk, but whose efforts are stymied by the intimidation and blackmail of Belarusian officials. A playwright, novelist and screenwriter Kureichik is not a Free Theatre member, but he was the first Belarusian dramatist to breakthrough internationally after the fall of Communism. At the time, though, his *Sky*, which was originally penned in Russian and was translated into Polish, was published in Poland's theatre magazine *Dialog* under the pseudonym Nikita Mitskevich. In that issue, Kureichik also wrote a 10-page essay that was critical of the Belarus government's repressive use of unofficial blacklists against its authors and songwriters. (I also interviewed Kureichik about the situation of theatre in Belarus for a similar article in *American Theatre* magazine. He later told me that the Ministry of Internal Affairs, in a private meeting, cited both articles as reasons for not allowing him to travel to Graz, Austria, to attend a reading of *Sky* in an international festival). Today Kureichik is considered a leading literary figure, with a commission from the state's Russian theatre named after Gorky.

By contrast, the Belarusian ministries of culture and education dole out no support to the Free Theatre. The reason? Except for a website (www.dramaturg.org), this theatre company does not exist in the official records. Inside Belarus, it exists in its own black hole. (Other Belarusian artists and cultural figures in the same boat include Ploschcha documentary filmmaker Yuri Khasche-

---

34 Aaron Landsman. Email correspondence to Natalia Koliada, March 26, 2006.

35 Landsman. Phone Interview, February 2009.

vatsky, oral-history author Svetlana Aleksievich [Voices of Chernobyl], singer Lyavon Volski and the rock group NRM, the music groups Krama and Nejra Dziubel and Liapis Trubetskoy, the painter Alexander Rodzin, the author and architect Artur Klinau, the photographer Andrei Liankevich, the satirical project "Sasha i Sirozha" of Alexey Khatskevich and Syarhey Mikhalok, the journalist and magazine editor Syarhey Sakharau, the musicians Vital Supranowytsch, and others.) In fact, Free Theatre, which was founded in March 2005, was barely a year old when it became a cause célèbre. Their first selection was the British writer Sarah Kane's 4.48 Psychosis. 'We tried everywhere to stage it but received rejection after rejection,' Koliada says. 'We were told, 'There is no psychosis in Belarus. There is no suicide in Belarus. There are no sexual minorities in Belarus.' "[36] And yet, although the Free Theatre runs the real risk of crackdowns and jail at home, the troupe has performed in more than 15 countries, including Sweden, the Netherlands, Finland, Belgium, France, Poland, Russia, Lithuania, Australia, the U.K. and the U.S. since the troupe's first touring gig at Alvis Hermanis's New Riga Theatre in Latvia in November 2005. The Free Theatre's status as guerilla artists forced to perform underground in a post-Soviet space while arguing openly for a regime change abroad has made it the darling of prominent and respected playwrights like Stoppard, the former president of the Czech Republic Václav Havel, Arthur Kopit (whose Oh Dad, Poor Dad, Mama's Hung You in the Closet and I'm Feeling So Sad is considered a landmark work in Belarus) and Mark Ravenhill (Shopping and Fucking). Later Harold Pinter and Rolling Stones singer Mick Jagger became Free Theatre trustees and patrons. Pinter, in particular, was so enamored of the Free Theatre's ferocious adaptation of his work, Being Harold Pinter, that he gave the company permission to perform his work anywhere in the world without paying royalties. 'We met Pinter,' remembers Khalezin in our conversation after the Nobel Prize–winning English dramatist died in December 2008. 'He told us that Britain was a dictatorship, too. We listened in respectful silence, and then we told him about our situation. He had to agree we had a far worse dictatorship.'[37]

Critics and international groups have followed suit—but not always to celebrate Free Theatre's artistry. In April 2007, the European Theatre Convention

---

36 Natalia Koliada. Interview, October 2008.

37 Nikolai Khalezin. Interview, May 2009.

waived its dues and invited the company to become a full member. The double irony of this largesse: no other official theatre company from Belarus is a member of this network of 40 European theatres, and Belarus is not a member of the European Union. In August 2007, not long after the group met with Havel at his country cottage in the Czech Republic, special police forces burst into the private apartment in Minsk where Free Theatre was holding its clandestine premiere of Edward Bond's *Eleven Vests*. Everyone, including the actors, director and audience members (among whom were theatre professionals from France and the Netherlands)—about 50 people—was hauled to a police station. All were released three hours later. 'One had hoped that the days when artists were arrested for free expression were buried with totalitarian states, but Belarus is as close to a totalitarian state as you can get in Europe,' Stoppard told the *Guardian* newspaper, accusing the authorities of a "grotesque" attack on human rights after learning of the raid through a text message sent by one of the Free Theatre's directors who was detained in Minsk.[38]

Such big-name advocacy has galvanized European bodies into action. In December 2007, the French republic awarded Free Theatre its Human Rights Prize—the first time this particular honor has gone to a cultural organization. In April 2008, at the instigation of Stoppard, Havel and Pinter, the European Union recognized the Belarus troupe with a special mention during the 2008 Europe Theatre Prize ceremonies, held in the Macedonian city of Thessaloniki in Greece, for the ensemble's 'opposition against the oppression of the Belarusian government.'[39] In November 2008, in a London presentation presided (again) by Tom Stoppard, Free Theatre was short-listed for ArtVenture's inaugural Freedom to Create Prize, winning a second-place prize of U.S. $15,000 for a group of four plays, titled *Campaign Stop Violence*, that 'confront the truths about government by standing up to censorship and repression.' (The main prize of $50,000 went to the Zimbabwean playwright Cont Mhlanga).

---

38 Tom Parfitt, "50 Arrested as Police Storm Play in Belarus," The Guardian, http://www.guardian.co.uk/world/2007/aug/24/theatrenews.theatre (August 24, 2007).

39 See the press release for the 2008 Freedom to Create Prize, http://www.freedomtocreateprize.com/press/2008percent20Freedompercent20topercent20Createpercent20Prizepercent20shortlist.pdf .

Let's put an even finer note on the anomaly of recognition faced by the Free Theatre. The quality of the artwork is not the defining criteria to earn a Freedom to Create Prize; what's deemed more significant is the impact of the artwork in achieving the prize's mission to support the lives of artists who promote social justice. Similarly, a complicated matrix of politics and theatre, dis-united Europe–style, obtained during the Europe Theatre Prize ceremony in Greece: Bestowed by a multinational jury of European critics, theatre scholars and European Union bureaucrats, the 2008 Europe Theatre Prize for new theatrical realities, a European Union Commission–funded award worth about 20,000 euros, went to the German choreographer Sasha Waltz, the German collective Rimini Protokoll and the Polish director Krzysztof Warlikowski. The special commendation that went to the Belarus troupe, however, came with no cash prize, as per the usual practice. It did come with an invitation to perform in Greece. When their names were announced during the ceremony itself, Free Theatre members flashed victory signs on behalf of all their Belarus friends and handed Jack Lang, the former French minister of culture and one of the creators of the prize, a European Union flag bearing the word 'Belarus' on it. Such huge political gestures did not go unnoticed or un-remarked in the media, and they were measured against the artistic qualities of the three shows (the monologue Generation Jeans, the excerpt-studded tribute *Being Harold Pinter* and the overly long three-act special creation *Zone of Silence*) that the Belarus troupe presented. Many international critics felt that, although the Free Theatre is being rightly touted as political theatre, not everything the troupe performed at Thessaloniki was of high artistic caliber. Free speech defenders praised the Belarus ensemble's sincerity and chutzpah in confronting life-and-death matters. In stating the reasons for the commendation, Jean-Claude Berutti, president of the European Theatre Convention, saluted the courage and resilience of the Free Theatre as an aesthetic of resistance, and it is instructive that Berutti compared Free Theatre's theatrical skills to that of African theatre. He wrote:

'We Europeans, over-indulged in culture, have got into the habit of applying a slightly pejorative description to those forms of theatre which do not exclusively conform to what we are used to call 'art theatre' for the simple reason that they have a pressing relationship with reality. I have often noticed this in Africa, in connection with what we call 'action theatre.' And yet this is what our friends from Minsk are practicing, with an exceptional determination and an acute sense of what art in a democracy ought to be. And the most extraordinary thing about their adventure is that they should have succeeded in so short a time in creating with each ensuing production a high-quality repertory in the image of their country and their language. They are making art theatre, urgent theatre and survival theatre (which theatre ought in the end to be for all of us) in the middle of the action. For them, the practice of their art, in conditions bordering on the impossible, is as important as breathing...In the midst of our lavish and not always dishonorable productions, their arrival on the European landscape comes as a breath of fresh air.'[40]

Note the slightly defensive and qualified tone of Berutti's citation, his hectoring of the sophisticated tastes of his elitist colleagues, the primitive-yet-lively making-it-up-as-you-go-along critical observation embedded in his deployment of an African-theatre comparison—all of that is compounded by the absence of a monetary reward that would have meant everything to a Belarusian troupe that receive not a single ruble of state funding.

Free Theatre's general manager Natalia Koliada herself can't help but note the disparity in the significance of the recent spate of accolades. She says: 'It's very important for Belarusian artists to feel they are protected by the international community, but it is very sad that the Europe Theatre Prize's special mention was given not for artistic choice. It was given for our position against the Belarusian regime. It was very difficult, because we have received great reviews in all the places where we go.' The human-rights prize, signed by French president Nicolas Sarkozy, on the other hand, 'was an honor for us,' she continues. 'In this case, the prize was for our artistic work—they [the French] totally supported our aesthetic choices.' Nevertheless, Koliada remarks, 'The most vitally important point for us is that Belarus is now on the artistic agenda of European theatre. We've made it so that the name of this country and the situation of our country are given voice at the highest level of European theatre.'[41]

That conundrum which Koliada notes in our conversation—the tension between the necessity to express political opposition to a dictatorship and the

---

40 To read the full citation, see the European Theatre Convention's website for the Winners of XII Europe Theatre Prize and X Europe Prize New Theatrical Realities at http://premio-europa.org/open_page.php?id=105.

41 Natalia Koliada. Phone Interview, March 2009.

precarious role theatre plays in mirroring the contemporary realities of a people—cuts to the very heart of the dissident's dilemma in Belarus. For Landsman, the Free Theatre's existence raised question about 'how much can one accomplish with art alone, about assumptions one makes when working at a remove from one's colleagues, about the ways aesthetics are affected by political strictures and freedoms.' The process of becoming involved with the Free Theatre as a U.S. writer, Landsman adds, 'was more of a learning experience that raised a lot of questions than it was a simplistic triumph of moral purpose.'[42] Having seen Free Theatre's productions of *Generation Jeans*, *Zone of Silence* and *Being Harold Pinter* in the international circuits, and yet struck and deeply disturbed by how emboldened some older Europeans critics have been to carp and insist that whatever harsh repressions the Free Theatre have faced in their country they could not have been as terrible as those perpetrated by, say, the fascist elites in Italy, Spain and Portugal under the respective rules of Benito Mussolini, Francisco Franco and Antonio Salazar, I was motivated to travel to Minsk. I was troubled by questions similar to Landsman's but stated differently: In a post-Soviet space, what is the difference between creating new theatre for the sake of innovation versus creating new theatre for the sake of survival and self-expression under extreme conditions? Given that direct censorship in an independent Belarus is a recent phenomenon, how are the mechanisms of control actually put into practice? Based on the facts on the ground, what does it mean in today's Belarus to create an independent theatre scene outside the law?

You can't snap a photo of President Alexander Lukashenko's residence in central Minsk. Photography is not banned—but taking a photograph of this cube structure, built in the Stalinist Empire style, is simply forbidden, no questions asked. When I approach Lukashenko's residence with my camera, the KGB guards who patrol all four sides of the building shoo me away. I try to get a shot of the residence from behind a metal fence in the leafy public park across the street, but a KGB officer spots me, his face evincing such fury, his fist taking empty stabs in the air, that my young Belarusian interpreter freaks out and advises me to briskly walk away. A couple of times he looks back just to be certain that the KGB officer did not go running after us.

42 Landsman. Phone Interview, February 2009.

This grandiose building, surrounded by clean boulevards and shaded by the trees of a modest park, is supposed to be the most closely guarded place in the country, since all the roads leading to the area are sealed-off to vehicular traffic flows. The nearby October Square bears no physical traces I could recognize that a Denim Revolution, as memorialized by the play *Generation Jeans,* was snuffed out here or that it has sometimes morphed into a vast stage for organized protests and for symbolic actions that borrowed the logic of flash mobs. (An aside: During the March 2006 protests, the October Square was 'a stage for the collision of oppositional political views,' states Barykina, a professor who left Minsk for Canada in October 2003 after Lukashenko's government shut down the European Humanities University, where she was employed. In her book, *Architecture and Spatial Practices in Post-Communist Minsk: Urban Space under Authoritarian Control,* she states that the unusual activities and symbolic protests would show up in the unwelcoming public spaces of downtown Minsk and disrupt everyday routines and intensify daily events. 'The interesting aspect of such actions,' she writes, 'is that there is no central authority; participants are autonomously self-directed, the actions are relatively low-risk and aim at embarrassing power and making authorities nervous rather than directly confronting power in criminal acts of opposition'[43]). Look around the spacious streets of this sleepy capital, whose law-abiding citizens rarely jaywalk, and you can't help but be in awe of the stark monumentality and the reconstructed splendor of all of it. No trash, no graffiti, no mess, no broken glasses, no bottles, no cigarette butts, no stray dogs, few English-speaking tourists—nothing seems out of place. Minsk is beautiful and pristine. You would have to search way off the beaten path to see beggars. The place seems limpid and open. Still, 'Watch out for taking too many pictures of official-looking buildings' was the warning Landsman got when he traveled to Minsk in March 2008 to attend workshops for his own writing contribution to Free Theatre's international play project, the three-hour *Eurepica.Challenge,* in which 14 playwrights from 14 countries wrote short plays about the major challenges their countries are facing today. Landsman adds, 'When I saw the police headquarters and expressed

---

43   Natalia Barykina in "Architecture and Spatial Practices in Post-Communist Minsk: Urban Space under Authoritarian Control in Spaces of Identity," spacesofidentity.net, vol. 8, no. 2, 75. https://pi.library.yorku.ca/ojs/index.php/soi/article/viewFile/18121/16894 (2008).

the desire to photograph it, I was told not even to try.'[44] Several months later, Natalia Koliada tells me that according to the new rules, it is now forbidden to take a photo of the Minsk airport.[45]

Unlike the White House, which is separated from the hoi polloi by a gated park and an immense garden, Lukashenko's residence sits right on the curb. It was so close, so accessible, that I entertained the notion of making a house call—until I realized that this proximity and pristine façade maintain the illusion of order and wellbeing. 'The larger-than-life monuments cast shadows of secrecy over the territories of terror and the operations of power," states the writer Svetlana Boym in *Common Places: Mythologies of Everyday Life in Russia*.[46] As I watch and linger in the buildings across the street of the presidential palace, I observe the inverse relationship between the levels of urban control and the mass concentration of people: Minsk is walkable, but the long boulevards and the monumental architecture ultimately discourage citizens from conquering the city or staking claims on the city space. Unlike in most countries, tourists and Belarusian citizens alike avoid the immediate areas surrounding the residence of the head of state. The majority of citizens live in the suburbs—outer districts that spread farther and father from the city's political and public center. When the opposition stages demonstrations, the center of the city, where transport is highly regulated and already detoured, simply shuts down—or City Hall denies the opposition the right to protest downtown, no questions asked. Add to these zoning policies the skyrocketing prices of downtown Minsk properties since the privatization of housing in the 1990s, and you immediately understand that, through diverse visible and invisible power strategies, the urban architecture itself effectively redirects political gatherings and pushes expressions of community discontent to suburban parks, water reservoirs, private apartments and other places in the outer edges of Minsk.

At night, the lights soften considerably the unearthly-looking cube building where Lukashenko lives and works. Night is also when young people and counterculture artists spring to eager life. Young Belarusians like to party and have fun, yet the official culture (with its bureaucratic war on such fundamental

---

44 Landsman. Phone Interview, February 2009.

45 Koliada. Phone Interview, March 2009.

46 Svetlana Boym, *Common Places: Mythologies of Everyday Life in Russia* (Harvard University Press, 1995), 88.

rights as that of expression and association) does not adequately allow them the freedom to say what they want or behave in the way they see their peers are doing in parts of the world. The forces of social conservatism and a Soviet-era suspicion of the avant-garde or the experimental influence the ability of even apolitical artists to make live music. Rock bands flirt with being both above-board and clandestine. If the musicians play too many government-sanctioned gigs, young people would view them as morally bankrupt and refuse to buy their records. If they play too many underground gigs, the government cracks down. Persons who discreetly slide between the two cultures could easily be denounced as collaborators or infiltrators by either side. There are few inde-pendent clubs in Minsk available for performances; many so-called alternative venues have been forced to close down. To find a club willing to take a risk by supporting an informal gathering of musicians is difficult, since few clubs sur-vive more than one or two years, and the ridiculous bureaucratic obstacles put in place by Belarusian officials allow for a number of legal pretexts to stop musi-cians from performing. Each concert requires individual licenses, separate reg-istrations for venue owners and producers, as well as performer permits from the city authorities for either the rock group of the performer. The officials have the right to refuse a license for any number of reasons—and the right to with-draw it once it has been issued. Worse, no reasons for refusal need be offered or stated in writing—the decision, given orally, was simply that. There is no way to argue the case.

Beneath the veneer of Minsk's crime-free society, impressive civility and na-scent market forces is a tight system of tight control and limited personal free-doms. Since the rise of political opposition to Lukashenko in 2004, when presi-dential term limits were removed through a highly controversial and internationally condemned referendum allowing him to remain in power, Be-larusian writers, theatre artists and rock musicians began complaining of the difficulties of performing in Belarus or traveling abroad; many individual artists and independent groups claimed they had been unofficially banned or placed in an unofficial blacklist, because they had experienced severe obstacles related to their music recordings, their writings and stage performances. In 2008, Free-muse, an independent international organization advocating freedom of ex-pression for musicians and composers, published in Denmark a landmark re-port, 'Hidden Truths: Music, Politics and Censorship in Lukashenko's Belarus.'

Based on investigations done for six months around the time of the 2006 presidential elections in Belarus, the Freemuse report delves into the exact nature and effects of this unofficial blacklist, which was difficult to prove because no such list actually existed on paper. The following areas were researched and explored: 'the Soviet legacy of censorship, the national identity and freedom of expressions, the growth of political opposition music and moves to suppress it, legislation and the music industry, 'official music' and state propaganda, and the effects of music censorship.' The authors of the report, Lemez Lovas and Maya Medich, conclude: 'There is no Belarusian department of censorship per se as censorship is illegal under Article 33 of the Belarusian Constitution. Rather it is the bureaucratic structures controlling the performance, broadcast and distribution of music that make censorship both possible and difficult to investigate. While the reasons behind the 'ban' on live performance of the opposition rockers are clearly political, the ways in which it is implemented purposely avoid any mention of the political dimension—it is implied but never publicly proclaimed. Instead, a sophisticated and highly effective variety of legal and economic mechanisms are employed to prevent rock and underground bands from performing.'[47]

Not surprisingly, a lot of the mechanisms used by authorities to enforce music censorship in Belarus today, which are detailed in the Freemuse report, apply to the measures and scare tactics used to prevent live theatrical performances by politically active writers, directors and theatre artists, including the members of Free Theatre, during the same period. In addition to the last-minute revoking of licenses, for example, consultation with the KGB, Ministry of Culture or Ministry of Religious Affairs (the latter deemed necessary for goth and metal concerts) enables officials to refuse applications with the justification that they are simply observing "orders from above"—a vague explanation that Free Theatre members and its colleagues (whether local or from abroad) have repeatedly met. Because of the government's interest in restricting and regulating the free-flow of youth culture, because of the numerous tactics to cut off the oxygen of rock groups, Belarusian-language bands and theatre artists, a nefarious state policy is seen to have emerged. This policy divides Belarus' artistic

---

47 Lemez Lovas and Maya Medich, "Hidden Truths: Music, Politics and Censorship in Lukashenko's Belarus," Freemuse, Report no. 07/2006, http://www.freemuse.org (2008).

scene into two camps. On the one hand, official artists are actively supported
and promoted on state-owned television, radio and media, but on the other
hand, unofficial artists are either unofficially banned from the media or rendered *persona non grata* in the local scene or economically coerced so that they
cannot perform live at all. 'In Belarus today,' the Freemuse study reports, 'censorship and its avoidance is becoming an increasingly sophisticated game of cat
and mouse between the regime and the musicians—the authorities are learning
about these strategies and try to intercept them, pushing artists and promoters
to come up with new and ever more innovative and complex ideas in order to
keep ahead of the game.'[48]

Such polarization wreacks havoc on the artistic development of Belarus
Free Theatre. This company's brave stand against the Lukashenko regime—
based on the inherent belief that theatre can foment a denim revolution on the
world stage—makes their cultural productions elite phenomena inside Minsk.
With no place to rehearse, no permanent facilities to perform its shows, no ad-
ministrative offices to call its own—indeed, no means of a earning a ruble lo-
cally—Free Theatre has no choice but to perform in private apartments, and
even then those locations frequently change because of the risk of exposure
and persecution. 'If we sell one ticket," Koliada says, "we would be sent to jail
for two to six years.'[49]

The few times the Free Theatre has performed in clubs and street cafes during the first couple of years of its existence, the owners of those establishments
lost their business licenses. In the summer, this dynamic 18-member company
(10 actors, one professional dramatist, one director, four managers and two
technical assistants) resorts to performing in the woods. On that same October
night when I was wasting my time stealing photos of Lukashenko's residence in
central Minsk, I was actually waiting for a return call from Free Theatre's stage
manager; she was supposed to tell me where to meet a theatre representative,
who would then shepherd a group of us to the actual performance. Since sig-
nage in Minsk is in Cyrillic, it is a virtual necessity to know Russian or be accompanied by someone who does, particularly if you need to reach the outskirts of
Minsk. I had no choice but to retrieve my passport from my hotel (the precau-

48 Ibid., 67.
49 Koliada. Interview. October 2008.

tion is not in vain: in case of an arrest, I was informed, it could be the difference between being held in a police cell for a few hours to a few days); I unfortunately had to miss that evening's performance of *Numbers*, part of a larger production called *Zone of Silence*. 'It was good you didn't make it,' Koliada tells me later. 'Five policemen with guns came to the performance. Thank God, Nikolai and Vladimir somehow managed to solve it. The performance was stopped for 40 minutes.'

Free Theatre's underground performances, which have more or less settled recently in a condemned house in Minsk's outskirts, constitute the very essence of poor theatre. 'We walked through a whole ton of muddy streets,' Landsman says, recalling his own experience of attending a Free Theatre performance. 'We went into a backyard and entered a back door. Someone lent them the house. There were 15 or 20 people outside smoking. You go in an entryway. There were cookies and coffee in a makeshift kitchen. The troupe used two main rooms, probably both 15 feet by 18 feet. An arched wall had been knocked out between them. The audience is on one side. Styrofoam white blocks were placed on three windows. It was a white space. The actors performed with one bare light bulb overhead and a small black curtain on the door.'

Witnessing the fierce, naked Belarusian actors bring Numbers to life through mime, dance, projection and metaphor in a stark, white room in a dilapidated house on the edges of this former Soviet city completely alters the polemical context and poetical meaning of Free Theater's unregistered performances. The body of the Belarusian actor itself becomes profoundly politicized. No doubt the covert process of simply getting to the venue itself increases the milieu of danger, anxiety and apprehension. In the freer and safer confines of American and Western European auditoriums, Free Theater performances somehow look more exposed, rougher and, at moments, threadbare. At the Joseph Papp Public Theater in New York City, *Generation Jeans* aroused a great deal of interest and curiosity, but while Khalezin's autobiographical narrative about his experiences during a 15-day jail detention after being arrested at an anti-Lukashenko demonstration perked ears among sympathetic advocates of free speech, its lack of form definitely suffered in comparison to the wealth of usually one-person plays to which New Yorkers have become inured, from the commercial spectacles of Spalding Gray, Eric Bogosian and John Leguizamo to the naughty downtown antics of Holly Hughes, Tim Miller and John Fleck. In my conversations with Khalezin's wife, Natalia Koliada, I was not surprised to learn that Khalezin never actually put his solo piece on its feet in a rehearsal room in Minsk. 'He rehearsed all of it in his head,' she says.[50] A more critical determining factor shaping the antigovernment, counterculture environment in which Free Theatre audaciously moves is the intense international scrutiny. Lately, Free Theatre members have taken more and more to rehearsing abroad, usually in other Eastern European countries. For a good part of the year, the troupe goes out on tour. Particularly now that that it has received an array of international accolades, it would be a rare occurrence for foreign visitors to see Belarus's most world-renowned ensemble in its own turf.

So much international notoriety concerning the political attributes of the Free Theatre is not necessarily a good thing. Despite the strong protection it has afforded the group, all Free Theatre actors have been sacked from their regular jobs at state-run theatres. Foreign collaborators have been stopped at the border and detained at the Minsk airport and summarily sent back home—and if they do manage to enter the country, they risk being arrested. The publicity generated by the Freedom to Create Prize have raised the group's profile and won them global respect, it is helping drive a new documentary project (and possibly other initiatives as well), but it has also caused the dismissal of Koliada's father, Andrei, from his position teaching acting at the Belarusian Arts Academy where he thought he had lifetime tenure. He and his children were told that they are 'a disgrace to Belarus.'[51] Vladimir Scherban, who stages all Free Theatre productions, was fired from his position at the Yanka Kupala National Academic Drama Theatre—not only is he forbidden to direct at any state theatre in Belarus, but all of the productions he worked on before joining the Free Theatre have been cancelled. 'Belarus is completely isolated from the rest of the world,' Scherban states. 'Promoting our productions and inserting them into the European context is both necessary and indispensable. Our tours abroad are a means of overcoming the censorship that we are victims of at home. The set we use has become one of the only free spaces for promoting

---

50 Ibid.

51 Koliada. Phone interview. March 2009.

Belarusian culture abroad. We recruit writers, all under 30 years old, by means of a competition. Some of them are starting to become well-known in Russia.'[52]

Scherban's last remark, about the increasing visibility of young Belarusian writers in Russia, is worth briefly revisiting and interrogating further. Through an annual international competition of contemporary drama as well as through collaborations with actors and writers from the Netherlands, Sweden, England, Amsterdam and other countries, the Free Theatre gives exposure to a new generation of Belarusian playwrights who are not being produced or acknowledged by the state theatres. As I have illustrated above, the Internet has been an essential gateway—and focus—for the troupe's dissidence and countercultural activism. What is less clear to me, however, is how the group situates the specific promotion of Belarusian language in its play initiatives. Most Free Theatre productions are written and performed in Russian. Its Belarusian audiences in Minsk grew up in Russian as well and generally speak it at home and in public. Since there is not a huge demand for Belarusian writing outside of the country, Belarusian writers and musicians clearly target the Russian, Ukrainian and Lithuanian markets, where they can earn a better living by writing in Russian. Some authors have emigrated there permanently.

The decision *not* to write or *not* to perform in Russian may have considerable financial implications both inside and outside Belarus. For many counterculture artists and underground musicians, performing in Belarusian has become increasingly commonplace, because it signifies a resurgent sense of national identity and a conscious act of resistance against the former Soviet occupier's language. Performing in Belarusian can also represent an oppositional stance against the higher status that Lukashenko has accorded Russian, marked by his noticeable disdain for the Belarusian language (save for those occasions when it suits his political purpose to project a folksy paternalistic image of himself as a *khozyain* or a communal leader). In my conversations with Koliada, it was not clear how the Belarusian language itself operates as a clear mark of opposition in Free Theatre productions or the Belarusian plays it supports. In the opinion of many intellectuals, writers and artists I have spoken to, with respect to literature and language, Belarusians suffer from a severe iden-

---

52 Vladimir Scherban as quoted in "Free Theatre of Minsk: Onstage Resistance," http://democraticbelarus.eu/taxonomy/term/64 (June 4, 2007)

tity crisis. This problematic matrix of language and politics, beyond the scope of my own resources and knowledge, is worth deeper and prolonged study, perhaps by a bilingual critic more intimately familiar with how the Belarusian language has been marginalized and disadvantaged historically. In the current rock-music scene, the restrictions on musicians have helped popularize Belarusian-language music among young people and dozens of rocks bands across the country, some of whom perform in Belarusian without a politically conscious valence. But have those censorious restrictions had long-term effects on the development of music in Belarusian language? Have Free Theatre's promotion of Belarusian culture also had an effect on the future of the Belarusian language in the wider cultural battle?

What has been evident to me, as a critic of the world theatre, is that Free Theatre members revel in the notoriety it has achieved in the West. Today it functions thanks to the money the group earns in tours and foreign commissions. I would like to complicate that picture further by adding a cautionary tale. While the group's aim of promoting cultural freedom in Belarus has been rightly welcomed, the politics of money and international funding associated with its busy international activities abroad has been treated with some skepticism in some quarters. The paradox is that the kind of smear campaign that Communist dictatorships used to sully and slander its dissident artists (including disciples of Havel's anti-politics politics)—that somehow they were all in the pockets of Western NGOs and U.S. interests—is once again being hurled at Free Theatre, whose freedom-fighting stance and antigovernment opposition credentials have been criticized as somehow necessarily compromised simply because they accept prize monies and move freely in the international circuit. And it remains next to impossible to access material support for democratization from sources inside the country. To live inside such precarious truths involves an amazing balancing act. While relying on Western individuals and organizations marks the Free Theatre as dangerous and suspicious in the eyes of its critics and of Belarus authorities, the company has effectively leveraged its international renown to escape (so far) the worst possible consequences. 'We have a very great teacher,' Koliada says. 'Václav Havel told us that we need to speak very loudly and openly in order to stop dictatorship. Otherwise we would just prolong this dictatorship.'[53]

Koliada's remark, along with Khalezin's most recent statements in the international media, leads me to a related cautionary observation. In a *New York Times* article that appeared on September 22, 2009, Khalezin was asked about Free Theater's political agenda, and he was quoted to have said, 'This not political theatre—political theatre looks different. This is 'relevant theatre,' which deals with issues that people are used to keeping silent about.'[54] The *Times* article, in which Khalezin describes himself as a 'freedom fighter,' dovetails with numerous media reports in which both Koliada and Khalezin balk at the label of political theatre. In a 2006 Radio Free Europe interview, Khalezin offers what is by now an almost standard retort: 'The actors, the directors, and us, the theatre's founders, do not consider ourselves [to be] political theatre,' Khalezin said. 'Political theatre is boring. The fact that our aesthetical position and our views on the freedom in art differ from those of the authorities have enabled journalists and society to say: 'This is political theatre.' No, we do not declare any political idea. The only thing we declare is freedom in art and the morality of those involved in theatre. In a sense, the slave looking after his master is freer than the latter, since he has the option of running away from him. The master, however, cannot hide from himself.'[55]

These statements strike me as evasive and disingenuous. There is a kernel of truth of Khalezin's statements. (To show why and how, this essay will later shift to a critical analysis of Free Theatre's repertoire, which details its beginnings and its evolution to become a theatre of necessary politics.) At worst, however, these statements are awkward and convoluted, since they contradict the troupe's own admission on its website that the Free Theatre project will cease when 'Belarus will be changed from dictatorial regime to democracy.'[56] Despite its founders' protestations, there is no question that Free Theatre uses the arts as a form of political expression to undermine the current Belarusian regime. Moreover, in an authentic but fraught campaign to continually attract

53 David L. Stern, "In Belarus, Theatre as Activism," September 22, 2009.

54 Koliada. Phone interview. March 2009.

55 Claire Bigg, "Belarus: underground Troupe Brings Cutting-Edge Theater to Moscow," *Radio Free Europe/Radio Liberty*, http://www.rferl.org/content/article/1065395 html (February 3, 2006).

56 See www.dramaturg.org.

international support, some Free Theatre members sometimes resort to feeding the international media's ravenous maw with oversimplified stories about what is banned and what is permitted onstage in Belarus today. Although it is true, for example, that independent artists aren't allowed to draw candid and critical portraits of the social and political reality of Belarus today, it is not true, as Free Theatre members often insist in interviews, that Belarusian authorities have completely left the repertory of its own state theatres to remain dusky, stagnant and mired in total conservatism.

When a foreigner scans a state theatre's repertory and is unable to recognize any famous names in a season of current productions, it seems to me that this lack of recognition cannot be endemic only of the cultural isolation or narrow-mindedness of the country's state theatres. Profoundly, I think, it also exposes that foreigner's ignorance, insularity or lack of curiosity of Belarusian affairs. Operating in an atmosphere that is increasingly hostile to alternative voices, Belarus artists are struggling to keep themselves in business and sometimes out of politics, but, based on my own admittedly limited theatrical experiences in Minsk, Belarus is not a country of losers and miserable people. Free Theatre members are themselves impressive representatives of a yearning underground culture that is dynamic, modern, brimming with life and interesting. Using black-and-white stereotypes and sweeping generalizations when speaking to the international media—a species that is already predisposed to tell uniformly negative stories on Belarus—may be necessary to engage an apathetic world in that country's increasingly repressive climate, but when even the most outspoken opponents of the regime also participate in this media spin, their statements are irritatingly self-serving and frustratingly un-nuanced and ultimately self-defeating. Perhaps we can see in such cynical statements a filtering down and internalization of state propaganda even by those most obviously opposed to it. Certainly in my experience there was some discrepancy between what I expected to find and the reality on the ground. Western journalists must acknowledge the propaganda role we play.

At the end of every performance of *Generation Jeans*, Khalezin loudly shares his desire to be free and, with a pair of scissors, he slices a pair of denim jeans, the pieces of which he hands out to members of the audience. It is an inspiring action, this cut piece—an optimistic gesture that although the longed-for Denim Revolution did not succeed, we, too, can be part of a generation that aspires for freedom. This patriotism, a key feature of the political opposition to Lukashenko, brims as an artistic and intellectual source of motivation for the Free Theatre. At the same time, the negative international image of Belarus is a cause of shame. With the country's steady descent over the last decade into what increasingly resembles a full-blown totalitarian system, even the most optimistic voices, both inside and outside the country, see any changes for the better as a distant prospect.

Sometimes, as in the works of Khalezin and Koliada, Free Theatre exposes this ugly side of life in Belarus under Lukashenko. *Discover Love*, for example, poetically interweaves the real-life story of Irina Krasovskaya, whose dissident husband Anatoly Krasovsky was kidnapped and murdered, with similar stories of political prisoners and forced disappearances from Asia and South America, including France's Ingrid Betancourt, who was recently released. Recently performed in Washington, D.C., San Diego and Los Angeles to mark the 10th anniversary of the enforced disappearances of Krasovsky and his pro-democracy colleague Viktor Gonchar, the play unravels as a stream of disconnected memories chronicling a woman's childhood, marriage and eventual descent into political nightmare.

Culture and memory play an important role in the nation-building project of Lukashenko's Belarus. Sadly, Lukashenko has been tragically deaf to what his country's writers and artists have been trying to express. In the beginning, however, Khalezin's efforts (*Here I Am* and *Thanksgiving Day*) dealt with broader existential questions concerning family relationships, domestic life and immigrant struggles. These scripts were socially relevant and intimate works that earned him a few youth-theatre awards outside of his country. But as Lukashenko's repressive grip tightened and Free Theatre's political struggles become more desperate, the ensemble's stripped-down, rough-hewn, sometimes dated, in-your-face aesthetic has assumed more journalistic motives and autobiographical plots. The three-part *Zone of Silence*, dubbed "a modern Belarusian epic," was tortuous to sit through, if you're inured to the accessible forms of Western dramaturgy, but it was riveting and insightful as an earnest attempt at documentary-theatre self-exposure. In the confessional first part (*Childhood Legends*), four actors air the pain and trauma of their own childhood losses: a suicide attempt due to an unfulfilled romance, the humiliations of kindergarten, the scars of twice witnessing the imprisonment of a father, a child's last encounter with a mother in a hospital, and the anguish of a ten-year old orphan girl held captive in a rigid Belarusian system that separated her from the Italian father who raised her. *Diverse*, the video-infused second part (based on real-life interviews), reveals the daily costs of existing in the shadow-life of Belarus: a black Belarusian gay man who is frequently harassed, an eccentric old woman for whom Stalin and Lenin remain romantic heroes, a homeless man with a passion for vulgar dancing in a city that prides itself of its spotless streets and hobo-free parks. *Numbers*, the almost wordless concluding section, juxtaposes an array of statistical facts about Belarus (How many are unemployed? How many newborn babies are left in maternity homes? How many died in World War II?) with stunning physicality; this meditation on the naked persistence of Belarusian bodies lifts the lethal sincerity of *Zones of Silence* into the realms of stage poetry.

Free Theatre is fortunate to have Vladimir Scherban at its disposal. He is a breathtakingly good director who knows that simply broadcasting taboo subjects is not enough to counteract the official ideological mythology, as personified in the figure of a dictator. Nowhere is his originality more evident than in his prismatic treatment of *Being Harold Pinter*, which he skillfully assembled from excerpts of six Pinter plays (*Old Times*, *The Homecoming*, *One for the Road*, *Ashes to Ashes*, *New World Order* and *Mountain Language*), using Pinter's Nobel Prize speech as a spine and concluding with touching letters from Belarusian political prisoners. The actors' performances in this 90-minute masterpiece of montage run roughshod over those famous Pinter pauses yet mines the oblique, more intimate dramas for their global resonance and overt violence. Fierce and relentless, the Belarusian actors push the later, more political Pinter works to expressionistic intensity: A woman brandishes a flaming torch over a male victim's naked body in *One for the Road*. An actor transforms himself into a vicious guard dog in *Mountain Language*. At one point, the entire company is trapped inside a plastic sheet as if gasping to breathe the air of freedom.

The Free Theatre took risks by turning Pinter's plays into a mirror of their underground life in Belarus. 'When you have children at home,' says Koliada, whose got two of her own, ages 10 and 15, 'and suddenly the door bell rings and your daughter opens the door, and she sees the police there and your daughter, who is five years old, asks, 'Did you come to arrest my mum?', the situation becomes very complicated and painful. We have two girls who have never lived in a democratic country. We want our children to live in a free country.' And if that's not possible? "We want our children to understand what it means to think freely."[57]

Ironically, Free Theatre's righteous mission to be a potent voice of artistic dissent limits and marginalizes its very real ability to reach out to the Belarusian citizens who are the source of their creativity, even as its producers claim to have several thousands on its audience waiting list for every performance. And yet Free Theatre's story inspires. Says Koliada: 'What Free Theatre does, first of all, is create. This has never done by any Belarusian theatre before: a Belarusian theatre talking about Belarusian issues and written by Belarusian authors and performed by Belarusian artists. We create a new way of art in Belarus. We don't want people to think about Belarus only in political terms. We want people to know that there are artists in Belarus and they are contemporary artists. This is a time of national revival.'[58]

In waging a subversive campaign through drama in the shadows of the official culture, the Free Theatre suffers from and struggles with the impossibility of separating their artistic choices from their own political troubles. Because everything that is different is criminalized, true Belarusian renewal can only be realized if the current regime is removed from power (an unlikely prospect).

'At the press conference after our reading,' Landsman recalls, 'a reporter asks me if there was anything one could do onstage in New York that would get you arrested. I said I didn't think so—that after the Patriot Act was passed, a few artists produced shows they claimed would lead to their arrest, but as far as I know no playwright, actor or audience members were incarcerated, though by aesthetic standards, perhaps we'd have been better off had a couple of them been. I mentioned a friend's joke that if a dictator really wanted to neutralize the subversive effects of experimental theatre in Belarus, he should do what we do in the States: Ignore it.'

To which Khalezin instantly said, 'I think that is called democracy.'

Landsman continues: 'The speed with which he came with that remark'—suggesting that the Free Theatre would love to be ignored like that— 'is

57 Koliada. Phone interview. March 2009.

58 Ibid.

illustrative one of the more profound moments I encountered in Belarus.'[59] To which I would add that at this historical moment, questions about Free Theatre's aesthetic merits or its political agenda—even if they are not wholly irrelevant— are beside the point. What matters is that in Belarus it exists at all.

---

59 Landsman. Phone Interview, February 2009.

4

Performing in "the zones of silence"
A conversation between Gabriela Salgado and Guillermo Gómez-Peña

[In this ongoing conversation/blog, Argentine curator Gabriela Salgado and Post-Mexican performance artist Guillermo Gómez-Peña, both living and working away from their original homelands and language, discuss the politics of exclusion in the "international" art world and its visible and invisible cartographies. They elaborate on the concept of "Zones of Silence," the countries and cities that exist beyond the radars of the art world. Gabriela's English is 'British' while Gómez-Peña's is more 'American.' A few phrases and words here and there—in italics—have been left in Spanish.]

GP: The map of the self-proclaimed 'international art world' clearly does not include all countries. *Stricto sensu* it's not an international map, but rather a very exclusive club that involves a few European countries, the U.S., some secondary partners like Canada, Australia and Japan, and some seasonal partners like Mexico, Cuba, Brazil, Russia, China or South Africa, and only when they are in vogue. Entire regions of the world are erased from that map. It's like the IMF (International Monetary Fund) of culture, *que no?*

GS: Definitely; this idea of internationalism is very problematic. It has historically drawn maps out of colonial dependency and trade interests which have guided cultural policies and the collecting priorities of museums. Did you know, for instance, that MOMA New York bought works by Latin American artists during the Second World War and in the post-war period, which remained dormant in unopened crates in their storage rooms until decades later?

GP: *No me sorprende nada.*

GS: That 'internationalist will' of the U.S. government prompted Rockefeller to fund the Americas Society as one of the branches of a major project to 'include' the countries south of the U.S.-Mexican border in a Pan-American plan: it was called the 'Good Neighbour Policy'.

GP: Art as a form of conservative diplomacy, or rather as an innocent front for interventionism.

GS: Yes, and in the same way today, countries are incorporated or excluded from the 'international' tag depending on fashion, cultural parasitism and the voyeuristic impulses that are created mainly by economic and political trends. It's as if we were always the prey of new tendencies to develop in order to become visible...

GP: The cost of visibility, unfortunately, is good behaviour. If Latin American artists wish to be included in the club we must be willing to paraphrase, 'represent,' mimic, and echo the stylistic trends set by the North.

GS: ...with slight variations.

GP: Sure. We are allowed to deviate a bit, but not too much. What we have to contribute to the great international delicatessen is our ability to generate desire for the global cultural consumer...

GS: and perhaps a bit of fear...

GP: We are allowed to perform our stylized difference with an obvious understanding of Western sophistication and current art trends. Only the mildly ethnic sophisticates are allowed. Certain 'Third World' art products are seasonally fashionable so long as they pass the quality control tests imposed by the cultural centres. But our temporary inclusion is always on *their* terms. They've got the key and they choose the door by which we enter. Then they tell us when to leave. The new Third World 'minority' or 'outsider' artist is expected to perform transcultural sophistication; to perform unpredictable eclecticism and cool hybridity. If we perform well, we are in...for a short while. Soon we will be replaced by another seasonal other, another designer primitive. There is always a long line of willing others in the *maquiladora* of international art. It's a never-ending ritual, a revolving door. Curators make sure that the revolving door moves fast.

GS: And that is a response to the art world's high demand for exotica and its obsession with innovation. You also need to live in the right place to be part of the club.

GP: True. When it comes to Latin American artists, one must live and work in a "major" country like Mexico, Brazil, Cuba or Argentina. We must live in countries embellished with exotic mythologies that appeal to the desire of the North. It's the Buena Vista Social Club syndrome; the Frida [Kahlo] syndrome. But if you come from, say, Paraguay, *estás jodido*.

GS: No tag no joy...

GP: Artists from certain countries like Paraguay, Uruguay, Ecuador...

GS: Honduras, Costa Rica, El Salvador, Bolivia...

GP: ...they complain bitterly about the fact that they don't belong to any world imaginary. They claim that they live and work in invisible countries, in which not even a negative stereotype exists to signify them. *Es una chinga.* This Ecuadorian friend of mine told me recently: "At least Colombians have the mythology of drugs, *Macondo* and *cumbia* music; and the Peruvians, the powerful mythology of the Incas and Machu Picchu; even Bolivia now has Evo (Morales), and Venezuela has (Hugo) Chavez, who is a consumate performance artist...but what about Ecuador? What mythical iconography and fetishes can we evoke that can make us attractive to a German curator or a British art critic?" It's the

Latino ultra-periphery; the margins of the margins so to speak, and from *there*, countries like Mexico or Brazil are understandably perceived as culturally hegemonic. I understand their predicament. These *vatos* suffer from a double *bronca*: The deadly combo of Latin American internalized colonialism and the lack of interest from the Northern producers of culture, who are only seasonally interested in certain milieus that fulfil their desire for exotic otherness. Their claims are real. And we should broker on their behalf.

GS: The split is due to the fact that the Latin American hegemonic countries you mentioned have a strong presence in the historical imagination. This was produced by the insertion of their *avant-garde* artists in the circuits of the European modern movements. That insertion, in turn, was made possible thanks to the circulation of intellectuals and artists between those peripheral but somehow hegemonic capitals in Latin America and the much desired European centres of production. It is true that a regrettable invisibility affects many countries of our region. But we have to be realistic here: the art history taught outside of Latin America is only now beginning to incorporate other modernities to its so-far monolithic discourse, and that also affects the culturally hegemonic nations that you mentioned, whose artists are still under-represented in the European/North American history of art...

There is a succinct but powerful conceptual piece by London-based Colombian artist Fernando Arias: *La Historia de Arias*, which summarises that struggle with a great deal of humour. The work consists of a volume of Sir Gombrich's *The Story of Art* (1950)—the Bible of North European art historians—pierced by metal poles and made into a plinth to support another, smaller publication with identical cover and typography that reads *La Historia de Arias,* a catalogue of the artist's own work. We are still trying to insert a huge part of the 20th century's creative thought produced by amazing artists and intellectuals from our continent into the European and North American *historia oficial*, validated for centuries as the only ruling one.

The other problem is our own lack of communication. Researchers based in the UK or New York can easily access specialised literature on those cultural movements and histories across the board, but within each Latin American country that is virtually impossible; with the occasional exception of Mexico and Argentina, exhibition catalogues do not circulate.

GP: This endemic problem of lack of documentation affects experimental artists and rebel intellectuals even more. The more established institutions (museums, festivals and art schools) concentrated in the main Latin American urban centres tend to document and catalogue the work of the best known artists, mostly painters and sculptors whose aesthetics agree with official policies and international trends. And they will promote this small cadre of artists as a package for export with the generous financial help of their governments and some corporations working for those governments. But the pioneering artists responding viscerally to their immediate political and cultural conditions tend to be overlooked.

GS: Who are you referring to?

GP: I'm talking about the wildest performance and installation artists; the more edgy and politicized conceptual *locos and locas*; the independent-minded ones who don't belong to any *clicas*.

GS: *Continúa*.

GP: I'm referring to those who don't receive direct instructions from *Art Forum* or *Flash Art*. These *locos* are never promoted by their country's institutions. Paradoxically, many of them end up migrating to the U.S. or Europe in search of freedom, visibility and community. My lost generation was part of this migratory phenomenon. We were artistic exiles, forced to leave our country in order to find the tone and volume of our voice and the true shape of our madness. And once we migrate, we begin to lose communication with those who stay. Even when we make an extraordinary effort, the lines of communication become thinner and thinner, year after year...

GS: The communication problem seriously affects our capacity to generate efficient strategies for ourselves...

GP: Very seriously...There exist clear lines of communication between the main cultural capitals (Mexico City, São Paulo, Buenos Aires, etc.), and the European and North American cities which are part of the self-proclaimed "international art world," but these direct lines do not exist amongst Latin American countries, or between homeland and diaspora. In other words, the *chic* Mexico City artists and curators are more closely connected to their New York, London or Parisian peers than to their South American colleagues or to their distant Chicano relatives. So the crucial question is where and how do we meet? The European and U.S. critics, curators and producers are always brokering and framing the dialogue amongst us, and even speaking on our behalf. They perform the role of impresarios and ventriloquists for the so-called Third World. And we only get to meet amongst ourselves when they invite us to participate in the platforms and events they stage.

GS: ...we let them discover us, speak on our behalf, be our hosts and promoters and then take us to their metaphorical beds, so we can breed their exotic, mixed-cultured children.

GP: And we love to partake in this bizarre ritual.

GS: Yes...a kind of *Malinchismo atávico* which dates back to the first encounters between the indigenous cultures and their Spanish conquistadors.

GP: This Faustian deal is at the core of Latin American culture. The original goals of the Latin American and African biennales were precisely to create a more inclusive cartography and to nurture multiple self-sustained art worlds, parallel art worlds with direct communication lines; but throughout the years, I guess they forgot their *raison d'être* and ended up emulating the European and American Biennales. Once you are part of the club, you tend to forget why you are even there. It's bizarre, *que no?*

GS: It is due to our internalised colonialism that the only opportunities to create our own cartographies—like in the example of the biennales you mentioned—are replaced by the emulation of mainstream models.

GP: In order to belong, to be part of the *onda,* the South ends up reproducing the same behaviour of the North. Frantz Fanon and Eduardo Galeano wrote about this phenomenon extensively. But tell me, Gabriela, how did you arrive at the notion of 'The Zones of Silence'?

GS: The expression was originally coined by the Dutch organisation Prince Claus Fund to signal those areas of the world that remain in the shadows of the cultural mainstream. I found it appropriate to define the situation of many areas of Latin America, the zones that have a strong cultural production but do not host biennales, triennials or mega art fairs. In the zones of silence there exists an acute sense of isolation among artists and organisations, accompanied by a frustrating lack of communication with the region's multiple cultural scenes. This alienation from each other not only helps to maintain the negative dependency from the Western mirror to validate our own productions, but also takes away the possibility of creating necessary networks of collaboration. I envisage stimulating new cartographies as a possible tool for the empowerment of creative communities outside of the established maps. And you? Tell me about the concept of 'X-Centris' which is at the core of La Pocha Nostra's art production.

GP: My performance troupe (La Pocha Nostra) is working on a long-term project to decentralize 'Art.' We don't talk much about it, but we are very committed to it.

GS: How did it all begin?

GP: Until the early 90s, performance artists of my generation were trapped within a solipsistic art circuit that encompassed a handful of U.S. cultural centres. They would tour from Los Angeles to San Francisco, and then to Chicago, New York, and a few other cities and back, over and over again. And their audiences were strictly comprised of artists, intellectuals, cultural organizers and students. But as politicized Chicanos and U.S. Latinos, our "American" art map was much wider. Besides presenting work in the Anglo experimental art circuit, we regularly visited Latino barrios and Indian reservations. Our map included the whole U.S. Southwest...what I term, *Chicanolandia*...and other U.S. Latino *milieus* like Nuyo Rico, Miami and South Chicago. We also toured our Latin

American homelands. Because of this, we had access to much more diversified audiences and cultural experiences than our Anglo colleagues.

By 1993, my collaborators and I decided to expand our cartographic project and to begin touring other non-Chicano USAs, places where they had never seen a Mexican as a speaking subject, much less radical Mexican performance artists. We started touring conservative states, what we thought were scary places like Montana, Georgia, Indiana, Louisiana...and that became part of our political project: to bring our border art and hybrid aesthetics beyond the *terra ignota of Chicanolandia*. In doing so, we started performing for non-art audiences, and realized the incredible impact performance art can have on the lives of regular people or even people who disagree with us.

In the mid 90s, we expanded our decentralization project to an international level. We put special emphasis on countries that were either generators of migration to the so-called First World, or host of those migrations. In the process, we created our own routes, our own bridges and tunnels. So in a sense we arrived at our concept of an 'X-Centris' type of internationalism empirically: by travelling to those places and engaging in a dialogue with artists from those very sites. The theory came later.

Since then, my performance troupe has made an extraordinary effort to tour to places that exist beyond the radars and telescopes of the so called "international art world." And we continue to find amazing artists and vibrant art milieus in these places. I guess we confront our own ethnocentrism by doing it.

GS: Why is La Pocha's office still located in California and not somewhere in Latin America?

GP: It's a political decision and a direct response to an ironic global phenomenon, immigrants from so called 'third-world' countries live inside the much touted First World, and by living and working within this First World, we are redefining its culture. The great paradox is that our host country is often responsible for our homeland's hardships. Most of the members of La Pocha are social protagonists of this border phenomenon.

GS: And for you personally, what does this mean?

GP: It's a very personal matter. My family and friends are divided by the U.S./Mexico border. And we did not choose this predicament. To me, it is clear that one of the main reasons Mexicans are in the U.S. is that the U.S. has messed with Mexico's economy and resources, including the cultural resources.

GS: Besides, 1/3 of the U.S., what is now California, Arizona, New Mexico, Texas, and parts of Utah, Nevada and Colorado used to belong to Mexico.

GP: *Absolutamente*. These territories were taken by force through an expansionist war (1846-48). And the memory of the old border is still in our psyche. It's like the Kirlan effect of an amputated limb. We all somehow remember. It's an archeo-typal memory. So in a sense I am migrating in reverse. I came to the U.S. following the footprints and memories of my ancestors and seeking my lost family. Originally it was an unconscious process, but eventually as I became politicized within the Chicano movement, I realized that I was part of a much larger cultural project. Unfortunately, the memory of that territorial theft only exists on the Mexican side. The gringos have conveniently erased that memory, as they conveniently erase all unpleasant memories. It's a quintessential feature of U.S. culture: to consciously forget...or pretend to forget, and then to rewrite history in their own terms.

GS: What kind of activities does la Pocha engage within these 'silent' places you go?

GP: We make a lot of noise. Our basic idea has been to present workshops leading to performances that incorporate young rebel artists from those communities. The workshop becomes the nerve centre of activity during these residencies. And around the workshop we present different kinds of satellite activities including lectures, public dialogues like this one, street interventions, and video screenings. The idea is to engage with the local communities in multiple fronts and using multiple strategies and languages. The basic premise of these collaborations is founded on an ideal: If we learn to cross borders within the art space, we may learn how to do so in larger social spheres.

But this cannot happen in two weeks. In order to attain this, we must develop long-term collaborative projects with these communities. Continuity is an important part of this project. After twelve years of engaging in this 'X-Centris' artistic praxis, La Pocha has become good at it. We now have long-term projects with multiethnic artists residing in other 'border zones,' in the Other Europe, the Other U.S., Canada and Australia, as well as with several Latin American communities living in cities outside of the centres. We have developed robust connections in all these places. Artists we have met during these residencies often end up touring with La Pocha in future projects. It's an open and fluid system, an ever-changing entity. By now, we have Pocha 'chapters and collaborators in different parts of the world. In a sense you can say that we are a virtual community, and our website is both our matrix and operational centre.

GS: In the past years you have been putting a lot of emphasis on pedagogy.

GP: Yes, it's the core of our new political praxis. We even have a summer school in Oaxaca, and are hoping to develop more sustainable workshops in other parts of Latin America. And your curatorial work has definitely influenced this new phase of La Pocha. We are particularly interested in the 'invisible regions' existing within the borders of the semi-visible countries; the otherness within so to speak; what you term 'the zones of silence.' I would love to develop ongoing collaborations with places like Tucuman and Rosario in Argentina; Medellin and Cali in Colombia; etc. The problem as you know is that, with a few exceptions, government bureaucracies and foundations don't really see the importance of this kind of work. It's perplexing to them. Funders constantly ask me: 'Gómez-Peña, why do you want to work in Yucatan or Oaxaca, instead of Mexico City? They don't even have a performance art milieu down there!' It's like trying to explain to a corporate real estate agent why you are interested in the *barrio*. Good luck! What about you Gabriela? Why did you end up in Europe?

GS: At the time of the last dictatorship in Argentina (1976-1983), there existed not only a deep fear in relation to our physical integrity as individuals, but also an invisible pact of silence that implicated the whole society, which mutated into a long standing culture of denial as a means of survival. This pact suppressed at once social solidarity and all possibilities of developing any kind of cultural response. Against that backdrop, hope ran low for many.

I initially conceived Barcelona as a stepping-stone, but it turned to be home for many years. When I arrived in Spain, the country was learning its own lesson on freedom after the obscurantism of Franco's regime, so it felt like an appropriate option.

By the 1980s, South Americans had lived in several European and North American cities for decades, having been expelled by the numerous military dictatorships that the CIA planted in most of our countries, as a response against the expansion of socialist ideology. However, despite that large South American immigration, it became clear to me that still in 1983, to speak with a 'sudaca' accent wasn't a door opener in Spain.

GP: Is that why you moved to England?

GS: I moved to England to study. London gave me the chance to be part of a wider cultural landscape and that in turn has nurtured my will to work beyond its shores. I have been increasingly interested in opening more platforms for interaction between the other Latin America—the one that we saw springing out of our experience in Tucumán—to other cities in the subcontinent. Not only are our countries culturally isolated from each other—except by the almighty power of music, literature and *telenovelas*—but they are also unaware of our relatively new culture, the one born out of the displacement of millions of Latin Americans in Europe, the U.S. and Australia. That floating Latin America is composed of people whose experience is that of being in between cultures, in the fractures of all definitions, and that liminality interests me deeply. Surely because when dealing with it I place a mirror in front of my own self. That other Latin America in the UK is mainly composed of near one million Colombians and Brazilians, but there are also Ecuadorians, Chileans, Cubans, Venezuelans and Peruvians who settled here. Our colonial past does not link us with the larger, more established communities of Asians, Caribbeans and Africans, but our present does. In Brixton (a popular neighbourhood situated south of the river), the second spoken language is Yoruba and the third Portuguese. How did that happen? That incredible hybridity transpires language and is expanding through music, film and visual art and is slowly reaching the shores of mass culture.

You see, after decades of multiculturalism these other communities are growing so fast and are so embedded in the British social fabric that for some sectors of society the very notion of Britishness is at stake, and they are beginning to react in the worst way possible by signing up to a fascist agenda. In the last local election, one of London's popular boroughs saw National Front—now conveniently re-branded British National Party—candidates obtaining a majority of votes...

GP: How will artists deal with this new threat?

GS: This is the kind of material that feeds La Pocha Nostra's public performances, and to me, it works cathartically, as you are opening symbolic valves that are very necessary to maintain society's mental sanity. I believe that when you put all those socio-cultural forces together in performance combined with radical pedagogy, the complexity of our realities surpasses what you have sharply called the 'mainstream bizarre.' In the staging of our realities as immigrants here and there, we cannot be de-politicised as the mainstream needs to be. But what price do you pay as artists who dare speak about these very hot issues? Are you and your colleagues given chances to act beyond the marginal land of otherness?

GP: Our job in this respect is to be coyotes. We are trying to broker and open doors for those who don't have access, and when possible, invite them to tour with us...The artists living in these hidden cartographies are rarely part of the 'official packages' of their countries. So we perform the role of alternative travel agents.

GS: Tell me about the Mexican 'official packages.'

GP: The cultural production that Mexico packages, brands and exports as 'contemporary Mexican art' is really circumscribed to a handful of privileged artists from Mexico City, and perhaps one or two from other large cities. And that's about it. *Es una micro-clica con mucho poder.* But the thousands of artists that live in 'the other Mexicos,' inside and outside the national borders: these *vatos* seem to live in another time and place...

GS: But things have been definitely changing in the past years. These artists are beginning to raise the volume of their voices. In Argentina there are remarkable examples of a strong will to disconnect from that dependency, like what has been happening in the city of Tucumán in the last ten years, thanks to the tenacity of a group of artists who have tried to insert themselves in international networks, bypassing the mighty power of Buenos Aires. Rosario is also a good example, with a scene that is growing in reputation, a good museum of contemporary art with an interesting collection and programme...

GP: Same situation in Mexico and Chicanolandia. In places like Oaxaca, Tijuana, San Antonio, and East LA, artists are creating their own *movida*; their own institutions; their own aesthetic. They are developing the means and capability to broadcast their voice and image. We are definitely witnessing a new cultural phenomenon: loud voices broadcasting from the imposed margins of their national cultures.

GS: I suppose that these initiatives contain in themselves the seed that was planted in those areas back in the 1960s, when a lot of very politicised, conceptual, non-objectual and time-based practises were explored with incredible intensity. We worked together in the workshop 'Tucumán Chicano' in 2005; didn't you perceive while we were there that Tucumán (Northern Argentina) was in its own right ready for interaction with the wider world?

GP: It was definitely a strange feeling to discover that my conceptual concerns as a Chicano or post-Mexican artist were closer to the Tucumán artists, and to the artists from other regions of Argentina, than to those of Buenos Aires. Now in retrospect it is more clear to me: We both are fighting similar battles in different cultural contexts. We both have consciously assumed the strategic positionality of the insider/outsider. We both are embarked in the great project of decentralization of culture. Last week, Roberto (Sifuentes) and I conducted a workshop here in London sponsored by Live Art Development Agency. Same thing: The 20 participants were all amazing artists from every imaginable hybrid and immigrant community of contemporary London. Caribbean, Arabic, Sri Lankan, Latino, pan-European...and the material we all developed was strangely, strangely familiar. It is as if we were having a collective dream...or nightmare. Soon I am hoping that we will have the capability to speak directly to one another, bypassing the brokers and ventriloquists from the North.

One of the cultural organizations I respect the most is the Hemispheric Institute of Performance and Politics, a unique organization created about eight years ago by theorists from the New York University Performance Studies Department. The basic premise was to develop a trans-continental network of theorists and performance artists bypassing the main cultural centres. Every other year, we gather in places like Lima, Rio de Janeiro, Belo Horizonte, Monterrey...and for two weeks, we talk, think out loud, debate, and present work. Many utopian initiatives have emerged out of these hemispheric dialogues. It's a good model.

GS: Tell me more about the similarities and differences of attitude between U.S. and European 'floating' communities when taking part in your performance work.

GP: As far as artists are concerned I don't see much difference. *Neta*. Whether it is Chicanos from the U.S. Southwest, Black & Asian British artists, German Turks or *Sudacas* and Canarians in Spain, we all seem to be bound by a sense of partial orphan hood, by the condition of being partial outsiders to both the art world in capitals and to society at large. Beyond the obvious cultural differences amongst us, there is this rebellious attitude and bifocal understanding of culture that help create a common ground for our collaborations. We are all post-national artists in search of a new conceptual nation capable of containing our aspirations and complex identities, our rage and *locura*. We are an unusual milieu of border-crossers, exiles, nomads and hybrids of sorts. I call our tribe, The New Barbarians. And our job is to cross the borders we are told we shouldn't cross; to infect the ethos and aesthetics of the West; to smuggle ideas from one community to another; from one country to another; and from the streets into the museum and back. Performance art is our common language; our *lingua franca*; our communication strategy.

Regarding audiences it's a quite a different matter. At the risk of generalizing, I'd say that U.S. audiences tend to be more racially mixed; more participatory and bold; less self-conscious. It's part of the American character. European audiences are more intellectually savvy and shy...and more specialized. The gap between high and low culture is wider in Europe. Of course there are always exceptions to the rule. Spain is a major exception. Spanish audiences behave in a very outrageous manner, sometimes to the point of being insensitive and a bit racist...But I like that rawness. It's a challenge.

Do you see any major differences between Latin artists living and working in the UK, versus other Latino diasporic communities, say in the U.S. or Canada or other parts of Europe?

GS: It is very difficult to avoid bold generalisation when analysing these questions, but I would say that the main difference resides in numbers. With thirty-five million Mexicans contributing substantially to the U.S. economy, omnipresent Latino TV channels and a significant span of Latin American communities living in major U.S. cities, the difference of perception is apparent. We can't equate that with any European country, where the percentages shift toward other communities, such as Arabs, Africans, Middle Eastern and Asians.

Let me give you an example: in the UK, when filling the so called 'equal opportunities monitoring forms' (forms that one is required to complete when looking for employment or applying to study), you are presented with a list of 'other' ethnic groups that does not include Latin Americans. We simply do not exist in their classification system. Latin Americans are still seen as an exotic minority in the UK, despite being a steadily growing migrant community. This exoticism is highlighted by the increasing and dangerous fascination that our countries generate through the impact of the tourist and cultural industries here: films by Latin American directors are in fashion, concerts and exhibitions of Latin American artists slowly gain increasing media coverage, and so on. It's the *Favela Chic* syndrome. In this climate, artists can fit in different contexts, without the need to make decisions about entering or separating themselves from a wider, inclusive identity discourse, such as the one that exists in the U.S.

Latin American art workers in the UK are testing the multicultural waters and finding their individual place in relation to personal interests rather than political agendas, as the mighty help of the equal opportunities policies does not affect them as much as other more established 'minorities.'

Of course you can also look at the case of Spain—where most economic migrants from Latin America choose to live due to the common language—and that process of exoticising does not happen: Dominican, Cuban or Ecuadorians are not seen as exotic or sophisticated, but as the noisy and far too widespread presence of a second-class immigration in an until recently very levelled mono-racial, mono-cultural society that is beginning to change very rapidly. Nowadays, I perceive Spain as being in a state of shock: facing the huge immigration tsunami brought by global changes, without the tools to understand the complexity of religious and racial diversity, and with frail and insufficient policies to deal with multiculturalism.

Where do you think lies the difference of the impact of your work in the U.S. today, in relation to Latin America, Spain and the rest of Europe?

GP: The theoretical aspects of my work perhaps have more impact in English-speaking countries. This is due to the fact that six out of my eight books were written in English, and also because I publish regularly in the English-speaking press. In the U.S., the work of La Pocha Nostra has been part of the national debates on race and culture for more than a decade, and since 9/11 we have been active participants in the debates around immigration, censorship in the arts and the cultural struggle for a more tolerant and open society. We are present in academia, and we also operate at a grassroots level. Our positionality is one of temporary insiders, or rather insiders/outsiders at the same time. We treasure this border condition.

GS: What about Mexico?

GP: In Mexico, I'd say that my work falls under the conceptual rubric of border culture and immigration. Mexico is finally interested in understanding "the other Mexicos" I was talking about earlier. The relationship with the Mexico that exists on the other side of the border (the U.S.) is particularly important, and border and Chicano artists and writers often perform the role of brokers, interpreters, and intercultural translators. Our Mexican audiences tend to be young. The Mexican youth is very much part of the international robo-youth culture. They are bilingual, fluent in global pop and cyber-technologies, and geographically quite mobile. A huge percentage of that youth has crossed the border several times. And most of them have relatives on the U.S. side, so they understand our Spanglish praxis and hybrid aesthetics at a very guttural level. To them it's not an intellectual exercise. It's part of their *lingo* and their cultural praxis. My

book, *Bitacora del Cruce,* published in Mexico (2007), is all about this phenomenon of trans-national Mexican culture. La Pocha's problem in Mexico is mostly
financial and bureaucratic. Despite the fact that we have huge audiences down
there, there is very little money to support the kind of work we do.

GS: Why?

GP: Mexican cultural functionaries are very Euro- and New York-centric, and
they would rather spend their money bringing European and U.S. art into Mexico than, say, bringing outspoken Chicanos who will remind them of their own
shortcomings and racism. But this does not stop my troupe from going down
there to present work at least twice a year. If at the end of the project we end up
even, we are lucky, but we love it. It's a highly charged context and we really like
the challenge. When I return to Mexico to present work I always go with other
Chicano and U.S. Latino colleagues, and we tend to overstate our Chicanismo,
our otherness. It's a conceptual strategy which grants us special powers; again,
it's the power of the partial outsider.

GS: What about the impact of La Pocha in other Latin American countries?

GP: Curiously, in other Latin American countries, we are perceived and
treated as Latin Americans and not as border, diasporic or "minority" artists. In
Brazil, Cuba, and Colombia, people are familiar with our work, because we have
performed there several times, and the experimental art scene is quite developed in these countries. I just presented *Mapa/Corpo* in Bogotá and I was happily surprised to see hundreds of young artists and students storming the gallery. They were extremely open, curious and sophisticated in their understanding
of our work.

My relationship to Argentina has changed dramatically. When I first went
down there in the early 1990s to present *The Couple in the Cage* with Coco Fus-
co, our audiences were very racist, arrogant and Eurocentric. We felt there was
no context for our work. Recently, however, when La Pocha went to Tucumán
invited by you, our experience was completely different. As I mentioned earlier,
we encountered a new society, rapidly becoming conscious of its multi-hybrid

soul, and a very exciting *movida*. It was as if the whole country was awakening. I think that Argentina is now one of the most exciting places on the continent.

GS: I agree. Argentina has gone to hell and back in various occasions, but the most recent economic collapse of 2001 seemed to prepare the ground for a more realistic perception of what the country is really like, and not what it aspires to be. How about your work in Spain?

GP: Our entry to Spain has been…bumpier. Until recently, Spain had been quite snobbish toward U.S. Latino artists. We were perceived as 'minority artists.' Most Spaniards seemed to be more interested in New York and the UK. It was a *nouveau riche* mentality over there. Though we have been presenting work in Spain since the early 90s (*The Couple in the Cage* caused a major stir in Madrid), it's only been in the past years, and thanks to the efforts of a new generation of curators like Canarian Orlando Britto and new initiatives like Zaragoza Latina, that Spain has finally become interested in matters of hybridity, migration and border art. La Pocha now enters Spain via the Canary Islands. It makes more sense. We call it 'the Chicanarian project.' We have also entered Spain through the side doors of Catalonia, the Basque country and Cantabria. Madrid is also slowly becoming aware of its border condition. Two years ago, we presented a project in Arco and encountered a much hipper Madrid.

GS: What about the UK?

GP: Our relationship with the UK is more complex. Thanks to the British post-colonial debates and the black British phenomenon, Chicanos started visiting the UK in the mid- to late 80s, and publishing in magazines like *Third Text*. La Pocha has also had a very robust and ongoing relationship with many UK-based performance artists through the amazing Live Art Development Agency (London) and the Centre for Performance Research (Wales). Producers like Lois Keidan and Richard Gough have been incredible allies in creating bridges between non-Anglo U.S.-based performance artists and our peers in the UK. It's strange to realize that there might be more of a context for our work in the UK than in Spain.

GS: It is indeed strange but understandable, as it has to do with an historical question, or rather, a matter of timing. The UK has been exposed to issues of diversity for decades, while Spain is just getting there. While some new organisations are now venturing into exploring wider artistic territories, like in the case of the young project 'Zaragoza Latina,' the main cities, such as Madrid or even more Barcelona, suffer of an endogamous syndrome that affects museum programming very badly. Of course in the streets, reality is much richer and more plural, but the museum and the streets are pretty disconnected...which is to say the museum world bubble is, as usual, outside reality.

GS: What strategies does La Pocha use, given its radical proposals, to penetrate the bubble of the museum?

GP: La Pocha has always had one foot in the museum world and one foot in the *barrio*. We have a very unique positionality *vis à vis* the international art world. It's a love and hate *onda*; a macabre dance. They pretend to ignore us, but we are always present. We get *there* through side doors, back doors and tunnels. We are the unwanted but necessary guests, the sexy *refusniks*, the mariachis with a big mouth. We are the kind of artists that get invited, with sterilized pincers and reservations, because we are very politically minded and are always questioning power relations. And we don't do this because it's fashionable to be political. We've always been. It's part of our Chicano condition.

The relationship between live art and the big institutions has always been very complex. One year we are 'in' (if our aesthetics, ethnicity, or gender politics coincide with their trends); the next one we are 'out.' We get welcomed and deported back and forth so constantly that we have grown used to it. And it is only when the art world is in a deep crisis of ideas that we get asked to participate.

GS: It is the same with otherness. That is what binds live art with cultural difference.

GP: Then, when the art market recovers, they tell us goodbye and don't call us back for a couple of years. Then they invite us back as if we were recently discovered. It's a bizarre ritual, but I kind of like this insider/outsider positionality. It's more congruent with our beliefs. And it really doesn't affect us much, because we operate in multiple art worlds. So if we get temporarily ousted from one circuit, we just move to another one and continue doing what we do. We make a point to always operate multi-contextually. It's our saving grace. And you, how do you see your work as a curator and writer functioning in the UK, versus in Latin America. I bet you perform different kinds of roles in both worlds.

GS: Of course, that insider/outsider condition you were referring to occurs at many levels. As a 'specialist' in Latin American art in the UK, I am often perceived as someone capable of providing the colourful, exotic experience of a less known 'otherness' so dear to the curious British spirit. That is obviously a caricature of reality, and fortunately, I don't need or wish to oblige. But when opportunities are created for an open dialogue in a similar level with my European peers, good collaborations emerge, and then, I consider my task as a broker complete. I do this mainly through exhibitions, participation in education events in museums and galleries and through my writing.

On the other hand, in Latin America, and especially in Argentina, my otherness is given by my long absence from the realities that people there have confronted all these years, so I have to humble myself and keep learning about the changes in a place that is not my current "home" in the sense of belonging, but in an emotional level because of the blood ties that link me to it. My writing and curatorial work are enriched by and characterised by this 'life in the border,' the state of being inside and outside at the same time. It is precisely this life experience that attracted me to your theoretical work, which I started to read nearly fifteen years ago, and which opened the door to a border territory within the vast field of contemporary culture.

I articulated these ideas in a proposal for an exhibition made of artworks and events by artists who are on the move, physically or metaphorically displaced; I called it *Dancing with aliens on a moving platform*. The title was inspired by an image that remained in my head for a long time after watching a performance by Pocha Nostra performance artists Juan Ybarra and Silvia Antolin: his naked body painted green, his head covered by an alien mask... an alien graciously dancing with a flamenco dancer...

But for me, this image does not refer to migration only: If you look at the state of things within the mainstream, you realise that displacement is a fundamental symptom, for instance, of the presentation of artists in contexts that are completely artificial, like biennales, triennials, etc. I constantly question myself about whom we are dancing for and how this exotic dance is perceived. Context has always been one the most difficult topics associated with the presentation of art, and not only artists, but also artworks and ideas need fertile ground to fully manifest.

GP: The mainstream always feeds off the margins and borders, and the theory and practice developed in the so called margins eventually becomes mainstream. Five years later that is...Border culture and hybridity became *lingua franca* years after they were everyday praxis for so many communities. This happened in the early to mid-90s. Then the paradigms of border culture and hybridity were replaced by techno-art and cyber-culture as the new 'isms.' Now, it's a new ball game. The new praxis seems to be engaging in a stylistically radical, but thoroughly apolitical type of transnational multiculturalism that indulges in mild difference and stylized displacement. The new praxis flattens and consumes all thorny edges, alternative expressions, antisocial behaviour, glamorous kink, and revolutionary kitsch. One trend or style will follow or overlap with the other as perplexed artists patiently wait to be discovered, this time under a new light—one without implications, continuity or context. Conscious decontextualization is now desirable. The definition of the photo is much sharper; the text and the context, much vaguer. And the question for us is always how to generate fresh and sharp-edged proposals that can't be easily commodified and immediately turned into a master discourse. Is this even possible? What do you think?

GS: I think that no matter how edgy the proposal, the mainstream will eventually digest it and vomit it back to the world as an innocuous *prêt à porter* commodity. It is the mainstream role to process what is meaningful into flat banality in order to make it consumable...to feed the beast, as it were. But in my opinion art is a survivor of all domestications, finding its way through this demonic process with new forms, until the next trend absorbs it and makes it palatable, and so on, and so forth. But then it will come back with new ideas, and will leave a mark, like a stubborn river that flows among the rocks, carving a path patiently, eroding the hard surface. Your work has suffered that process of commodification, but you have come back many times with fresher proposals.

Don't you think that, after all, that has benefited your practise, as it has forced you to move restlessly, not to conform to your own image but to reinvent the message once and again?

GP: Definitely. Permanent reinvention becomes a survival strategy in the experimental art world. And this involves reinventing not only our artistic praxis, but also the very language and framing devices we utilize to name our praxis. It's a merciless semantic war, *sin tregua*. If you re-signify and reframe (and therefore reconstitute) your work into the new trend you may have a chance to outlive the vertiginous cult of innovation. If not, you are out of the game and deported overnight back to the barrio or to your Latin American homeland. In this sense, the performance art world is not much different than the merciless world of pop. Only a handful are granted the privilege of having several reincarnations. I guess I am lucky....or maybe very stubborn. *No se.* And you, Gabriela, tell me, within the milieu of the Latin American curators of your generation, which are the colleagues of yours interested in creating a more inclusive art cartography?

GS: There are many ways of articulating similar ideas, therefore each individual brings a piece to the puzzle. José Ignacio Roca, a curator working in Bogotá, has been involved in very interesting cross cultural projects, like a collaboration with conceptual Japanese artist On Kawara in the Amazonian jungle. It consisted of hanging his conceptual timepieces in a couple of primary schools in deprived, isolated areas of Colombia. I liked that very much, it touched another chord.

The zones of silence need sustainable collaborations that would contribute to expand the reach of our projects, instead of competing with each other in the illusory battle for the curatorial role in the next São Paulo Biennale, or Documenta.

GP: You just got back from Cuba. What was the art temperature down there?

GS: The current Havana Biennale is a good example of how an event of historical relevance can decline due to the lack of contact both with the Cuban reality and a plurality of curatorial voices. It has become a self-contained discourse that ultimately does not serve artists. Thematically, the last biennale dealt with the *Urban*, but few projects reached the outside world. The main exhibitions delivered a literal approach to the dynamics of the city: endless photographs and videos shot in urban centres of the world. However, during the opening days, the city was a set for parallel events that opened up a dialogue with emerging artists, like the one hosted by Tania Bruguera for her students from the ISA. There was also a project by graffiti artists from Brazil and Cuba scattered around the streets, and a fashion workshop using recycled materials in the environment of a community.

GS: I was rereading a Border Arts Workshop publication which you contributed to in the late 80s. In it you stated: *"En este momento histórico tan delicado, tanto los artistas e intelectuales mexicanos como los chicanos y anglosajones debemos intentar recontextualizarnos, es decir, buscar un territorio común y dentro de él, poner en práctica nuevos modelos de comunicación y asociación."*[1]

Twenty years later, it still seems necessary to recontextualise our work, to look for a common territory nurtured by a multiplicity of voices, beyond the stereotype, doesn't it?

GP: I totally agree with you: Twenty years later the challenges are still the same, perhaps even more formidable. Among other challenges, we badly need to look for a more inclusive context in which to operate: a conceptual zone in which all kinds of voices are allowed to coexist and dialogue. This "territory" must be considerably wider than the existing art world, and much more accepting of cultural difference. The theorists and the curators with their binoculars must descend from the top of their mountain and hang out with us down here. And the artists...we have to recapture our compass and understand once and for all why we're making art. It is certainly not just to be accepted by Documenta, or to get a chic New York gallery to represent us. We must attempt to

---

1   Gómez-Peña, Guillermo, Wacha esa border, son; *The Border Art Workshop* (BAW/TAF), 1984-1989, p.31

recapture a more central place in society as vernacular thinkers, intercultural brokers, experimental chroniclers of our times and critics of power. We must be seated at the table of debates. The re-vindication of the voice of the artist seems to be the ultimate task.

GS: The other task is clearly to debunk all the stereotypes that get in the way of dialogue.

GP: True. Only by cleaning the mirror, so to speak, can we have a more direct and complex cross-border understanding of one another. However, the problem is that the North continues to project stereotypes onto the South, as the center does unto its perceived margins. Meanwhile, the South and/or the margins continue to embody these stereotypes in order to appeal to the North, to be accepted at the table. How to break away from this neocolonial game of reflections and refractions? I don't know. Any ideas? Do you have a joke?

GS: ...Yes, perhaps a text I came across recently, in a conceptual piece by Luis Camnitzer: *"La estética vende; la ética derrocha."*

GP: The slippery nature of performance—its reticence to be domesticated and defined—may be another way to combat neocolonial models and art elitism. I've got a joke: What do you get when you cross a performance artist and a comedian? (Long pause) A joke that no one understands.

Sound and Silence

A Conversation between Joanna Laurens and Caridad Svich

[Joanna Laurens grew up on the UK Channel Island of Jersey. Her first play, *The Three Birds,* opened at the Gate Theatre, London, in October 2000. It won the Critics' Circle Theatre Award for 'Most Promising Playwright 2001' and a *Time Out* award for 'Most Outstanding New Talent 2000'. *Five Gold Rings* opened at the Almeida Theatre, London, in December 2003. *Poor Beck* was produced by the RSC, opening at The Other Place, Stratford, in October 2004. Joanna has just completed a commission for the RSC called *Jay and Haitch.* She has been writer-in-residence for the RSC and writer-on-attachment at the National Theatre. This conversation was conducted via e-mail throughout winter and spring of 2006.]

Caridad Svich: So much of this volume is about the power of language: to construct realities, enforce ideologies and silence others, about the collisions and meeting places between and among different verbal languages and cultures, and about the many languages that are part of the world of theatre and performance (related to censorship and self-censorship). In theatre, although many languages are possible (pictorial, emotional, linguistic) for dramatists especially there seem to be societal restrictions as to the languages that are allowed to tell a story. In Britain, there is already a notice-able sea change evident in text-based work. If the mid to late 1990s saw the emergence of radical possibilities for text and story, the trend now seems to be toward moving away from form to content, content to form experimentation and pushing of boundaries and toward event-centred, site-specific work (i.e. Shunt, Punchdrunk), imagistic storytelling (i.e. Kneehigh), continued work with pop languages (i.e. Frantic Assembly), and a desire for the epic (i.e. the Monsterists). For dramatists the restrictions seem to have narrowed again perhaps, ironically so, because of the proliferation of documentary and verbatim theatre. Authenticity equated with a recognisable "truth" is demanded more of dramatists now than, say, even five years ago. Poetic work, transformative work (that is not in translation from Germany or France), non-realistic text-based work is having harder time of it (despite the recent Beckett celebration). And of course other forms, no doubt, suffer as well, as a result. I'd like to ask you first about restrictions (imposed or apparent in the industry given what gets put on and what doesn't) and how as a writer you deal with them or not. I know some writers find restrictions liberating, or perceive them as a site certainly for rebellion.

Joanna Laurens: What gets put on is what has been successful in the past, generally speaking. If a particular writer has been very successful with their last play, they are likely to find it easy to place the next one. Or it goes for a genre. If a writer has been successful writing in a particular style, and a new writer comes along who writes generally within the same style, but makes it their own as well - that will probably be welcomed too. We are in a culture that encourages sameness.

What is hard to get on is work which is 'different' in some way and so therefore unproven. What is even harder than that to get on is new work by writers whose previous pieces have been slammed by critics. I have experience of this from both angles. The success: After my first play, which received rave reviews, I then received several offers of commissions: all wanting me to 'do' *The Three Birds* on a different text. Implicitly so that these companies could all then enjoy the same success which the company which produced *The Three Birds* did. It is such an uncreative way to look at the situation, to ask a writer to repeat the same process in application to a different text. Do they think we're some sort of input-output machine, and they feed a text into us and this version of it comes out the other end?

And the failure: After the second play, which received reviews as terrible as the first play's were good, I had a theatre in Germany try to pull out of a contracted German premiere of my next play, and was told, via my German agents, that they had lost faith in the play. When really they just saw the reviews of the previous play in the UK! (And, similarly, they had become interested in my work after seeing the great reviews of the first play!)

Well, I was naive and a newcomer when the first play got such good reviews. It's hard to hear such praise and not listen, especially if you don't know what the press are like and are new to theatre writing, and everything is so exciting when you start anyway. So I opened up to it. And then the second play got such shit, dismissive, patronising, awful reviews, and yes, I was all opened up to the press and what they had to say because of the success of the first. If they'd tried to throw a harder punch, they couldn't have. So of course it just hit home. I'd let my defences down. I didn't really know what to make of it all and spent a while trying to figure out what the truth was, amongst all this conflicting information. I mean, if you read some of the reviews from the first play alongside some from the second play, you'd see what I mean. It's hard to believe they are talking about the same writer. But if you define yourself and your ability by the critical reception of it, it will screw with your head and make you lose yourself. Which 'you' are you? Which labels apply? How can both the positive and negative be true?

As a result of this, and the self-examination which came after, I accepted that actually I am independent of these reviews. I have my own judgment of my work. I believe in what I am trying to do. When the reviews came out for the third play, I didn't really care what they said. I read them, yes, but the positive parts no longer made me happy, no longer were applied to who I felt I was. And the negative parts didn't make me upset, and I didn't apply them to myself either. In fact, it was quite a neutral, "oh, so that's what they are" kind of reaction. I think that's healthy. Although you do also lose something in this process. You lose the pleasure and sense of success when you read a good review, and that's inevitable because it's what protects you from the bad ones. Really, you just have to stay focussed on the production and on the play itself and see the reviews as something extraneous to it. Take pleasure in what you see on stage. It sounds so obvious that this is the way to perceive the situation, and a lot of people at the time were telling me to do this, but you can't make someone go through an emotional process at a speed faster than they are ready for, or that they can take themselves at. I think it's interesting to define 'failure' anyway.

There are pieces in theatre which are hugely successful with critics, but don't draw the audiences and play to half empty houses. And there are pieces which get critically slammed but play to full houses. My second play was one of these latter. Which of these defines success? The response of a small number of people with a lot of power, or the response of many more people, with no power? That's not a rhetorical question, I don't know the answer.

There are two actions evident here: the action of the reviews on the theatres and the action of them on the writer. The first is definitely a restriction in that it limits the work which theatres will consider. The second, I'm not sure if it is a restriction or a liberation. I'm not writing very much at the moment and I'm not really sure why. It feels like it's because I just don't have anything to say. If we're going to talk about censorship, then we have to talk about self-censorship. Like all writers, I write to communicate. But I don't feel that people are 'hearing' what I'm saying. I feel like I am writing "entertainment," in their eyes, because that's what all theatre is (they think). That's not what I'm doing, or not what I'm intending to do. I want to write deeper than that and to reach them in a profound way. I don't want to provide entertainment for an evening out, which they can forget about as soon as they've seen it.

CS: Secondly, although theoretically the notion of authenticity is hardly up for debate, it's interesting to me that in the text-based theatre (unlike performance) it continues to hold sway especially in terms of content and its presentation. And yet, this mirror of the authentic often acts as a censor, thus disallowing other authentic experiences from being represented. It's interesting you say we live in a culture that encourages sameness especially since at the same time it proclaims a commitment to diversity and difference (the two buzz-words in the US, anyway). Why do you think seeking the same is encouraged? Do you think it has to do with staying in the comfort zone? And a fear of unknown (which leads me to think about 'foreign-ness' and alienation)? Or is it more about the corporate, mass-produced mind-set: in the Hollywood-movie mentality: what sold before can sell again? So that we are basically talking about the expectation of profit equated with success.

JL: I don't think that seeking *exactly* the same is encouraged. If all plays used exactly the same plot, exactly the same style, to communicate exactly the same concepts, audiences would get very bored and things would be very pre-dictable. But at the same time, to go to the other extreme and to have some-thing which is very different in terms of either plot, style, concepts means that, sometimes, some audience members can be quite resistant. I think you are right, this is something to do with the larger human issue of being afraid of, or distrusting of the unknown. With anything which is very 'different,' there is a tendency for people to react extremely, one way or another, and either to pro-claim they love it and it's the next big thing, or to be very resistant towards it and wary of it. With theatre in particular, as an audience member, you can't be resistant. If you are, you will set up a barrier between yourself and the piece, and it will fail to move or engage you, for sure. In terms of: 'what sold before can sell again.' I do think this is true with young writers, just starting to write for the stage. Inevitably they want their work to be produced and performed, and it is only natural for them to look at what has previously been successful, and even if unconsciously, emulate that in some way.

CS: I look at, for example, the many different kinds of works that get put on in other art forms, and whilst the culture of sameness factor does surface, I think it's more pernicious perhaps in the theatre, especially text-based theatre. Has this to do with language? And perception? Are certain languages (of telling story) more allowed than others?

What happens when a writer disrupts culturally accepted linguistic and/or pictorial planes? In Britain, for instance, the 1990s new writing boom, which is often characterised as "in-yer-face" (coined by critic Aleks Sierz), yielded many different kinds of writers who were working in varied ways, but most of the time the writers were conveniently branded as part of a one writing movement. Cer-tainly there were commonalities amongst the themes, and dramatic strategies these writers (Ravenhill, Neilson, Kane, Upton, etc.) were employing in their works, but there were and are significant differences. Obviously Kane's work is the clearest to discuss in this regard, as her writing was more Artaudian and classical at one and the same. But, for example, Patrick Marber is often classi-fied as part of this new writing movement, and I think his work is far more tradi-tional in its concerns as well as its structures. In Britain now it seems that there has been not quite a backlash against the kind of work that was produced in the 1990s but certainly a sense of "well, that was a navel-gazing, adolescent phase we had to get through and now we can move on and write Big Important Plays again," while at the same time there is this hunger (which is both a good and bad thing) to discover the next Kane or Ravenhill. So, writers as different as Debbie Tucker Green and Laura Wade, for example, are seen alternately as heirs to the throne, which I think is not only unfair to these writers and their particular gifts and pursuits, but to the climate of new writing in general. (I know in Kane's case the issue is complicated because of her suicide, which heightens the desire for who is the anointed writer that will follow in her footsteps - and interestingly enough also at a time when her work in the UK isn't seen that often. Her writing in the last five years has been more successful in Germany, France and non-English-language-speaking countries.)

My concern has been always (speaking Stateside now) with branding and how playwrights are readily branded by critics and audiences, and what happens when that happens, and how to work under the weight of the brand? Whether the brand is the 'success' of the previous play and the sometimes unconscious desire to replicate that success, which is impossible, or to counter a perceived 'failure.' The brand can be internalized by a dramatist too. I don't want to say that the pressures are all external. Sometimes your own need to match the level of a previous work can get you into writing trouble or make you scale even greater heights. Either way you are reacting to something, and this is the question.

What happens to your ability to actually just listen to yourself, to your impulses, to your voice, to the world, to truly listen and respond (which is a very delicate and sensitive process because it has to do with being alert and awake and attuned to impulse in a direct way) if you are in a state of reactive-ness? And what happens to the work as a result?

JL: Well, speaking from my own experience, it is hard to write if you are in a state of reactive-ness. I could only do it after a period of time had gone by and I felt distanced from the event and from the critical feedback. Time is a great healer. We gradually become different people, the more time passes by, and can eventually look back at events in our past as though they happened to another. For me, that was what I had to wait for, before I could write again.

CS: I've been grappling with two questions lately: one has to do with politics and theatre and the other has to do with form and content. On the latter, I've been wrestling with the privileged stance urban and urbane works have other rural-set plays. It seems that when it comes down to it, the industrial world continues to dominate in the media and the agrarian one is too often presented as 'quaint' or 'backward.' And in terms of new writing there is a clear privilege given to producing works that are either urban or deal with the upper-middle-class.

JL: The upper middle class wields the power these days, and the voice. So does the urban over the agrarian, in theatre. More people live in cities than in the country, and these people like to see their own lives reflected through art. With the threat of theatre seeming unfashionable or dull (Shakespeare, the classics, etc.), theatres have responded to this by trendying it up a bit, so you get urban themes: drugs, parties, socialites, groups of young people hanging out and so on.

CS: But moreover what does this do to our continuing disconnection to the land, to the earth and its care? To the voices and bodies that inhabit the country rather than the city? And basically how do we make our stages more equitable to the range of experiences in our towns, villages, cities and the world too?

JL: Theatre's never really been about the land, the earth or farming. Poetry and prose, yes. Theatre? Hasn't theatre always been for the masses, didn't it start as common entertainment? And where are the masses, but in the villages and towns? Right from touring theatre companies in medieval times in Europe, theatre needs an audience, the audience is in the village or town, so that's where they go and put the theatre on. As theatre and towns have grown larger and more urban, so theatre plays for these audiences. What does this audience want to see? Their own lives reflected and identified with. This need for an audience sets theatre apart from prose or poetry. Romantic poets can go off and write poems about daffodils and self-absorption, but no theatre is going to work in front of participatory medieval and Renaissance audiences unless it engages with their lives, and as they would be invariably townsfolk, perhaps that's why theatre has continued to be urban. Even today, theatres exist in cities, so the audience is largely drawn from cities, and again, people like to see their own lives, or characters they can identify with, onstage. Perhaps if theatres existed in the middle of no where, like country churches, the subject matter would change, but then how many people would be in the audience?

CS: In the US, for instance, there has been a steady aversion over the last few years toward work that uses heightened language, that is poetic or even lyrical, in favour of works that are excessively plain-spoken, blunt even. Perhaps this reaction has to do with the more general reaction against misperceptions of the avant-garde or experimental and an attempt to place trust in the Recognizable, the Comfortable, the Known, or the Seemingly Known.

JL: I'm not really sure why, let's call it, 'lyrical' language isn't more widely accepted in theatres. Certainly this is similar in the UK, although perhaps there are still a few theatres around which are more welcoming to this sort of writing. It seems to be that there is a large body of people who consider lyrical language to be the antithesis of 'sincerity.' In that, they believe that the writer who uses such language is almost hiding behind a superfluity of words which are largely devoid of meaning, in the vain hope that the audience won't notice that the words are empty and will instead be impressed by this use of language. Instead, they prefer writers who just use blunt, plain-spoken language, as they believe this equates to emotional honesty, truth and in some way, reaches deeper. Personally, I think it's all just a matter of perspective. When a writer uses lyrical language effectively, words and sentences can often carry more than one meaning and, in this way, can often say two opposing things at once, sometimes up to three or four things at once. Rather than being just 'words for the sake of words' and devoid of meaning, they are packed with meanings which are much more complex than anything which can be communicated in a more plain-spoken language. If an audience can access this, to any degree, even if not all meanings come across in performance, it results in a much more complex and interesting play than one written in a more plain-spoken or blunt language. But this does require some amount of interpretative effort on the part of the audience, which, in today's world of TV and films and increasingly naturalistic (plain-spoken) theatre, is asking a lot. Today, audiences expect to do less work and put less "into" a theatrical experience than they have done in the past, and instead expect to consume theatre passively, rather than actively. When they try to do this (consume passively) with a piece of lyrical theatre, it just doesn't work. They won't 'get' the complexity of meanings, it will all appear a self-indulgent mess and they will withdraw from it, and then the play has lost them.

I think it's really important always to remember what "play" is. Play is something which starts when we're kids. When I was a kid, I was always creating stories. I played with my (ahem!) "My Little Ponies" (yes, really), I played with my brother's collection of cars, I played with my brother's "He-Man" figures...but I was always creating elaborate story lines. That was the fun part of it. Deciding what was going to happen. The storylines continued from one play session to the next. It was even more fun to play with someone else, who controlled some of the figures while I controlled the others because I couldn't predict what input into the game the other person would have, and it was fun to have surprises sprung on you or suggestions made for an event in the game which you hadn't thought of. My point is that at no point in this process is it important what you're doing. At no point does 'play' have to be of a certain quality or standard. The people who are consuming the 'play' are also the ones creating it (kids). I remember, there was nothing more inhibiting when play-ing to look up and see an adult watching, someone you hadn't noticed. In fact, I think I was incapable of playing if someone was watching, although I could play with endless numbers of participants.

From my point of view, the speed with which I wrote *The Three Birds* is also due to the fact that I had no idea or expectations that it would ever be produced (watched). I'm not sure whether it's now ever possible to regain that ease of composition. There is nothing which highlights this more than rewrites in rehearsals. The process of making changes, writing out new sections, then bringing them into rehearsal, often just the next day, or even making changes in the theatre and immediately hearing them - that process really obliterates any barrier between private and public, psychologically, for me. It brings the public into the writing process, which is as inhibiting as being a kid and knowing your mum is watching you play. It's not just about rewrites though, but also just the experience of being produced. That can never be undone, or taken away, and in turn it does rob me of some of the privacy I experienced as a writer, before. It's easier to take risks in private than in public. And it's easier to write for the sheer sake of it, because you're play-ing, in private than in public.

CS: What happens when playwrights break down language to the structure and form/grammar of words themselves. Do we need permission to break it down?

JL: No, we don't need permission to break anything down. As writers we have not only license to do that, but an obligation.

I Know not How to Tell Thee Who I Am

MATTHEW GOULISH

[Matthew Goulish co-founded Goat Island in 1987, and has performed in all the group's works. Routledge published his *39 MICROLECTURES in proximity of performance* in 2000, and *Small Acts of Repair: Performance, Ecology, and Goat Island* (co-edited with Stephen Bottoms) in 2007. He teaches at the School of the Art Institute of Chicago, and was awarded a Lannan Foundation writer's residency in 2004/5.]

In Roman times the censor took the census, assessing citizenship in numbers, words, and laws. On April 16th, 2007 a student named Seung Hui Cho shot and killed 32 people and himself on the campus of Virginia Polytechnic Institute and State University in Blacksburg, Virginia. In the aftermath of the massacre, many observed violent imagery in his adolescent creative writing. On April 23rd, at Cary-Grove High School in Illinois, first-year teacher Nora Capron asked her students to write freely for 30 minutes. "Be creative; there will be no judgment and no censorship." Allen Lee, a student with a 4.2 grade point average, wrote a 342-word essay that contained the following passage: "So I had this dream last night where I went into a building, pulled out two P90s and started shooting everyone, then I had sex with the dead bodies. Well, not really, but it would be funny if I did." Lee was arrested the next morning on his way to class. Capron had shared the essay with her superiors, who notified police, in a series of acts of "judgment and censorship." Possibly Lee knew of P90s, compact submachine guns, because he had enlisted in the Marines as he was scheduled to graduate in May. The arrest nullified his enlistment. On May 24th all charges

against him were dropped after the efforts of his attorney. The Marines are re-
considering his enlistment. In the 1950s, attempting to theorise the conditions
from which schizophrenia arises, Gregory Bateson coined the term "double
bind" to describe a situation in which a subject, in relation to powerful familial
or social forces, encounters two conflicting demands, both of which must be
met. For a double bind to be effective, the subject cannot plainly see that the
primary injunction's demand directly conflicts with that of the secondary injunction. In this sense the double bind differentiates itself from a simple contradiction, as a more inexpressible internal conflict. The subject vigorously wants
to meet the demands of the primary injunction but fails each time by failing to
see the incompatibility of the situation with the demands of the secondary injunction. A delusional system provides the escape. To maintain a grade average
.2 points above perfect, a student must write something that proves he has followed the assignment of applying no judgment or censorship. Yet to write with
no judgment or censorship negates this injunction by applying the judgment of
noncensorship. The solution is to envelop the signifier of non-censorship – unspeakable acts described in the wake of similar unspeakable acts – in multiple
layers of unreality – a dream that was never dreamed, but if it had been, would
have been funny (insignificant). Unlike Lee's undreamed dream P90s, Seung
Hui Cho's P22 semi-automatic pistol was real, and purchased on eBay from Elk
Ridge Shooting Supplies in Idaho in violation of Federal law. On December 13th,
2005, a physician at New River Valley Community Services Board found Cho
"mentally ill and in need of hospitalisation." Virginia Special Justice Paul Barnett
certified in an order that Cho "[presented] an imminent danger to himself as a
result of mental illness." On December 14th, Cho was released from the mental
health facility after Judge Barnett issued a directive for the "court-ordered [out-
patient] to follow all recommended treatments." Virginia state law on mental
health disqualifications to firearms purchases was worded slightly differently
than the federal statute. The form that Virginia courts used for a mental health
disqualification addressed only the state criteria, which listed two categories
that would warrant state police notification: someone who was "involuntarily
committed" or ruled mentally "incapacitated." Because Cho was not involuntarily committed to a mental health facility as an inpatient, he was still legally
eligible to buy guns under Virginia law. However, according to Virginia law, "A
magistrate has the authority to issue a detention order upon a finding that a

person is mentally ill and in need of hospitalisation or treatment," and also must find that the person is an imminent danger to himself or others. Virginia officials and other law experts have argued that Justice Barnett's order meant that Cho had been "adjudicated as a mental defective" and was thus ineligible to purchase firearms under the United States federal law that remained unenforced. What sort of nation of censors have we become, moving so swiftly to monitor our words, so slowly to monitor our laws? A December 13th stalking incident had triggered Cho's examination and subsequent diagnosis. On that day he frightened a female student by writing on her door board a line from *Romeo and Juliet*, Act 2, scene II.

My name, dear saint, is hateful to myself ...
Had I it written, I would tear the word.

Making The World Strange Again

RINDE ECKERT

[Rinde Eckert is a composer, writer, performer, and director. His Opera / New Music Theatre productions have toured throughout America, and to major festivals in Europe and Asia. His recent work includes *And God Created Great Whales* (Obie Award 2002), *Horizon.* (prem. 2006), and *Orpheus X* (Pulitzer Prize finalist 2007). He received the Marc Blitzstein Memorial Award from the American Academy of Arts and Letters in 2005, and a Guggenheim Fellowship in 2007.]

I take censorship to be an artifact of complex society: an official or un-official limit on freedom of expression or interpretation.

Of the official limits, there is little to say, in general. If one believes in the cause of the censor, one is unfazed by the censorship. If not, not. In civil society, all sorts of defamatory and libelous expression is, quite right-ly, censored. The lewd, lurid, incendiary, or sadistic are similarly interdict-ed or curtailed.

The difficulty is that in protecting a social norm from some countercul-tural ethos one might drive away prophet and solipsist alike, kill God's messenger (so to speak) because one lacks the imagination to see a bene-factor in the stranger at the door. One needs a healthy respect for one's ignorance, here, a faculty of self-criticism.

What follows is what I might call a theatrical essay. It means to sug-gest that the enlightened censor must acknowledge the intrinsic mystery of ultimate ends (God, Science, Utopia) while attending to the demands of the moment (balance, meaning, beauty). It suggests that the convention-

al benchmarks (manifesto, bible, tradition) of the censor can dull the imagination and lose us the opportunity of renewal, refreshment, and clarity.

On the back cover of *Company of Moths*, one of Michael Palmer's extraordinary books of poetry, a critic proclaims that Palmer's 'genius is for making the world strange again.' I love this idea: returning strangeness, as if strangeness has been misplaced or lost or (more likely) run off.

I'm hunting again today, in and around the field of religion. By religion I don't mean the political organizations that dominate the air waves these days. They aren't religious at all, of course, whatever disguise they adopt. They are purely political. God is simply useful to them. No. I mean earnest religion, reverence before the mystery, humility, compassion, and reason. Here in this field one can still make colossal mistakes. One can carry the bare frame of an umbrella in a rainstorm and imagine one isn't getting soaked. One can even have one's choice of viable shelter and choose to carry this pathetic umbrella skeleton instead, simply because it was grandad's umbrella. No matter that it's in tatters. With enough faith, it is assumed, you will be protected from the rain.

This is my hunting ground, then. This is what I call my reading: Hunting, not gathering. Gathering is about opening one's focus, recognizing the familiar, ignoring the blood track: see the gooseberry, the wild fennel, the mint – whatever is edible and within reach. The day old deer track does the gatherer no good. The deer is long gone. I'm hunting, looking for something unusual, something that leads in a singular direction away from camp and all the trampled ground. I'm looking to return the strangeness that fled when the invaders put up the fort.

I'm not sure why I continue to hunt here; this particular hunt has already resulted in a piece of theatre: *Horizon*. It was finished in 2005. The piece revolves around a theologian named Reinhart Poole, a seminary teacher who, having been fired (censorship, in effect), is working on his lecture on Ethics the night before his last class. During this night he will converse with his wife, imagine his lecture, remember and invent conversations with his dead brother, and take long breaks to reread a play he's been writing, an allegory involving two ancient masons (with not-quite-convincing Irish/Scottish accents) who have been busy building the same cinderblock church foundation for 1750 years.

Poole will recite from the Bible, invent parables all his own, and watch his play unfold. He will occasionally sing. One time he will fall asleep and wake up at a kind of 'last supper' with his fictional masons. They will be appalled at this visitation.

I play Poole, the central character in *Horizon*, an irony that will surface over and over in the image of the creator as his own creation.

Poole: You've got a bit of the preacher in you. Theatre is your church

RE: That seems a fraught analogy.

Poole: That doesn't mean it isn't useful. Look. Theatre, by acknowledging the lie at its centre may be closer to religious truth than most liturgies. Theatre says, "We cannot be speaking truly for we are not who we say we are, but it is only in this way we may speak the truth; we are not who we seem to be, yet we are truly who we say we are." So I am fictional and utterly true, while you are real and utterly lost.

RE: I don't understand.

Poole: Exactly.

Poole has been hanging around. Reminding me I'm not quite done hunting even though the piece is finished.

Poole: The piece is done, yes, but the story isn't finished.

The story began when I read an interview with Al Gore in the *New Yorker* in which he referred to Reinhold Niebuhr. I recalled having heard the name on a number of occasions, most notably, around the dinner table of a high school chum whose father taught theology at The University of Iowa, in Iowa City where I grew up.

I picked up the first book by Niebuhr I could find, which turned out to be *The Irony of American History*. From then on I was hooked. I read all of Niebuhr's major work. I read half of his brother H. Richard Niebuhr's work. I read some Spong, Barth, Tillich, Spinoza, Bonhoeffer, Kierkegaard, Josiah Royce.

Let's talk about magic for a moment. I believe in magical thinking. Any hunter worth a damn does. The art of magical thinking seems critical to a process of discovery. The hunter believes he must let the animal possess him, let the sign be an omen, say to himself, the hunter is no longer separate from what he seeks.

Poole: Who authors? Who censors? Who is writing? Who is written? These are the religious questions. I'm comfortable with these questions. But, being fictional, I have nothing to lose. You, on the other hand, have a great deal at stake.

Horizon, of course, is a comedy with a capital C. That is, it seeks to wed high and low irony. It has a Niebuhresque understanding of philosophical perils of the eroticism of love as opposed to agape. Passionate feeling seen as the acme of spiritual animation, turns one's body into the ultimate end. One's psyche is asked to be the whole point of evolution, the ultimate arrival. Of course, the psyche is no such thing and can't bear the assignment. So it either organizes itself in the form of a despotic utopianism which seeks to add weight to its claims through a body of worshipers or it turns inward as the hermetic/artistic and consumes itself, sometimes becoming quite literally consumptive. Modern tragedy continues to suffer from this romantic hubris, the body as the end of history. It's irony deficient. Comedy ensues in the light of the realization that we may not be the end of history as our modern and largely romantic world suggests. It takes the form of low irony (sentimentality, nostalgia, camp, wit, etc.) and high irony (art, philosophy, religion, marriage, etc.). Low irony chronicles the local slapstick of our romantic miscalculations. High irony explores the contextual ramifications of those miscalculations.

Poole: I'm a character of essentially low ironic origins (a witticism or joke) breathing the air of high irony.

RE: What? An ironic irony?

Poole: Let's take *Too Loud a Solitude,* for example.

RE: The Hrabal?

Poole: Yes, Bohumil Hrabal's novella. The main character is shovelling waste paper and discarded or condemned books into a compactor in this subterranean vault. The paper and books are shovelled in from above through a hole through which it is possible to see a little patch of sky. While doing his job, he has also been preserving books, making a dense library of his small apartment. He's also been opening books to certain passages then inserting them into the middle of the wastepaper bales. It's a kind of conceptual art project, if you will. He is the hermetic/artistic romantic type. One has to suspect he won't survive the end of the story. He is subsequently invited to tour a new compacting plant that, he sees, will make his little operation obsolete. The state's program of waste disposal and, of course, censorship, has been made terribly efficient. Our hero, then, returns to his crude little compactor and promptly throws himself into it.

RE: What are you driving at?

Poole: That Hrabal's project is high irony in the guise of low irony — a truth embedded in a witticism, a transfiguration disguised as a suicide. What seems reduced is ramifying. The author, buried, (or seriously obscured within the particular character and context of the story) is transfigured by the story's higher allegorical functions. So the witticism, ignored as trivial by the censorious pedantry of the state, is the seed of a revolutionary thought.

RE: You are my higher self, disguised as my lower self?

Poole: Yes, more or less. Let's call it 'the dynamics of the real.' I am, literally, a thought, an idea. I am a resonance in the mind of the reader or auditor. Let's call this resonance 'Reinhart Poole'. Every time this resonance (or a resonance indistinguishable from it in the form of this exact argument) occurs, I am active, alive. The problem with you, Rinde, is that you are under the cynical misapprehension that you are a provisional solution when, in fact, you are a universal truth.

RE: What?

Poole: Believing yourself to be provisional you believe you need to exaggerate your claims, inflate your provisional aspect in a tragically confused mimicry of truth. This is the neurotic lie at the heart of most religions, the pathetic fig leaf that separates us from the truth of our eternal souls. And indeed, it is also at the heart of a devout secularism which assumes redemption through history, or more accurately, progress. 'Progress' is the Messiah of the acolytes of secularism.

RE: We've strayed pretty far from theatre, I think.

Poole: Not at all. We're right in the middle of it, in fact.

By the time I was ready to start exploring *Horizon* with my cast (David Barlow, and Howard Swain) and my director (David Schweizer) I had written some 240 pages of dialogues, parables, observations, essays, and homilies.

When we all gathered in Lincoln, Nebraska at The Lied Center (the lead commissioner of the work) I plopped this huge wad of writing in front of my colleagues. We read for three days, then went to work. The set was in place at the beginning – seven easels each with a chalkboard on it, three six foot tables on metal saw horse legs, a dozen cinder blocks. Plenty to play with, I thought. After a day with the cinder blocks we agreed we needed more blocks. Eventually there would be close to fifty, enough to build a substantial wall. So we built a substantial wall.

Poole: With one brick missing in the middle

Eckert: Yes. David B. and Howard came up with that.

Poole: The child of an observation and a parable

The observation: Any foundation contains flaws, no matter how precisely one measures or how meticulously one builds. If the foundation is presumed to be flawless, no adjustments for the subsequent expression of these intrinsic flaws will be made. Each layer built on the assumption of the perfection of the previous layer amplifies the original flaw. Each layer inherits the lie of perfection from the previous layer and adds the weight of its own lie. The higher the un-amended construction towers the more grotesque the expression of error. It's an elegant metaphor, and more than a little true.

The parable can't be paraphrased I'm afraid; parables by their nature are fiercely efficient:

Once upon a time there were a people living in a large house without windows or doors. No one had ever been outside. They only knew the inside of the house, its walls and rooms. One day a young man among them, while wandering through the halls of this sprawling house, stumbled into a dark corner and through a hidden door to the outside world. He marvelled at the horizon, the open air, and the trees and flowers. He couldn't have imagined such a wonder. "I must go and tell the others," he thought. Retracing his steps he found his way once again to the windowless living room of his fellows. "I have stumbled on an extraordinary truth" he said to them. "There is a vast world outside this house, without walls. It is full of marvellous things."

Of course no one believed him for they could not conceive of such a world. "No walls? Impossible! Something outside this house? Ridiculous!" they said. And so he said,

"Wait. Let me show you." And he took some paper with which he fashioned a paper flower. "There," he said, "this is something like one thing I saw." And all the people of the dark house stared in wonder at the paper flower. "This is marvellous indeed!" they said. "But," said the young man, "this is just paper, not the thing itself." "This is a revelation," said the people. "No," said the young man, "the revelation is not to be found in this room. The revelation isn't made by hand out of paper in a dark house." But no one was listening, so mesmerized were they by the paper flower. "Give us this marvellous thing," they demanded, "give it here, or we will take it from you."

And the young man saw that it was useless to explain. "They couldn't possibly understand," he thought. "They must stumble through the door themselves before they can see." And so he backed toward the dark corner and the unnoticed door, drawing them on with the promise of the paper flower. "Come," he urged them, "follow me. Come take this marvel from my hand." And so they all advanced with him toward the dark corner, toward the door, and freedom from their ignorance.

But just as he reached the door; just as he was about to stumble with them through the door into the air and light, he paused to adjust his footing, to make sure of the way. And in that moment one impatient housemate struck him with a hard and heavy book, snapping his neck and crumpling his body to the floor. All were appalled and turned on the killer. "You have killed the bearer of the revelation," they cried, falling on him and tearing him to pieces.

When all was calm again a child among them plucked the paper flower from the hand of the dead young man. "See," said the child's mother, noticing, "see what my child is saying? We have lost the man, certainly, but the revelation is in hand."

And all happily agreed and the paper flower was placed at the centre of the windowless house and worshipped.

So far all this seems necessary: the odd form, the desultory story-telling, Poole's appearance, religious questions and statements. The author, as god of his little world, knows something about the promise and peril of creation. One is defined by the forces one sets in motion; one is characterized in one's own characters, censored oneself by what one censors.

How does one proceed? Does one make an outline, a skeleton, an armature? Does one proceed rationally, block on block, to build the house. Certainly one must have some formal parameters; one must understand the physics of wall building; one must have technical strengths, muscle, to lift the bricks, math, to mix the mortar in the correct proportions – only so much sand, so much cement. One must know what one is building, surely.

Poole: Or one is at the mercy of some whim, the interruption of the methodical wall building by some stray insight or caprice that reveals itself in time to be an important admission of error.

Poole implies that God as pre-determiner rules a dead world of self-congratulatory witticisms and insipid tautologies, whereas God as continually reformed by unexpected outcomes is a living revelation.

Poole: God invented error in order that he might not know himself and therefore be recreated.

Let's get back to the making of *Horizon:* the 240 pages, the text, the literary event as the heart of the process. It pumps the blood, the river of oxygen, to the brain. Or, rather, it's a vital little fist of words – ideas, riddles, parables, subtle jokes, obvious jokes, doggerel, and verse – promising the open hand. It is the little bible of our devout house. I am its scribe. But the liturgy is a communal affair, the litany is the unfolding surprise, the theatre, the unexpected outcome, a surrender to the communal ideal informed by doctrine but not its slave.

Theatre is an adjustment of the wall on the basis of the imagined edifice but mindful of the flaws, or strangeness, natural to all foundations. Forget to adjust for the strangeness and you build a grotesque monument not a house of worship.

Idolize a text and you are lost to the great mystery. The play, as realization of the word is a raising of the dead, a kind of futile demonstration of power. Lazarus was the unfortunate pawn in Christ's demonstration of mastery. He must die again of course, and probably soon, the grief his family seeks to avoid, faced again. So Lazarus escapes nothing. His family escapes nothing. They are left in anxious suspension, their awful fear of death made all the more awful by this cheat of death. We may be ruled by desire, but we don't have to be buried by it. Lazarus' grieving family gets what they desire, and what they desire is going to haunt them. Christ raises the body of Lazarus, showing him off like a carnival geek, as if to say, "Here he is. Now, what is it you hoped to avoid?"

A great and terrible lesson that.

Let's get back to the idea of the hunt, the room, the cast as a moving camp on the hunt, following the blood track, needing the original text only on occasion, the majority of occasions demanding of the writer new text in response to the discovered territory. The writer improvises a structure, a jerry-built bridge, a song, a confession, a new wish:

> Jim: Are you awake, Harrison?

> Harrison: (sleepily) Mmm.

> Jim: What do you think of the sky?

> Harrison: Mmm.

> Jim: Do you suppose we're headed toward some revelation, you know, some saving grace. I'm <u>not</u> talkin' about Christ on a flaming toast gliding from the clouds, to hover in the church parking lot with his apron full of magic beans. I'm thinkin' of something a little less fabulous: a feller on a bicycle, with eyes as clear as water, who stops in the field, opens up his basket and invites us to join him in a little light supper.
> I was hoping the word wouldn't get out, that we could just have a private affair, you know, just the three of us, a last supper kind of thing, nothing fancy. If it's just the Christ on a bicycle we could keep it quiet. I think the rest of the world would be lookin' for somethin' a bit more Hollywood, golden chariots, virgins on swans. They wouldn't be inclined to believe in such a humble visitation.

> Harrison: If you would kindly move off to a remote corner of the earth a body could nap in peace on the hallowed ground.

> Jim: Right. I'm closing my eyes now.

These are the mason's in *Horizon*, in a scene that was cut. They speak with accents of dubious consistency – one doesn't quite know which of the ancient

Celtic tribes is intended. They are a part of a play within the play, supposedly
written by Reinhart Poole.

Poole: They need to be a little strange - a little out-of-this-world. I couldn't
have them speaking in regionally accurate dialects. That would have been commentary. They would represent some specific political history. They are philosophical allegory.

Once there was a man who began an article intending to say something
about the process of making a theatre that wasn't conceived as the physical
realization of the literary (text as dictator or bible) but was responsive to the
exigencies of the hunt, a theatre willing to change direction, follow the blood
track, so to speak, the scent, with no certainty of finding a way back: one follows the strangeness, one loses oneself, only to find one has circled back, or
rather that the original camp has found the hunter; one finds oneself gathering
berries in a glade, imagining the vaulted trees as a cathedral, in a religious
mood, worshiping ancestors, making sacrifices to the unseen gods.

Concerning Censorship

ALEKS SIERZ

[Aleks Sierz is a journalist, broadcaster and a university lecturer. He is theatre critic of *Tribune* and his bestselling seminal study, *In-Yer-Face Theatre*, defined a new generation of 1990s British writers.]

I

Censorship appears to be simple, but is actually quite complicated. It is a
slippery beast, bristling with paradox and contradiction. One reason for its
seeming simplicity is that censorship makes liberals look good. It is so obviously
wrong that fighting it confers on the fighters the laurels of moral rectitude, aesthetic modernity and plain common sense. Doesn't it feel great to have right on
your side? If censorship did not already exist, in so many different forms, liberals
would have had to invent it.

II

Censorship is universal, in the sense that all societies practice it, in one way
or another. But its anthropological commonality should not conceal the fact
that censorship always has a history. In British theatre, for example, one of the
great sea-changes occurred in the 1960s, when a profession that was mainly
conservative (socially as well as aesthetically; in its audiences as well as its key
figures) became increasingly liberal. In 1968, when stage censorship was abolished in Britain, this looked like a triumph. But isn't there something a bit too
comforting, not to say complacent, in this narrative?

So before we pat ourselves on the back for abolishing censorship forty years
ago, it's worth pointing out that Britain was one of the last countries in what

was then called the Free World to abolish such controls. Since most other countries managed to do it long before, it's best to avoid crowing too loudly.

Abolition is usually constructed as a narrative of cultural liberation. Before 1968, the story goes, an authoritarian model of censorship ruled British theatre. True, before they could be performed, all plays had to get a licence from the Lord Chamberlain's office, but if in theory the censor was authoritarian, unaccountable and undemocratic, in practice the process was one of negotiation — his edicts were contested by liberal artists, and a compromise reached. One of the paradoxes is that while progressive opinion argued that censorship was a bad thing, the late 1950s and 1960s were a golden age for British dramatists. Was the conflict with the censor one element that contributed to creativity?

Another problem with the narrative of cultural liberation is that it ignores the fact that the will to censor remains alive and well, reborn in every generation. Since 1968, the nation's moral guardians are no longer concentrated in the centre, but are diffused throughout society. The authoritarian model has been replaced by the plaintiff model. Over the past forty years, there has been a spawning of censorious activity by religious groups and reactionary newspapers, by pressure groups and moral vigilantes. Open censorship is replaced by invisible censorship, whose aim is mental closure.

For theatre, the problem is that while you can contest moral absolutism by appealing to reason, there's very little you can do about rhetoric which effectively closes down debate, when the argument is reduced to the discourse, current in many areas of culture since the 1980s, of "bums on seats" and "give the public what it wants". When dumbing down and anti-intellectualism rule the roost. This kind of discourse marginalises the voices of artists who might want to take risks, to investigate or to criticise.

III

Abolishing censorship doesn't stop people being censorious, it merely makes them more ingenious, or crass, in their methods. The paradox is that although British theatre has moved from being one of the most heavily controlled art forms to one of the least censored, the stage is still affected by a whole variety of restrictions. When the law on censorship is abolished, other legislation can act as the continuation of censorship by other means.

For example, laws which were originally meant to control morality can be used to impede theatrical work. In the case of Howard Brenton's *The Romans in Britain*, the play's director, Michael Bogdanov, was charged under Section 13 of the Sexual Offences Act of 1956, a law usually used to charge people having sex in a public place. In the case of Mark Ravenhill's *Shopping and Fucking*, the law which bans part of its title is the Indecent Advertisements Act of 1981, which updated the original Indecent Advertisements Act of 1889, a Victorian law designed to stamp out the adverts that prostitutes used to put in shop windows. In this way, laws designed to police real-life activities are used to attack the representation of other, if similar, activities. (This assumes confusion between real life and fiction that would disgrace a ten-year-old. Or maybe it is adult plain bad faith.)

IV

Censorship's best weapon today is psychological war. Censorious groups constantly wage a mental campaign against anything they regard as too dangerous, too immoral, or too experimental to be subsidised by the state. A psychological climate may be harder to document than the use of laws but it can be equally effective. One area where the creation of a negative psychological climate — or public mentality — can interfere with freedom of artistic expression is to libel a play, in other words, to give it a bad image. For example, Shakespeare's *The Merchant of Venice* is racist; John Ford's *'Tis Pity She's a Whore* is dodgy; Howard Barker empties theatres.

These psychological aspects of the creation of a negative public mood also suggest that morality is a sharply contested terrain. With the diffusion of the censorious impulse, concerned citizens now use a variety of threats: and authoritarian populism gradually suffocates liberalism. Its rhetoric is simple, indeed crude, but apparently effective. Instead of discussing moral choices and justifying values, the discourse has shifted to more practical grounds: the impulse to censor accepts that the battle over traditional morality is increasingly hard to win, and moves on to dispute the right of artists to get state funds for work that may offend the sensibilities.

V

Theatre is a live art form — that is its most distinctive characteristic. Does this mean that it is inherently uncensorable? If only.

VI

The most universal censorship is performed by language. Language is always being policed by usage, convention and censorious social codes. However, because language is inherently fertile, fluid, alive with new metaphors and new meanings, it can always outwit the censor. In so far as liberal society tolerates jokes and slips of the tongue, it more effectively controls all cultural products. On the other hand, because of the instability of language, the most brutal censorship — the cutting out of a tongue or the banning of a language — is doomed to fail.

VII

The stricter a system of censorship, the more fragile it is. The more puritanical the system, the more vulnerable it is to unconscious subversion. The slip of the tongue, the mispelt word and the irreverent joke are all terroristic devices wherever severe controls are in place. Whether or not the unconscious is structured as a language, it will always disrupt language. The fart that echoes in a church is more effective than the treatise that moulders in a library.

VIII

There is no such thing as an unshockable audience, or an unshockable person. So don't kid yourself. By its very nature, shock comes as a surprise; it happens when least expected, when your defences are down. When you experience it, however momentarily, it serves to redefine your sense of self. It draws a boundary; it punctuates illusion. And who is to say when the next shock will come?

IX

Can censorship be avoided by allowing anything and everything? A stupid question: this permissive fallacy assumes that tolerance can be extended indefinitely. History, however, suggests that toleration, permissiveness and indifference can only react to, rub up against, some idea of prohibition (whether legal, mental or imaginary). Without such boundaries, freedom has no meaning. In fact, in all societies, one can only imagine what freedom is by actively looking for prohibition.

X

One of the best methods of censorship is to ignore, to turn your back, to deprive something of the oxygen of publicity. But the more strongly you ban, the more interest you attract. Of course, censors have no choice. They are motivated solely by the desire to ban. If the censor could ignore the offensive, they would not be a censor. They would be simply banning themselves. Joining the dole queue.

The most effective form of censorship is self-censorship. The idea that one can be against all censorship, or believe in the absolute freedom of the individual is a powerful, but pitiful, illusion. (Indeed, plagiarism would inevitably result from complete artistic freedom.) What the confident declaration of total freedom always ignores is the power of self-censorship. This is perhaps the most beautiful form of control since it requires no blue pencils, no office buildings and no legislation. All it needs is the faltering of individual bravery, supported by a collapse of collective courage.

The second most effective form of censorship is economic. It's quiet, it's safe and it's highly effective. Because economic censorship is so effective, it is so rarely discussed. After all, there is simply too much to say.

XI

Liberals have hitherto only defended themselves from censorship; the point is to provoke it.

Come on liberals, one more push and you will become radicals!

SELECTED BIBLIOGRAPHY

Aldgate, Anthony and James T. Robinson, *Censorship in Theatre and Cinema*, Edinburgh: Edinburgh University Press, 2005.

Aldgate, Anthony, *Censorship and Permissive Society: British Cinema and Theatre 1955-1965*, Oxford and New York: Oxford University Press, 1995.

Badiou, Alain, *Being and Event*, trans. Oliver Feltham, London & New York: Continuum, 2007.

Becker, Carol, *The Subversive Imagination: The Artist, Society and Social Responsibility*, London and New York: Routledge, 1994.

Bevan, Robert, *The Destruction of Memory: Architecture at War*, Chicago: University of Chicago Press, 2007.

Boal, Augusto, *Theater of the Oppressed*, Sidmouth: Pluto Press, 1979.

Davis, Mike, *Buda's Wagon: A Brief History of the Car Bomb*, New York: Verso, 2007.

Davis, Walter A., *Art and Politics: Psychoanalysis, Ideology and Theatre*, London and NY: Pluto Press, 2007.

Delgado, Maria M. and Paul Heritage (eds), *In Contact with the Gods? Directors Talk Theatre*, Manchester: MUP 1997.

Deutsche, Rosalyn, *Evictions: Art and Spatial Politics*, Cambridge: MIT Press, 1996.

Duncombe, Stephen, *Dream: Re-imagining Progressive Politics in an Age of Fantasy*, New York: New Press, 2007

Forche, Carolyn (ed.), *Against Forgetting: Twentieth Century Poetry of Witness*, New York: W.W. Norton and Co., 1993.

Genet, Jean, 'That Strange Word', in *Fragments of the Artwork*, trans. Charlotte Mandell, Stanford: Stanford University Press, 2003, pp. 103-112.

Gómez-Peña, Guillermo, *Ethno-Techno: Writing on Performance, Activism and Pedagogy*, London and New York: Routledge, 2005.

Goulish, Matthew, *39 Microlectures: in proximity of performance*, London and New York: Routledge, 2000.

Haedicke, Susan Chandler and Tobin Nellhaus (eds), *Performing Democracy*, Ann Arbor: Univ of Michigan Press, 2001.

Hallward, Peter, 'Staging Equality: On Ranciere's Theatocracy', *New Left Review*, 37, 2006, pp. 1-12, Accessed on-line, (http://www.brunel.ac.uk/dap) 15 November, 2007.

Heathfield, Adrian, *Live: Art and Performance*, London and New York: Routledge, 2004.

Houchin, John H., *Censorship of the American Theatre in the Twentieth Century*, Cambridge: Cambridge U Press 2003

Jameson, Frederic, *Postmodernism or The Cultural Logic of Late Capitalism*, Chapel Hill, NC: Duke University Press, 1991.

Jakovljevic, Branislav, 'The Space Specific Theatre: Skewed Visions' *The City Itself'*, *The Drama Review*, 49: 3 2005, pp. 96-106.

Kershaw, Baz, *The Politics of Performance: Radical Theatre as Cultural Intervention*, London and NY: Routledge, 1992.

Kester, Grant, *Art, Activism, and Oppositionality*, Chapel Hill, NC: Duke University Press, 1998

Krauss, Rosalind, *A Voyage on the North Sea: Art in the Age of the Post-Medium Condition*, London: Thames&Hudson. 1999.

Kwon, Miwon, *One Place After Another: Site-Specific Art and Locational Identity*, Cambridge: MIT Press, 2004.

Lavery, 'The Pepys of Ell: The Politics of *Linked,'* New Theatre Quarterly, 82, 2005, 148-60.

—— 'Performance Writing, Narrative and Walking', in *Theatres of Thought: Theatre, Performance and Philosophy*, eds. Daniel Meyer-Dinkgrafe and Dan Watt, Cambridge: Cambridge Scholars, 2007, pp. 95-110.

Mitchell, W. J.T. ed., *Landscape and Power*, Chicago: Chicago University Press, 1994.

Montgomery, David R., *Dirt: The Erosion of Civilizations*, Berkeley, University of California Press, 2007.

Parkes, Adam, *Modernism and the Theater of Censorship*, Oxford and New York: Oxford University Press, 1996.

Patterson, Michael, *Strategies of Political Theatre: Post-War British Playwrights*, Cambridge: Cambridge University Press, 2003.

Rancière, Jacques, *Short Voyages to The Land of The People*, trans. James B. Swenson, Stanford: Stanford University Press, 2003.

——, *Disagreement: Politics and Philosophy*, trans. Julie Rose, Minneapolis: University of Minnesota Press, 1999.

——, *Nights of Labour: The Worker's Dream in Nineteenth- Century France*, trans. John Drury, Philadelphia: Temple University Press, 1989.

Read, Alan, *Theatre and Everyday Life: An Ethics of Performance*, London and New York: Routledge, 1993.

Reinelt, Janelle, 'The Limits of Censorship', *Theatre Research International*, 32:1, 2007, pp .3-15

Schutzman, Mady and Jan Cohen-Cruz (eds), *A Boal Companion: Dialogues on Theatre and Cultural Politics*, London and New York: Routledge, 2006.

Sinfield, Alan, *Out on Stage: Lesbian and Gay Theatre in the 20th Century*, New Haven: Yale University Press, 1999.

Solnit, Rebecca, *Storming the Gates of Paradise: Landscapes for Politics*, Berkeley: University of CA Press, 2007.

Thompson, Michael, *Performing Spanishness: History, Cultural Identity and Censorship in the Theatre of Jose Maria Rodriguez Mendez*, London: Intellect Ltd, 2007.

Žižek, Slavoj, *The Parallax View*, Cambridge, MA: MIT Press, 2006.

Lightning Source UK Ltd.
Milton Keynes UK
UKOW050513220312

189385UK00002B/53/P